THE RECEDING SHADOW
OF THE PROPHET

THE RECEDING SHADOW
OF THE PROPHET

The Rise and Fall of Radical Political Islam

Ray Takeyh and Nikolas K. Gvosdev

Westport, Connecticut
London

Library of Congress Cataloging-in-Publication Data

Takeyh, Ray, 1966–

The receding shadow of the prophet : the rise and fall of radical political Islam / Ray Takeyh and Nikolas K. Gvosdev.

p. cm.

Includes bibliographical references and index.

ISBN 0–275–97628–9 (alk. paper) — ISBN 0–275–97629–7 (pbk. : alk. paper)

1. Islam and politics—Islamic countries. 2. Religion and politics—Islamic countries. 3. Islamic countries—Politics and government. 4. Islamic fundamentalism—Islamic countries. 5. Islam—21st century. I. Gvosdev, Nikolas K., 1969– II. Title.

BP173.7.T34 2004

320.5'57--dc22   2003062253

British Library Cataloguing in Publication Data is available.

Library of Congress Catalog Card Number: 2003062253

ISBN: 0–275–97628–9
    0–275–97629–7 (pbk.)

First published in 2004

Praeger Publishers, 88 Post Road West, Westport, CT 06881
An imprint of Greenwood Publishing Group, Inc.
www.praeger.com

Printed in the United States of America

The paper used in this book complies with the Permanent Paper Standard issued by the National Information Standards Organization (Z39.48–1984).

10 9 8 7 6 5 4 3 2 1

To our wives

Contents

Acknowledgments

Ray Takeyh wishes to thank John Gaddis and Paul Kennedy of Yale for granting me a most hospitable place to work.

Nikolas K. Gvosdev extends his thanks to Derek Davis of the J. M. Dawson Institute (Baylor University) where this project was first conceived and subsequently to Dimitri K. Simes, president of The Nixon Center, and Adam Garfinkle, editor of *The National Interest*, for their encouragement of this project.

Introduction

When the two authors of this study first began their collaboration in 1994, radical Islamism seemed to be on the upsurge in both regions of the world that formed our respective areas of study—the Middle East and Southwestern Asia for Ray Takeyh as well as the Balkans and Eurasia for Nikolas K. Gvosdev. Iran remained in the grip of hard-line Islamist revolutionaries. The defeat of the Soviets in Afghanistan had energized a worldwide movement of Islamist revolutionaries, who dispersed to continuing fighting around the world. Debilitating internal low-intensity conflicts convulsed both Egypt and Algeria. Civil wars were underway in both Bosnia and Tajikistan, and the first Chechen war erupted in that year as well. Christopher Ross, a senior U.S. diplomat who served in Algeria and Syria, predicted "Regretfully, that the region is fated to witness a wave of Islamist revolutions, successful or failed, over the next decade."[1]

Yet, despite a vast amount of prima facie evidence that radical Islamism was poised to assume power in significant portions of the Middle East and across the Eurasian landmass,[2] the first arguments were already being propounded that Islamism was a hollow ideology that was certainly capable of fomenting rebellion and channeling unrest and popular wrath, but it was fundamentally flawed in terms of providing a workable template for governance. Scholars such as Olivier Roy[3] and Gilles Kepel[4] argued that, while radical Islamists could certainly destabilize and disrupt a society, especially by utilizing violence and terror, they could not, in the long run, hope to gain and effectively wield state power to construct viable political and economic institutions based on their utopian vision of Islam. Radicals would increasingly be marginalized or would have to moderate their stance to gain greater public support. At the same time, other observers warned about not underestimating the capabilities of existing regimes, both in the Middle East and in Central Asia, to cope with the challenges posted by the radicals.

This book was first envisioned in Spring 2001 as a way to revisit those areas that had been considered to be such at risk for Islamist revolution in the early 1990s—Egypt and Algeria in the Middle East in addition to Bosnia and the countries of the former Soviet Union—as well as to assess the course of the Iranian revolution. To us, it did appear as if radical political Islam—revolutionary, messianic, and utopian—was on the wane. Islamist revolutionaries had been unable to overthrow the Egyptian and Algerian regimes despite the use of terrorism and violence. The ideological basis of the Iranian revolution was increasingly being called into question after the election of the reformer Mohammed Khatami as president in 1997. In Fall 2000, a nonnationalist coalition of parties had ejected the Islamist-inspired Party of Democratic Action (SDA) from power within the Muslim-Croat Federation in Bosnia; although, the SDA subsequently won a slim majority in the Fall 2002 elections. The 1997 cease-fire in Tajikistan, which ended that country's five-year civil war between ex-Communist and Islamist forces, was holding. Islamist regimes in Sudan and Afghanistan were increasingly isolated from the world community. Chechnya remained a festering trouble spot as the second war launched in 1999 ground on, but the rest of the Muslim regions of the North Caucasus remained quiet. There appeared to be only two real exceptions. The first was the role of Islamists in helping to mobilize Palestinian resistance to Israel. The second was a certain unease in parts of Central Asia as a shadowy guerilla organization, the Islamic Movement of Uzbekistan (IMU), mounted a campaign to overthrow the regime of Islam Karimov.

The horrific events of September 11 seemed to throw the conclusions of this book into grave doubt. If radical Islamism was indeed "everywhere on the retreat" and no longer an "immediate peril,"[5] why were the World Trade Center towers in ruins, the Pentagon damaged, and thousands dead? Yet, it was precisely because the radicals were—to a large extent—driven out of their native societies that they shifted tactics. "The most dangerous of the Islamists—Osama bin Laden and crowd," Martin Kramer observes," found refuge in remote corners of east Africa and south Asia. From there, they did unfurl terrorist tentacles into Europe and America. But, Islamists no longer threaten any of the region's rulers."[6] It is to examine how and why this has come about that this book was written.

Radical Islamism may indeed remain a dangerous threat to the peace and security of the Western world and provide the ideological underpinnings for an international terrorist network. This is a conclusion neither of us would contest. Nevertheless, it is increasingly clear that radical political Islam cannot seize control of modern or modernizing states within the Islamic heartland and construct an effective alternative model of governance capable of meeting the political and economic problems faced by the Muslim world—lack of economic development, the need to modernize the infrastructure, and extending basic social and political freedoms. Where radical movements have taken control, their legitimacy is increasingly being undermined by a crisis of legitimacy engendered by their inability to deliver on their promises of a just and fair society. Indeed, in Iran, a December 2002 open letter to Supreme Leader Ali Khamenei authored by Dr. Qassem Sho'le-Ye Sa'adi, a leading academic and reformist politician, warned,

In any event, the natural and logical result of such behavior [on your part] and of such a poor image of the religious regime (because of which there is a sense that your religious regime in Iran has failed) is that the end will [bring about] not only the fall of the religious regime, but, ultimately, the establishment of a secular regime in the form of a genuine republic.[7]

It is quite striking the degree to which Islamism has been transformed over the last decade. Although radicals native to particular countries have moderated their stances—either as a result of defeat by the security forces, as in Egypt, or through pragmatic political considerations, as in Turkey—it is the exiles dispersed to the fringes of the Muslim world—the failing states of southeastern Asia—or to the diaspora of the West who continue to embrace radicalism. Radical Islamism's efforts to seize control of Muslim-majority states have largely failed. By the late 1990s, the Islamist revolution had been "forcibly thrown back." As a result, "It is the gaunt losers in that combat who have now emigrated to London and Paris."[8] As David Martin Jones concluded, "Islamism's active nodes and cells are not located in Arab countries. As we have seen, many are evolving in southeast Asia, but the most dangerous networks are located in the West."[9] In fact, the real danger now lies in a radicalism incubated in the West "being deliberately and systematically re-exported to Muslim countries,"[10] but this is a subject best addressed separately.

The first part of this book opens with a discussion of what distinguishes radical political Islam from other forms of Muslim politics. In the popular mind, any application of Islamic principles to social or political life equals Islamism. We recognize that the fundamentalist/Islamist label has been "attached to groups as diverse as Hamas in Israel/Palestine; Hizbollah in Lebanon; the Refah (Welfare) Party in Turkey; the al-Nahda Party in Tunisia; the Muslim Brotherhood in Egypt, Jordan, and Syria; the Armed Islamic Group (GIA) in Algeria; and the Jamaat-i-Islami in Pakistan."[11] However, for us, radical Islamism is a distinctive political force, a radical, utopian, messianic movement that rejects the status quo and employs violence to further its agenda. Radical Islamists themselves draw clear distinctions between themselves and Muslim reformers or traditionalists. It may be useful to keep in mind the twentieth-century distinction between socialists and communists. While the communists were a socialist political movement and shared a common origin in Marxist principles with social democrats, communists took great pains to distinguish themselves from other socialists and indeed viewed more moderate socialists as their principal rivals for power.

We then proceed to examine the three bookends of the Middle East—Iran, Algeria and Egypt.[12] The Iranian revolution was an Islamist one, and the post-1979 Islamic Republic was the first attempt to take Islamist theory and apply it in actual governance. The gradual erosion of Islamist fervor is of special importance because Iran's fate points to the likely trajectory of Islamist movements in other states. The cases of Algeria and Egypt are critical because these were, in essence, the test cases for the entire Arab world. As Andrew J. Pierre and William Quandt observed at a time when it looked as if Islamists might seize power in Algeria (and the same could have been said of Egypt during this period as well), "Algeria's fate will influence the future of its immediate neighbors . . . as well as democratization and development efforts in the Arab world, the role that Islamist movements will play in the politics of the Middle East and even the chances for Arab-Israeli peace."[13] However, in both Algeria and Egypt, Islamist revolutionaries proved unable to spark mass uprisings even against corrupt regimes. Idealism and terror could not win out against determined and ruthless regimes prepared to meet force with even deadlier force.

This book then examines how Islamist movements gained toeholds in the Balkans and across Eurasia, but they proved unable to consolidate and expand them beyond isolated villages and valleys, despite the influence and support of the international Islamist movement, including refugees from the failed campaigns in Egypt and Algeria.[14] A discerning reader will notice that the chapters on the Balkans and Eurasia contain much more background information on Islam in those regions than in the chapters on the Middle East. This is because, while Islam is generally well known in its Middle Eastern/Arab context, one of the great mistakes made during the 1990s was to assume that the Middle Eastern experience was the norm for all Muslims. One of the reasons Islam in the Balkans and across Eurasia, especially in Central Asia, has proven more resistant to radical political Islam is its different experience with modernity.

The book closes with some general conclusions about the trajectory of radical Islamism. Islamism is an ideology of wrath that is capable of mobilizing the masses, but it provides little guidance for actual governance. As Islamists are given responsibility—whether to an electorate in a professional association, as in Egypt, or for the administration of the state, as in Iran—the realities of politics have generally forced change and evolution in Islamist movements. In large part, this is because the dilemmas of institutional decay, maldistribution of wealth, and the absence of democracy throughout the Muslim world were and remain problems that cannot be solved by empty ideological formulations and the use of violence. We agree with Kepel when he concluded, "But violence in itself . . . has proven to be a death trap for Islamists as a whole, precluding any capacity to hold and mobilize the range of constituencies they need to seize political power."[15] This is why, throughout the Muslim world, former militants have abandoned their comrades and have sought to reconcile Islamic precepts with modern liberalism. This is why we believe that, despite the terrorist attacks of September 11, 2001, the moment of radical political Islam has passed and genuine political liberalization and economic modernization remain the only viable means of transcending the predicament in which much of the Muslim world finds itself.

Finally, a stylistic note. Translations and transliterations, especially from Arabic and Farsi, can assume a variety of forms in English. Linguistic purists will no doubt find many examples in this work with which they would disagree. We have made no attempt to impose a standard form, but we have followed two general principles. The first is that we have chosen not to change the forms used by sources from which we directly quote. The second has been to arbitrarily choose, in the case of each country and region, what we feel is the most recognizable forms of names—recognizing that differences in dialect and pronunciation will produce different spellings. However, what we have hoped to avoid is a situation in which a reader might conclude that "Usama ben Ladin" was a different individual from "Osama bin Laden." We ask the reader's indulgence.

NOTES

1. Christopher Ross, "Political Islam: Myths, Realities, and Policy Implications." Speech delivered to the Salzburg Conference of Near Eastern Affairs Public Affairs Officers, September 21, 1993.

2. See, for example, Robin Wright, "Islam, Democracy and the West," *Foreign Affairs* (July/August 1992) and Stanley Reed, "The Battle for Egypt," *Foreign Affairs* (September/October 1993).

3. Olivier Roy, *The Failure of Political Islam* (Cambridge, MA: Harvard University Press, 1994).

4. Kepel began his exhaustive research during this period and published his findings in 2000; the English translation of his *Jihad: expansion et déclin de 'islamisme* (Paris: Gallimard, 2000) was published two years later.

5. Ray Takeyh, "Islamism: RIP," *The National Interest*, no. 63 (Spring 2001): 97.

6. Martin Kramer, "Islamist Bubbles," *The National Interest*, no. 68 (Summer 2002): 133.

7. Ayelet Savyon, "Iranian Intellectuals Against Khamenei - Dr. Qassem Sa'adi: 'Your Regime Is Illegitimate, Your Foreign and Domestic Policies Are Failing and Despotic'", MEMRI *Inquiry and Analysis Series - No. 125* (February 28, 2003).

8. Christopher Hitchens, "Holy Writ," *The Atlantic Monthly* (April 2003): 98, 100.

9. David Martin Jones, "Out of Bali: Cybercaliphate Rising," *The National Interest*, no. 71 (Spring 2003): 83. Take the example of Hizb ut-Tahrir, which has been active in Central Asia, seeking to rally support for the creation of a single caliphate

governed by Muslim law. Hizb ut-Tahrir is indeed an international Muslim movement, yet, effective control over the organization is exercised, not by Muslims in
any traditional part of the Islamic world, but "a group of militants based in London." Compare Olivier Roy, "EuroIslam: The Jihad Within?" *The National Interest*,
no. 71 (Spring 2003): 67.

10. Roy, "EuroIslam," 67.

11. Zachary Karabell, "Fundamental Misconceptions: Islamic Foreign Policy,"
Foreign Policy, no. 105 (Winter 1996/97): 79.

12. Takeyh, "Islamism RIP," 97.

13. Andrew J. Pierre and William B. Quandt, "Algeria's War on Itself," *Foreign
Policy*, no. 99 (Summer 1995): 131.

14. Algerians and Egyptians formed a number of the jihadists who came to
Bosnia, for example, to try and create an Islamic state in the Balkans. It is interesting the degree to which the international Islamist movement abandoned direct
action in the heartlands of the Muslim world to fight in its perceived periphery.
Olivier Roy noted, "Al-Qaeda and its likes have been fighting in the West (New
York, Paris, London) and Bosnia, Kosovo, Somalia, Chechnya, Afghanistan, Central Asia, Pakistan, Kashmir, the Philippines, Indonesia and East Africa—but not
in Egypt, Palestine, Lebanon, Saudi Arabia, Syria, or Algeria." Roy, "EuroIslam,"
71.

15. Gilles Kepel, *Jihad: The Trail of Political Islam*, trans. Anthony F. Roberts
(Cambridge, MA: Harvard University Press, 2002), 376.

Chapter 1

The Islamist Challenge

A September 1991 headline in the Russian newspaper *Izvestiia* neatly encapsulates the attitudes expressed by many policymakers and opinion-shapers in the West in the period following the dismantling of the Berlin Wall, and reinforced since the September 11 attacks: "The Red Flag of Communism or the Green Flag of Islam?"[1] Having triumphed over Communism, the Western system of free-market economics and liberal pluralist democracy was now seemingly under threat from a new rival, for "with the death of communism, Islam is the global alternative,"[2] energized into a mass movement following the Gulf War. Samuel P. Huntington warned his audience that "the Islamic Resurgence has manifested itself in every Muslim country; in almost all it has become a major social, cultural, and intellectual movement, and in most it has had a deep impact on politics."[3] Hassan al-Turabi of Sudan confidently predicted, "Objectively, the future is ours,"[4] and Western scholars began to echo his assessment by predicting that "the future of the Muslim world lies with the Islamic political alternative."[5] The emergence of an international radical Muslim network, epitomized by Al-Qaeda, an outgrowth of the guerilla struggle waged against the Soviet Union in Afghanistan during the 1980s, seemed to presage a new chapter in the struggle of militant Islam against the West.[6] Yet, despite manifestations of terror and fury, despite deadly attacks carried out by small cells of fanatics, and despite armed attempts to overthrow existing regimes (as in Algeria), the Green Peril has not emerged as a viable successor to the Red Menace in international affairs. Radical Islamist movements, even when successful in obtaining power, have not proven themselves as workable alternatives. Today, throughout the Middle East, as well as in the Balkans and the former Soviet Union, Islamism—radical political Islam—is everywhere on the retreat as a governing ideology. Indeed, the fury of recent Al-Qaeda attacks, especially those directed at the American heartland, are a manifestation of the frustration of radical Islamists at their seeming inability to seize power in the Muslim world.

The destruction wrought at the Pentagon and the World Trade Center on September 11, 2001, demonstrated that small groups of well-trained, motivated Islamists could strike even the American mainland. However, there was no wave of unrest in the Muslim *umma* (the worldwide community of Muslim believers). American-backed regimes in the Middle East and southern Asia did not collapse before a tidal wave of Islamist anger. Al-Qaeda and other groups can wreak destruction or exploit unrest; this does not mean, however, that radical Islamists are on the verge of taking control of governments. It may be useful to note the parallels with the fight against radical leftist terrorism during the 1960s and 1970s. Groups like the Baader-Meinhof gang, the Red Army Faction, or the Red Brigades posed a real security threat to business, political, and military elites throughout the Western world. Yet no one argued that the activities of those organizations meant that the liberal-democratic governments of France, West Germany, Belgium, or Italy were in imminent danger of being overthrown and replaced by radical Marxist-Leninist regimes. While acknowledging the potency of the terrorist threat emanating from radical Islamic groups, we want to draw a clear distinction between the activities of extremist groups and the ability of radical Islamist ideologies and movements to provide political alternatives at the national level.

ISLAMISM VERSUS MUSLIM POLITICS

One of the prevailing misconceptions in the West, which has led to a great deal of confusion in trying to assess the influence of Islamist movements in the world, is that any use of Muslim values, beliefs, or religiosity by a political movement or by a particular regime is a sign of Islamist influence. Robert H. Pelletreau, Jr., appropriately cautions us that terms such as *Islamist*, *Islamism*, and *Islamic movement* have been muddled as a result of popular misuse of the terms and the attempt by both the media and policymakers to use *Islamism* as a shorthand designation for a variety of social and political movements in the Muslim world.[7] After all, strictly speaking, all "social actions by Muslims, acting as Muslims (acceptors of the *sharia*)" can be considered Islamic in motivation.[8]

In areas where the majority of the population is Muslim, or Islam forms a key part of the cultural inheritance of the nation, it is to be expected that Islam will have an influence over social and political developments and that political dialogue will be conducted within an Islamic context. This point was stressed by Muso Dinorshoyev, vice-president of the Academy of Sciences of Tajikistan, when he noted that "The influence of Islam is determined by the fact that this religion is in essence a national phenomenon . . . insofar as the bulk of the population are Muslims, it is only natural that the influence of Islam on the sociopolitical life . . . is significant."[9] The revival of interest in Islam, its teachings and rituals (the *al-tayyar al-islami*, or Islamic trend), will certainly lead to an increase in the use of Islam in social and political discourse.[10] The mere use of Islamic rhetoric to justify social and economic policies, however, does not mean that a movement is Islamist; it is important to recall, as Charles Tripp notes, that

> Islamic themes and symbols have been used to shore up patrimonial, authoritarian systems of rule, supposedly lending them a coloration that augments their authority among predominantly Muslim members of the associated societies.[11]

Dale F. Eickelman and James Piscatori point out that "rulers, for their part, routinely invoke Islamic imagery and ideas to legitimize their rule and to defend themselves against Muslim critics."[12] This creates the phenomenon that they have labeled "Muslim politics":

> A symbol has been created and now is integral to the identity and aspirations of groups of like-minded individuals as well as to the self-defined mission of the authorities. These examples, then, are political in part because they involve challenges to the limits of state authority but also because they involve a contest over people's understandings of and wishes for social order. The examples are Muslim because they relate to a widely shared, although not doctrinally defined, tradition of ideas and practice.[13]

Islamism, therefore, forms only one subset of a larger pattern of Muslim politics, because the Islamic legacy remains open to continuous interpretation and reinterpretation. Eickelman and Piscatori thus conclude, "the result is a flexibility of ideas and divergence over time and space."[14] Throughout the Muslim world, the Islamic legacy is critical to "legitimizing the political (and economic) power of that class or elite which happens to be in control."[15] The Islamist attempt to appropriate the legacy of Islam, in fact, is in response to secularizing movements within the Muslim world, which, as Mehdi Mozaffari demonstrated, "while remaining part of the Muslim community, and still invoking authentic Islam as their authority, have tried variously to divest the seats of authority and power of their sacred quality."[16] Islamism is but one attempt to harness the motivating power of Islam, either employed from above to legitimatize a particular regime or used from below to provide a basis for opposition to the status quo.[17] Islamists are able to do this, in part, because of the changes wrought by modernization throughout the Middle East and Eurasia. Mass literacy and modern technology have given to Islamist groups the ability to propagate their message directly to the people, bypassing traditional channels of authority. There is now an entire new Islamic literature that has emerged—the production of works intended for the popular market. As a result,

> with the development of mass literacy—not to mention the secondary orality of electronically mediated Islamic cultural production—matters of philosophy can hardly be considered merely elitist without making the mistake of depriving non-elites of specifically cultural concerns.[18]

Islamists (in Arabic, *al-islamiyyun*) are those who believe that their particular vision of Islam must be implemented as a corrective to un-Islamic practices that have crept into the governments and economies of the states that compose the Muslim world. This study concerns itself with the role and activities of Islamists who maintain that there is a need for a constant struggle between what they define as the Islamic order (*'al-nizam al-islami'*) and a political and social order based on what they term ignorance[19] of true Islamic precepts (*'al-nizam al-jahili'*). Ignorance of what constitutes a correct Islamic state can be manifested not only by non-Muslims, but also by Muslims, even if they are personally pious and religious. Thus, in contrast to those who seek to accommodate Islam with modernity, to blend Islamic precepts with reform movements, or those who seek to reestablish premodern Muslim traditions, Islamists, or radical Islamists (in contrast to Islamist liberals or reformers) seek to distinguish their own views by referring to an essentialist and sometimes ahistorical core of Islam, in contrast to the *jahili* practices (i.e., practices based on non-Islamic sources) of other Muslim political groups, influenced either by national traditions or by Western ideas.[20]

Islamists believe in "transforming religious beliefs into a conscious system, broadening the scope of religious authority, and redrawing the boundaries of political community."[21] The charter of the Palestinian Islamist movement *Hamas* (the acronym for *Harakat Muqawama Islamiyya*, or Islamic Resistance Movement) sets forth its intention of creating an Islamic state with "the Quran its constitution, Jihad its means, death for the cause of Allah its sublimest aspiration."[22] Islamist movements developed in the twentieth century as a response to Westernization and modernization, especially to the Western notions of separating religion from public life and transforming religion from serving as a social force that shapes the life of the community into a private monitor over the personal conscience of the individual. Sayyid Qutb (1906–1966), one of the key thinkers of the Islamist movement, was quite clear: "It is not sufficient to *be* Muslim and to follow Muslim practices. One must reflect upon Islam and articulate it."[23] Qutb maintained that Islamism, as a political and social ideology, was

> a divine vision that proceeds from God in all its particularities and its essentials. It is received by man in its perfect condition . . . He is to appropriate it and implement all its essentials in his life . . . If Islam is to be effective, it is inevitable

that it must rule. This religion did not come only to remain in the corners of places of worship . . . It has come that it may govern life and administer it and mold society according to its total image of life, not by preaching or guidance alone, but also by setting of laws and regulations.[24]

A contemporary of Qutb, Hasan al-Banna (1906–1949), maintained that Islamic societies could only overcome their social, political, and economic problems by returning to the earliest sources of the Islamic tradition. As John Esposito pointed out, al-Banna

> called for the return to the *Quran* and the *Sunnah* of the Prophet as the primary sources for the reestablishment of an Islamic system of government. In addition to rejecting Western sources . . . al-Banna believed that Muslims must go back beyond all historical accretions, and return to the early normative period of Islamic history—the time of the Prophet and the first caliphs of Islam.[25]

A hallmark of all Islamist movements is the conviction that all modern socio-political ideologies, being man-made and elevating the sovereignty of the individual over that of the Divine, cannot succeed in forging a truly just society. At the founding congress of the Islamic Renaissance Party (IRP) in Astrakhan, Russia, in 1990, the participants declared that "invented schemes of social development have brought mankind to complete crisis in all spheres of life. We see salvation only in following the way of Allah."[26] Subsequently, the IRP rhetorically asked

> Can we Muslims follow the various secularist systems which are based on teachings, whether they are about the dictatorship of the proletariat and class warfare or about nationalism and racial exclusivity or about Western democracy and absolute freedom, which leave God's teachings to the side, the teachings which raised us to a high level of civilization?[27]

This is why some consider Islamist movements to be proponents of a type of totalitarianism, for, as Mawlanda Mawdudi (1903–1979), another one of the founding fathers of modern Islamism, pointed out, "no one can regard any field of his affairs as personal or private."[28]

Islamism, therefore, is a distinct movement, not simply an umbrella grouping for all Muslims who seek to filter political and economic life through a Muslim lens. Mawlana Taqu 'Uthmani draws this distinction in discussing the application of Islamic law in Pakistan; it does not consist of simply removing non-Islamic concepts, observing:

> Even if, hypothetically, everything that is explicitly in conflict with the Qur'an and the Sunna is excised from English law, that law can still not be characterized as Islamic law. For the former is the product of an entirely different context, and its guiding concepts cannot be separated from the framework in which it has evolved.[29]

As James Piscatori concluded, "Muslims within one state and from state to state continue to disagree on the ends and uses of power."[30]

Islamists have a certain outlook on social and political life that distinguishes them from other thinkers and politicians who have attempted to adapt liberal democracy, nationalism, or socialism to a Muslim context.

It is also important not to confuse Islamists with traditionalists. Islamists do not automatically use the past as a standard for judging what is correct or true. They do not assume that a return to a premodern Muslim society is the solution. Rashid al-Ghannoushi (b. 1941), a Tunisian Islamist, draws a very clear distinction between "living Islam," a dynamic faith capable of societal transformation, and "museum Islam," based on the repetition of past tradition. Most current Islamists would be comfortable with his criticisms of Muslim traditionalists: "I wonder how our students feels studying Islamic philosophy when it offers them a bunch of dead issues having nothing to do with the problems of today . . . I propose that these shrouds be returned to their graves, that these false problems be buried, and that we deal with our problems—economic, politics, sexual license."[31] Similarly, Dr. Ali Shariati (1933–1977), an Iranian Islamist scholar, in his 1969 work *Eslamshenasi*, contrasted a *genuine* Islam as manifested in its early years with the "obscurist and passive Islam" being propagated by the Muslim establishment (*ulama*) in the modern period, further noting that it was an obligation for all Muslims to "take up the original version."[32]

Other than an idealization of the period immediately following the revelation to the Prophet, Islamists have often been critical of past Muslim societies and of corrupt practices that have entered Islam. Jacques Waardenburg notes that Islamist movements "and their ideologies share a vivid protest against corrupt forms of Islam and the desire to realize by practical means the ideal society where true Islam reigns."[33] Sometimes, Islamists have come into conflict with those trying to restore traditional Islam, especially in the Caucasus, Central Asia, and Balkan regions, because traditional forms of Islam as practiced in those regions conflict with the interpretation of Islam advanced by Islamists.

Islamists also do not automatically recognize traditional authority as being legitimate within the Islamic world. In Egypt, the Muslim Brotherhood has consistently challenged the authority, status, and pronouncements of the official ulama and the scholars of al-Azhar University. In particular, Islamist movements have been critical of traditional leaders, either for their perceived surrender to Western interests, or because their views and interpretations of Islam are no longer relevant to the needs of Muslims living in the modern world.[34] Nor do Islamists necessarily advocate the restoration of past institutions in seeking to achieve their program. Bhikhu Parekh, in his comparison of Protestant Christian and Islamic fundamentalist movements, pointed out that a group like the Islamist organizations arises in a society widely believed to be degenerate and devoid of a sense of direction . . . Fundamentalism represents an attempt to regenerate it by comprehensively reconstituting it on a religious foundation. It rejects the tradition, offers a "dynamic" and activist reading of the scriptures, abstracts what it calls their essence or fundamentals, builds a moral and political programme around them, and uses the institution of the state to enforce the programme.[35]

Islamists are also not traditionalists in the sense that they reject modern technology or seek to return Islamic societies to a preindustrial state. From its founding in Egypt in 1928, the Muslim Brotherhood embraced modern technology and forms of organization—it functioned as a "modern-style party organization, using schools, youth groups, news media, national congresses, and social service provision to mobilize hundreds of thousands of active members."[36] Islamists have embraced the fruits of modernization, including mass literacy and the development of mass communications, as a means to spread their message.[37] Thus, many specialists would class Islamist movements as a synthesis of traditionalism and modernism[38] because Islamists are trying to cope with how a modern society can be reconfigured along Islamic lines, not trying to turn back the clock in terms of technology or organization. This distinction is critical because one of the principal errors made today by Western policymakers and analysts is to assume that Islamist movements represent traditional Islam attempting to reassert itself.[39]

Islamist movements are more properly described as radical, because Islamists see themselves in opposition to the constituted authority both in the religious establishment and in the political order.[40]

It is important also to note that this work draws a distinction between Islamists (or, in the popular parlance, radical Islamists) and Islamic liberals (sometimes also referred to as moderate Islamists or Islamic reformers). Unlike Islamists, Islamic reformers do not reject Western values out of hand; instead, they "espouse an indigenous response" and utilize an "indigenous vocabulary" to sanction democratic concepts of governance. Therefore, as Ray Takeyh noted, the reformers'

discourse gives democratic ideas the advantage of seeming novel and untarnished by the legacy of colonialism and failed secular rule. The reformers' doctrinal evolution brings their vision closer to Western ideas than they themselves would admit. The prominence of fringe groups in the media ought not to obscure the reality that Muslim reformers find themselves not repudiating the West, but selectively appropriating its benign ideals . . . The success of this enterprise can have profound implications as it bridges the gap between Western and Islamic political orders. In this context, the civilizations do not clash, but adapt and engage one another.[41]

This stands in opposition to the Islamist contention that Muslims need not look to the outside world, or to the ideologies or experiences of nonbelievers in the *dar al-harb* (the House of War, the non-Muslim civilizations) for inspiration. In fact, radical Islamists are critical of the Islamic reformers. Commenting on the reform movement, Dr. Mohammad Madadpur characterized the moderate Islamists as

> pursuing the Westernization of the society . . . What they want to negate is the guardianship of the religious jurisconsult . . . and defend secularization. They defend the separation of religion from politics . . . They want to separate the arena of religion from the public arena of the society.[42]

From the point of view of the Islamists, the moderates or liberals are confused; they are honest Muslims who are trying to reconcile Western ideology with Islam. Madapur said that "some of them are infidels in their minds but are faithful in their hearts. Many of the reformists have faithful hearts, but there has been disruption in their minds."[43]

Thus, although to some outside observers, radicals and moderates form one overall Islamist trend in the Middle East, radical or hardline Islamists reject any sort of compromise or admixture between Islam and Western values and institutions.

THE ISLAMIST OUTLOOK

Islamism sees itself as a complete and total social ideology, rooted in the Islamic experience. Although Islamist movements are, in some sense, rooted in the desire for a religious and spiritual revival, they are not primarily concerned with moral affairs but with politics. Islamism is first and foremost "an ideology, that is, a blueprint for political action."[44] It is not a reworking of a secular ideology in religious language, even if features or policy proposals resemble those found in other, secular systems (e.g. anti-imperialism). In fact, Islamists take as one of their first priorities the need to "disabuse the Muslim of the necessity of adopting one or the other of the two models projected by the First and Second Worlds . . . The Muslims are and should feel free to devise their own models for solving their problems."[45] This is an outgrowth of the Islamist view, first propounded by the Indian author Abu al-Hasan Ali al-Nadawi, that Western civilization must be considered both as *jahiliyya* (ignorant of the Divine precepts and thus violent and barbaric) and as *maddiyya* (materialistic), a view that was later echoed by Qutb and other Middle Eastern Islamists.[46] In fact, Qutb and his disciples equated all non-Islamist approaches to politics, economics, and ethics as polytheist—that is to say, pagan—in essence and orientation, and thus unacceptable as a basis for discussion or consideration.[47]

The fact that something (whether an idea or an institution) espoused by Islamists might have a counterpart in the non-Muslim world is irrelevant. Speaking about the institution of presidential elections in the Islamic

Republic of Iran, and asked to comment on the similarity of the election process in Iran with those of other states, Professor Hamid Mowlana pointed out the following:

> Presidential elections and campaigns today in many countries, including America, differ entirely from Islamic principles, world view, and customs . . . Within the framework of the Islamic system, presidential elections must be for service, not for power . . .[48]

Anwar Ibrahim, an Islamist spokesperson, summed it up bluntly: "We are not socialist, we are not capitalist, we are Islamic."[49] In other words,

> Islamism is the sum total of intellectual, economic, cultural, and political activities which spring from the comprehensive Islamic viewpoint, in order to support them in theory and apply them in practice in all spheres of life with the objective of establishing a new political and cultural entity.[50]

For the Islamist, "the Islamic Republic system is a religious and ideological regime."[51] The end goal of the Islamist is "to make the society Islamic."[52]

Islamism preaches the unity of *din* (religion) and *dawla* (the state, government), so that no distinction is to be drawn between religious and secular law, or between the citizen and the believer.[53] Islamist movements reject the division of social relations and affairs into those which are said to belong to the sphere of religion and that of mundane activities (or, in other words, secular or worldly matters). For Islamists, everything in society, from education to politics to economics, should be subjected to the "influence of the true faith."[54] Islamists strive to create an organic Islamic state and society.[55] This vision, in turn, is based on the concept of sharia (the path), the regulation not only of religious matters (*'ibadat*, the rules for worship and ritual) but also societal relations (*mu'amalat*). The end result of sharia (the *maqasid al-sharia*) is said to comprise social justice, equality, and everything considered to be in the interest and for the welfare of both the individual and the community as a whole.[56] Islamists believe that sharia is not intended simply to be an inspiration for legislators in a Muslim society, but that it itself should be "objectivated" into legislation.[57]

To maintain the harmonious interaction of religion and state, drawing upon the political philosophy of Mawdudi, state institutions, especially the legislature, must be made up of Muslim males "who are good Muslims and sufficiently Islamically trained to interpret and apply the sharia as well as to draft laws which are not contrary to the *Quran* and *Sunnah* of the Prophet."[58] In a fashion similar to Rousseau's concept of the general will, Islamists believe that if the state is staffed by virtuous and faithful Muslims who understand the tenets of the *Quran*, destructive conflicts in government can be avoided. This is in keeping with their view that, in the early days of Islam, "the Ministers and the Head of State were all along working in complete cooperation and harmony and the question of any-one resigning in protest never arose at all."[59] This follows from the assumption that, in a Muslim state, the ruler will be selected in accor-dance with two key qualifications:

In the first place, his own behavior must be, outwardly at any rate, in confor-mity with the law; that is to say, he must possess the quality of *'adala* or high moral probity. In the second place, he must have a specialist knowledge of the law, the ability to interpret it and apply it; in other words, the quality of *ijtihad*.[60]

Whether by community selection (the tendency found in Sunni Islamist thinking), or whether the government is to be guided by a supreme judge of the religious law (the jurisconsult, or *vilayat al-faqih*, a feature of Shiite Islamist thought), Islamists agree that a person's private religious life and his knowledge of Islamic law are critical points to consider in locating the personnel needed to create an Islamist state.

Properly staffed and structured, therefore, an Islamist government should be able to carry out a comprehensive program for the reorganiza-tion of socety. Article 3 of the Constitution of the Islamic Republic of Iran, in part, lays out some of the stated goals of an Islamist state, among which are the following:

1. The creation of a favorable environment for the growth of moral virtues based on faith and piety and the struggle against all forms of vice and corruption;
3. Free education and physical training for everyone at all levels, and the facilita-tion and expansion of higher education;
6. The elimination of all forms of despotism and autocracy and all attempts to monopolize power;
7. Ensuring political and social freedoms within the framework of the law;
8. The participation of the entire people in determining their political, economic, social, and cultural destiny;
9. The abolition of all forms of undesirable discrimination and the provision of equitable opportunities for all, in both the material and intellectual spheres;
12. The planning of a correct and just economic system, in accordance with Islamic criteria in order to create welfare, eliminate poverty, and abolish all forms of deprivation with respect to food, housing, work, health care, and the provision of social insurance for all;
15. The expansion and strengthening of Islamic brotherhood and public coopera-tion among all the people . . .[61]

Islamists claim that a society devoted to salvation will produce virtu-ous citizens willing to subordinate individual gain to the collective good and allow for the best people in society to emerge as rulers and gover-nors. Mawdudi maintained that, in a properly functioning Islamic society, the best man would naturally end up in political control of the state.[62]

Islamists claim that their ultimate goal is to create the system of *shura*, by which leaders would be in frequent contact with all members of society, would be obliged to inquire about their needs, solicit their input on policy, and be respectful of public opinion; however, they have provided few concrete details as to how this system would be maintained.

In matters of trade and commerce, Islamist thinkers have predicted only that "[they] will produce according to [their] capabilities and consume according to [their] virtue."[63] Even more detailed manifestoes have tended to focus on desired outcomes rather than chart practical policy measures that an Islamist state might undertake to reach those goals. One such document simply concludes that

In an Islamic society the government will guarantee the implementation of Islamic norms and regulations. For example, just as the government is bound to mobilize Muslims for *jihad*, it is also called to compel the citizens to guarantee the life of the needy. If the prosperous members of society do not wish to carry out their Islamic obligation as it concerns the fulfillment of their duties to their fellow members of society, then an Islamic government should utilize its own resources for the guaranteeing of this principle.[64]

Combating poverty, seeking to provide full employment, guaranteeing a basic social standard of living, promoting mutual aid and assistance among Muslims, focusing on internal development—all are worthwhile goals. However, without a clear understanding of what policies are or are not permissible to execute to achieve these goals, Islamist movements are left with vague pronouncements that may serve to mobilize the masses but that cannot effectively shape economic policy. Islamists stress that "Islam's way to social justice is the establishment of a brotherhood of believers" and that an Islamist system "does not prevent a man from acquiring or enjoying the just and lawful produce of his labor, but insists that what is earned be spent in a manner prescribed or approved by Allah,"[65] yet there are still no practical policy guidelines set forth to determine when a person has moved beyond the "just and lawful" produce of his labor, or how religious pronouncements can be translated into economic decisions.

This problem has become even more pronounced because the modern industrial economy raises issues that were never addressed or foreseen by the Prophet and the early leaders of Islam. Former Iranian president Hashemi Rafsanjani, in a recent interview, bluntly noted

With regard to economic issues, there was the issue, "What can the economic resources be?" One of the very serious issues was this very matter of banking . . . At the beginning of Islam banking in the form of international banking and financial relations with non-Muslim nations did not exist . . . These discussions were held in such a way that *if necessary they could be made to conform to Islam* [emphasis added]. Clinging to the dictum, "Muslims are held by their circumstances,"

which opens the way to the interpretation that suitable procedures should be promoted for the day for economic transactions and other affairs, was also widespread.[66]

This, then, is one of the major challenges facing Islamists: To what
extent, whether in economic matters or other practical policy areas, is it
legitimate to take existing non-Muslim institutions and practices and to
Islamify them in keeping with the ideological requirements of Islamism?[67]

The main problem with the Islamist outlook on society, in the end, is
that few practical details have ever been provided as to how the regenera-
tion of political and economic life will take place. They are to take place,
"simply, with a leap of faith."[68] The criterion often set forth for judging
whether a movement, party, or policy is truly Islamist is simply that of
righteousness.[69] Al-Banna indicates as much:

Our duty as Muslim Brothers is to work for the reform of selves [nufus], of
hearts and souls by joining them to God the all-high; then to organise our society
to be fit for the virtuous community which commands the good and forbids evil-
doing, then from the community will arise the good state.[70]

In commenting on the early Islamist thinkers, Esposito came to the following conclusion:

Early twentieth century Islamic activists . . . were pioneers, ideological vision-
aries rather than practicioners. Their writings on Islamic government and institutions tend to be sketchy, dealing more with general principles and ideals rather
than specific details.[71]

Such an assessment was also guardedly made by Rafsanjani, who
admitted,

I also said previously that when we say Islam has perfect effectiveness, we do
not mean that none of the existing religious decrees and expressions of opinion
that were made when [Islam] was isolated from the government and have not
been tried in the field of action are completely effective. Many of these views have
value in their own place . . . We now want to run a twenty-first century government . . . the conditions of the time are very different.[72]

This is especially problematic in attempting to deal with practical questions such as detailing how the political system will operate, what the
limits of dissent will be, or how power will be apportioned out, balanced,
and accounted for. Speaking to students in Alexandria in 1989, the Egyptian minister for religious endowments, Muhammad Ali Mahgub, made
the following statement:

There's a pretty slogan, "Islam is the Solution" [al-islam huwa al-hall, the campaign slogan of the Muslim Brotherhood] I say in all frankness: Yes, Islam is the
solution to all political, economic, and social problems. But it demands calm,

reflective planning, and is far from application until we have calmly, rationally ascertained the means we desire.[73]

Such issues have begun to surface more and more in discussions in Iran, ever since the elections of 1997 brought Muhammad Khatami to power. One Iranian scholar commented,

At this time, the mentioned topic abruptly showed itself acutely, and this question was raised: Where does the legitimacy of the Islamic Republic come from? Does it come from the people's vote or from religion? The consequences of [the election of 1997] are very important from a political philosophic point of view, because . . . the people actually showed that they do not always comply with the government's viewpoints. So what should be done in cases where the people's vote and choice are not in accordance with those of the government? Should the people's opinion be accepted or not? And where is the limit of the people's vote? The appearance of such questions was what turned the issue of the system's legitimacy and its source into the most important matter of political discussion among different intellectual and political camps . . .[74]

Islamism, like a number of medieval Christian political ideologies, assumes that rulers and government officials who are faithful adherents to true belief will, ipso facto, be honest, trustworthy, and reliable. Such an attitude was also reflected in the appeals made by the Islamic Revolution Devotees (isargaran) society, asking that the purity of the Islamic Revolution be preserved:

Therefore, should an effective and functional program be designed for this sacred crusade, the people would then become more hopeful and enthusiastic with regard to the country's management system, justice would replace discrimination, and corruption would be supplanted by honesty and soundness.[75]

Likewise, on the anniversary of the Islamic Revolution, an editorial in the Tehran newspaper Qods stated,

The people's Islamic revolution was aimed against administrative, economic, judicial, and executive corruption; they expect their officials not to rest for a minute before they have uprooted corruption from society.

The people of Iran are thirsty for justice. They consider the revolution, the Imam, and the leader to be the symbols of . . . justice. They expect their officials not to permit discrimination to slowly strangle their ideals. The quests for privileges, financial windfalls, and discrimination are the plagues of the Islamic Republic. A determined and relentless struggle against the ugly face of poverty, corruption, and discrimination in society would be a fitting reply from the heads of the three branches of government and the officials of the state to the greatness and generosity of this nation.[76]

However, as Esposito noted, Islamist thinkers, such as Mawdudi and others, do "not indicate how Muslims can safeguard against rulers who falsely use the banner of Islam to legitimate their rule, impose their will, and stifle dissent."[77] Islamist movements have not detailed how leaders, once in power, can be restrained from turning into tyrants or dictators.

ATTRACTIONS AND PITFALLS OF ISLAMISM

Radical Islam exploded on the global scene in the wake of the failures of other ideologies, such as nationalism or socialism, to solve profound social and economic ills in Muslim societies. Corruption, graft, and dictatorship, combined with external factors, such as Western economic and military intervention, or the Arab defeat in the 1967 Six-Day War, led many, disillusioned, to search for a new ideology—one rooted in religion.[78] All of this led to what is sometimes termed the "Islamic Awakening" (al-sahwa al-islamiyya). A. Nizar Hamzeh noted that

Islamic movements enjoyed tremendous growth due to crisis conditions that beset the region in recent years: Arab defeats by Israel, the failure to achieve balanced socioeconomic development, political oppression, gross maldistribution of wealth, and the disorienting impact of Westernization.[79]

Islamism was embraced by many as a viable "way of navigating the shoals of modernization."[80] It appealed to Muslim pride, as inheritors of a great past civilization that had, at one point, dominated much of the civilized world, and it suggested that Muslim societies could reenter the limelight of the global arena only by returning to those practices and methods that had marked Islamic lands during the first centuries of Islam.[81]

A key factor in the rise of Islamist movements has been the critique of the status quo that they provide. In its place, they have held forth as a solution the ancestral ways of the initial Islamic community under the Prophet. Reclaiming this mythical heritage, they maintained, would lead to the renewal of Islamic civilization. For the new disciples, the Quran alone offered all the solutions to properly guide modern societies. In Iran, for example, the Islamic Revolution Devotees maintain that that late Ayatollah Ruhollah Khomeini's position, drawn from his interpretation of the Quran, "are still today the subjective and practical guide for all the Muslims in the world . . . The correct and detailed recognition of the Iman's line could guide us through the complex and intricate labyrinths of government even today . . ."[82] Islamism has proven seductive to those on the margins of society, excluded from wealth and power, and the inequities in many Muslim societies have provided fertile fodder for Islamist agitation, especially when presented against an idealized picture of the first Islamic society based at Medina. Indeed, this desire to return to the purity of an earlier Islamic Golden Age has often proven to be one of the main ways in which Islamist movements recruit and gain members, who are disaffected with their current environment.[83]

By explicitly characterizing current governments and regimes as un-Islamic, therefore, Islamist groups maintain that there can be no long-term stability or any effective solutions to the region's social and economic ills until the Islamist alternative is embraced. Turabi makes this point plain:

An Islamic state cannot be isolated from society . . . In certain areas, progress towards an Islamic society may be frustrated by political suppression. Whenever religious energy is thus suppressed, it builds up and ultimately erupts either in isolated acts of struggle or resistance, which are called terrorist by those in power, or in a revolution. In circumstances where Islam is allowed free expression, social change takes place peacefully and gradually, and the Islamic movement develops programs of Islamization . . .[84]

Because of the corrupt and authoritarian nature of many Middle Eastern societies, as well as the post-Soviet republics of Central Asia and the Caucasus, Islamist movements, as John Esposito and John Voll have noted,

are more likely to emerge as the major opposition party when they are "the only game in town," that is, when they function in political environments in which they become the sole credible voice of opposition and thus attract the votes of those who simply wish to vote against the government or system, as well as the votes of their own members.[85]

Islamism often projects itself as an ideology of righteous and justifiable wrath, fulminating against the debilitating Western culture and the debased and acculturated local elites who have betrayed their heritage.[86] Dirk Vanderwalle has observed that the Islamist movement's "criticism of personal power, economic mismanagement, corruption, and moral laxity allowed it to become a symbol" and to become a focal point for opposition to the status quo.[87]

Islamist movements are characterized by their call to *jihad*, to struggle against evil, unrighteousness, and faithlessness. Islamists maintain that the call to fight against the enemies of Islam (whether by violence or by other means) must be answered by all pious and faithful Muslims. As long as corruption exists within the Muslim world and as long as forces external to the *Dar-al Islam* have a negative impact upon Islamic societies (whether through armed aggression, unequal terms of trade, promotion of secular liberalism, or foisting corrupt local elites to rule as their surrogates), it "becomes incumbent upon every individual Muslim to extinguish the fire with his own bucket . . . namely, to fight Jihad as a personally binding duty (*fard'ayn*)." Thus, by taking the right to struggle and fight away from existing authorities—those who maintain that individual Muslims have no need to engage in the fight as long as the Muslim community in general has discharged this obligation (*fardkifaya*)—Islamist movements can be very empowering to individuals dissatisfied with the status quo. Those who sacrifice themselves for the cause are justified as martyrs (*shuhada*) for a noble cause and for the sake of God Himself.[88] In fact, many Islamists agree with the sentiment expressed by Muhammad al-Farag in a pamphlet called *The Neglected Obligation*, in which Farag argued that jihad constituted a sixth pillar of Islam, and that "the first battlefield for jihad is the extermination of these infidel leaders and to replace them by a complete Islamic Order."[89]

Islamism thus has the capability to mobilize the disaffected, particularly the young, especially when there is a "lack of any convincing homegrown alternatives."[90] Indeed, an examination of the social bases of Islamist movements reveals that their greatest strength lies among students and members of the new middle classes—professionals, businessmen, and civil servants—in other words, people who by education and background are capable of analyzing the conditions of the societies in which they live, but who are not part of the ruling elite.[91]

Once political oppression or economic deprivation is added to the mix, Islamist movements have proven themselves quite capable of mobilizing mass action, protests, and armed insurrection. Whether in Iran, Egypt, Lebanon, or Tajikistan, Islamist parties have demonstrated that they can exert considerable influence over political developments, either in opposition (peaceful or armed) or by taking control of the political apparatus.[92]

However, the point that has often been overlooked is that Islamists often have misunderstood the demands of their constituents. The masses do not desire a return to the seventh century but rather political modernization and economic progress. In response to those who would postulate that religious fanaticism drives the political motivations of the masses of the Muslim world, Mehdi Mozaffari points out:

> People do not struggle for ideals or abstract notions. People struggle and accept sacrifices to obtain material advantages so as to be able to live in peace and prosperity. People want to see their lives progress and the future of their children assured.[93]

An ideology can only transform itself into a sustainable governing dogma if it can present a coherent and appealing policy platform. Interestingly enough, this was also the conclusion drawn by Rafsanjani:

> Unlike some people who say that they do not care whether Islamic government is effective or not, we believe that effectiveness is a serious matter. When our Koran and many of our religious sources deal with all aspects of individual and social life, why don't we talk about it? More important is the fact that if religious government is not effective, the people will not accept it. Does a human being want to follow any path other than that of his own happiness?[94]

The goal of this work is not to determine whether or not Islamism has had or will continue to have an impact as a movement capable of generating opposition to the status quo. That is not in dispute. Instead, the purpose is to examine whether Islamist movements have been capable of forging alternative political and economic institutions and policies capable of long-term survival. In essence, this book is taking up the challenge that Hashemi Rafsanjani laid out:

> My belief is that if the Islamic government is not successful in practice, we must determine if foreign and external factors have created obstacles, or if our understanding and our implementation have been bad. We must go back to our sources and study them again to see whether or not our understanding was bad. If a foreign element is not an obstacle and if we understand Islam correctly, and if at the same time the Islamic government is still not effective, then it is possible that the effectiveness of religion will be doubted, but I am confident that it will not reach that point.[95]

At the beginning of the twenty-first century, it is not clear that Islamism, however, has succeeded. In Egypt, militant Islamists opted for the formation of a vanguard party, which was to destabilize the state through sporadic acts of violence, and to prepare for the creation of an Islamic republic. Their efforts have met with failure. In Algeria, the Islamist challenge began with the formation of an Islamist party, but ended in an unspeakably vicious civil war. In Iran, a radicalized segment of the clergy came to power by harnessing religion and nationalism to mass discontent via a populist revolution, only to witness the disintegration of its mass base. In the end, they were forced to come to terms with the waves of economic globalization and political democratization sweeping the globe, including selective repression designed to keep intact the Islamist veneer of society. The triumph of the Taliban in Afghanistan, cited by some as proof of the vitality of Islamism, owes much more to the perpetual state of war Afghanistan has found itself in since 1979, as well as its use as a pawn and proxy battlefield during the Cold War, as it does to any sincere desire among most ordinary Afghanis for an Islamist society. Once faced with the hammer blows delivered by American airpower, it collapsed. Across Eastern Europe and the former Soviet Union, fears of a rising tide of militant Islam have receded as more moderate and secular forces have risen to the fore. As different as the Islamist experience has been in all these areas, in each case the reason for defeat or recession has been the same: Islamism has not succeeded in transforming itself from an ideology of revolution and opposition into a workable formula for running governments and economies. Islamism may continue to inspire malcontents and terrorists into committing destructive acts, but it cannot provide a viable template for the organization of society.

Islamist movements have either become fringe players in society, or are seeking, under more moderate leadership, to accommodate Western democratic and free-market ideologies—in essence, to promote pluralism within an Islamic context. Moderate or liberal Islamism may indeed have an important role to play in acting as midwife to the birth of democratic regimes in the Middle East—a subject that cannot be encompassed within the framework of this volume—but the very rise of Islamist-reform movements is testimony to the failure of Islamism to engineer radical change. Islamist movements are likely to have an impact only in those areas where, by moderating their demands and agreeing to work with secular parties, they can have some input in the overall direction of society.

This is an important point, especially at a time when gloomy assessments are being delivered about the likely triumph of radical Islamist movements in Africa and southeastern Asia. A decade ago, specialists were predicting that radical Islamism was on the ascendancy in the Middle East, the Balkans, and the former Soviet Union, citing many of the same trends. Those predictions came to naught. Why and how the Islamist wave crested in the Middle East, the former Soviet Union, and the Balkans—and the conclusions that can be drawn from this—will be examined in greater detail in the subsequent case studies presented in this work.

NOTES

1. Alexei V. Malashenko, "Islam versus Communism: The Experience of Coexistence," in *Russia's Muslim Frontiers: New Directions in Cross-Cultural Analysis*, ed. Dale F. Eickelman (Bloomington: Indiana University Press, 1993), 73.

2. "Symposium: Resurgent Islam in the Middle East," *Middle East Policy*, III:2 (1994), 9.

3. Samuel P. Huntington, "The West: Unique, Not Universal," *Foreign Affairs*, 75:6 (1996), 37.

4. Judith Miller, "Faces of Fundamentalism: Hassan al-Turabi and Muhammed Fadlallah," *Foreign Affairs*, 73:6 (1994), 127.

5. Statement of Richard Bulliet, quoted in Gregory Starrett, *Putting Islam to Work: Education, Politics, and Religious Transformation in Egypt* (Berkeley: University of California Press, 1998), 6.

6. Gerald Papy, "The American Boomerang," *La Libre Belgique*, August 11, 1998, 4.

7. "Symposium," 2. In the territories of the former Soviet Union, a similar confusion exists over the term "*Wahhabite*," which is often used to describe any Islamic political group that is in opposition to the state, but also used as an umbrella term to encompass Islamists. See A. A. Iarlykapov, *Problema Wahhabizma na Severnom Kavkaze* (Moscow: Russian Academy of Sciences, 2000), 3–4.

8. William R. Roff, "Islamic Movements: One or Many?" in *Islam and the Political Economy of Meaning*, ed. William R. Roff (Berkeley: University of California Press, 1987), 31.

9. Interview conducted by B. Turekhanova, and published in *Agenstvo Politicheskikh Issledovaniy* (Almaty), January 10, 2001.

10. Starrett, 90–91. In speaking about Egypt, he points out: "More people are praying, more people are reading about Islam and listening to its preachers, more

people are discovering consciously the salience of religious ideas and practices to their private and public lives, than did a generation ago." (91).

11. Quoted in Quintan Wikotrowicz, "State Power and the Regulation of Islam in Jordan," *Journal of Church and State*, 41:4 (1999), 678.

12. Dale F. Eickelman and James Piscatori, *Muslim Politics* (Princeton: Princeton University Press, 1996), 5.

13. Ibid., 4.

14. Ibid., 16.

15. Gorm Rye Olsen, "Islam: What Is Its Political Significance? The Cases of Egypt and Saudi Arabia," in *Islam: State, and Society*, eds. Klaus Ferdinand and Mehdi Mozaffari (London: Curzon Press, 1988), 127.

16. Mehdi Mozaffari, "Islam and Civil Society," in Ferdinand and Mozaffari, *Islam: State and Society*, 106.

17. Olsen, 129.

18. Starrett, 226.

19. The term used, *jahili*, also encompasses a sense that this ignorance is not simply a lack of knowledge, but a lack of enlightenment that creates conditions for violence, barbarism, and oppression. See Dale F. Eickelman, "Changing Interpretations of Islamic Movements," in Roff, *Islam and the Political Economy*, 14.

20. Ibid., 19–20.

21. Eickelman and Piscatori, 41–42.

22. The entire charter of *Hamas* can be found in English as translated and annotated by Raphael Israeli, "The Charter of Allah: The Platform of the Islamic Resistance Movement," in *The 1988–89 Annual of Terrorism*, ed. Y. Alexander (The Hague: Martinus Nijhoff, 1990), 99–134.

23. Ibid., 42.

24. Quoted in John Esposito, *Islam and Politics* (Syracuse, NY: Syracuse University Press, 1984), 136.

25. Ibid., 131–132.

26. Malashenko, 73.

27. Ibid., 74.

28. Esposito, *Politics*, 147.

29. Muhammad Qasim Zaman, *The Ulama in Contemporary Islam: Custodians of Change* (Princeton, NJ: Princeton University Press, 2002), 96.

30. James P. Piscatori, "Introduction," *Islam and the Political Process* (Cambridge, MA: Cambridge University Press, 1983), 9.

31. Quoted in John L. Esposito, *The Islamic Threat: Myth or Reality?* 2nd ed. (Oxford: Oxford University Press, 1992, 1995), 157–158.

32. Lawrence Davidson, *Islamic Fundamentalism* (Westport, CT: Greenwood Press, 1998), 105.

33. Quoted in Jonas Alwall, *Muslim Rights and Plights: The Religious Liberty Situation of a Minority in Sweden* (Lund: Lund University Press, 1998), 119.

34. Starrett, 63.

35. Alwall, 118.

36. Starrett, 63.

37. Ibid., 226.

38. Alwall, 118.

39. Starrett, 17.

40. Alwall, 117–118.

41. Ray Takeyh, "God's Will: Iranian Democracy and the Islamic Context," *Middle East Policy*, VII:4 (October 2000), 42, 43.

42. Khalil Esfandiari, "Reformists Seek a Religion That Does Not Interfere in Supervision and Policies," *Resalat*, August 28, 2000, 5.

43. Ibid.

44. Henry Munson, Jr., *Islam and Revolution in the Middle East* (New Haven, CT: Yale University Press, 1988), 37.

45. Khalid M. Ishaque, quoted in Davidson, 147.

46. Youssef M. Choueiri, *Islamic Fundamentalism*, rev. ed. (London: Pinter, 1990, 1997), 93.

47. Choueiri, 137.

48. Hamid Mowlana, "Tomorrow and the Next Four Years," *Keyhan*, June 7, 2001, 15–16.

49. "Symposium," 5.

50. Ray Takeyh, "Islamism: RIP," *National Interest*, Spring 2001, 97.

51. Ali Kosh Goftar, "Reactionism or Realism?" *Resalat*, March 17, 2001, 16.

52. Esfandiari, 5.

53. Iarlykapov, 7.

54. Alwall, 113.

55. Sami Zubaida, *Islam, the People and the State: Political Ideas and Movements in the Middle East* (London: I. B. Tauris, 1993), 33.

56. Alwall, 112.

57. Ibid., 110.

58. Esposito, *Politics*, 148.

59. Comments of Mawlanda Mawdudi, cited by Esposito, *Politics*, 147.

60. N. J. Coulson, "The State and the Individual in Islamic Law," *The Traditional Near East*, ed. J. Stewart-Robinson (Englewood Cliffs, NJ: Prentice-Hall, Inc., 1966), 123.

61. From the text as provided at http://www.SalamIran.org/IranInfo/State/Constitution/ .

62. Esposito, *Politics*, 146.

63. Takeyh, "Islamism," 98.

64. "A Short Exposition of the Tasks and Goals of an Islamic State," *Russia and the Muslim World*, 4(94) (2000), 115 [in Russian].

65. Quoting Ishaque, in Davidson, 153.

66. "Rafsanjani Assesses Islamic Government Two Decades After Revolution," *Hokumat-e Eslami*, Winter 2001, 25–73.

67. The reciprocal fear is that "Islamicization" of Western institutions will instead lead to the Westernization of Islamic institutions, a concern expressed by Hamid Mowlana, "Tomorrow and the Next."

68. Piscatori, 4.

69. "Journalism of the Islamic Revolution," *Abrar*, December 10, 2000, 6. In this article, Kazem Anbarlouie states: "The criteria for righteousness of an ideology and school of thought are clear and not an ambiguous manner . . . we consider the criterion stated in the [Iranian] constitution as righteous, if anyone deviates and separates from this path, then we consider that to be wrong."

70. Quoted in Zubaida, 33.

71. Esposito, *Politics*, 223.

72. "Rafsanjani Assesses," 25.

73. Quoted in Starrett, 185.

74. "Legitimacy in the Islamic Republic System," *Khorasan*, March 12, 2001.

75. "Islamic Revolution Devotees Society, on Eve of 22 Bahman: Enemy's Method Is Subversion from Within," *Resalat*, February 7, 2001.

76. "People's Loyalty and Sincerity and Our Response," *Qods*, February 11, 2001.

77. Ibid, 147.

78. Youssef Choueiri lists the stimuli for Islamist-radicalist movements as follows: (1) Consolidation of the Nation-State; (2) Marxism; (3) influx of rural migrants into towns and cities; (4) the oil boom; and (5) Israeli victories. See Choueiri, 181. John Esposito has identified several of the commonalities in the backgrounds of the major Islamist leaders in the Middle East, including: (1) A mix of a traditional and modern education; (2) youth participation in (secular) Arab nationalist movements; (3) disillusionment with the effectiveness of nationalism after the defeat in the Six-Day War (1967); (4) introduction to and acceptance of the ideological positions found in the writings of Qutb, al-Banna, and Mawdudi; (5) rejection of Western culture and values and a reassessment of the potential role of Islam in shaping a new social and political order. See Esposito, *Islamic Threat*, 154.

79. A. Nizar Hamzeh, "Islamism in Lebanon: A Guide," *Middle East Review of International Affairs*, 1(3) (1997), Internet version at http://www.biu.ac.il/SOC/besa/meria/journal/1997/issue3/jv1n3a2.html. Although Hamzeh's comments apply most directly to Lebanon, they are mirrored in the conditions in other parts of the world, especially the Middle East, where Islamist movements have found bases of support among the local populations and have taken root.

80. Quoted in Takeyh, "Islamism," 97.

81. Mohammad Madadpur maintains that Islamists, in combating Western values and globalization, "are trying to change these modern phenomena so that they would not destroy the essence of humanity and beliefs. Therefore, they are trying to create some sort of distance between themselves and the culture of the West." Esfandiari, 5.

82. "Islamic Revolution Devotees Society," 1.

83. Iarlykapov, 5.

84. Quoted in Davidson, 26.

85. John L. Esposito and John O. Voll, *Islam and Democracy* (Oxford: Oxford University Press, 1996), 196.

86. One of the Islamist texts circulating in the North Caucasus but obtained from Islamist sources in the Middle East, for example, describes Islam as a religion of "jihad and life," calling on all Muslims to be prepared to contribute their entire wealth and power to ensure the final victory of Islam. It declares that true Muslims are forbidden from believing in destructive doctrines, which include, among others, communism, Marxist socialism, secular democracy, a secular approach to life, and any sort of nationalist ideology that would deemphasize religion and assign equal rights to Muslim and non-Muslim citizens alike. It also condemns those who would seek to separate religion and politics, or maintain that religion is properly exercised in a private sphere apart from public life and policy,

proclaiming that such is a lie against the Quran, the Sunnah, and indeed the very life of the Prophet. See Iarlykapov, 6–7.

87. Quoted in Esposito, *Islamic Threat*, 161.

88. "The Charter of Allah: The Platform of the Islamic Resistance Movement," Alexander, *The 1988–89 Annual of Terrorism*. See also Raphael Israeli, "State and Religion in the Emerging Palestinian Entity," *Journal of Church and State*, 44:2 (Spring 2002).

89. Esposito, *Islamic Threat*, 96–97.

90. Miller, 125.

91. Munson, 95–104.

92. One of the lasting failures of American foreign policy has been the inability of most practicioners to grasp the ways in which a religiously based movement can transform itself into a political force. This was the damning conclusion drawn by the report prepared by Dr. Robert Jervis of Columbia University ("Iran: Post-mortem") for the Central Intelligence Agency in analyzing why the U.S. government was caught unawares by the rise of Khomeini. Americans focused so much attention on liberal nationalists and Soviet-backed Communist forces because, in part, they accepted a view of Islam as a traditional faith that could not be made relevant to modern life and thus provide a vehicle for expressing opposition to the Shah's regime. They also discounted the fact that religion could be used to mobilize a population in support of overtly political goals. See Bob Woodward, *Veil: The Secret Wars of the CIA, 1981–1987* (New York: Pocket Books, 1988), 106–109.

93. Mozaffari, 112.

94. "Rafsanjani Assesses," 25.

95. Ibid.

Chapter 2

Iran: The Islamist State and the Reformist Agenda

It is appropriate to begin this study of radical political Islam with an examination of Iran because "the Islamic Revolution is a most appropriate example of the very high degree of politicization of Islam."[1] Today, Iran is a society fully immersed in a dynamic debate regarding the essence of the Islamic Republic. Twenty-five years after the momentous 1979 revolution, a large segment of Iran's populace has grown weary with the failed economic policies and trite political slogans of the regime. As with many other places in the Islamic world, a combination of secular leaders and progressive Islamists are seeking to revamp the political order and introduce accountability and representation to a system struggling with mass disillusionment. For better or worse, Iran is likely to emerge as one of the most significant laboratories for the harmonization of democratic representative government with Islamic imperatives. As Iran's President Muhammad Khatami has observed,

A young and educated society, informed of its rights, and aware of the culture of the Islamic revolution, in an age of rapid changes in science and communications, cannot accept authoritarian, bureaucratic, and discriminatory relations within the realm of government. The people are informed and responsible citizens with rights. They welcome policies and programmes based on attention to individual and social rights, freedom and lawfulness, general respect for the constitution and a civil society, the recognition of the people's rights and opinions in all areas, as well as justice and an end to discrimination at all levels.[2]

An earlier version of this chapter appeared in the *Middle East Journal* (Winter 2003).

At first glance, one can argue that Iran's dynamic attempt to usher in an Islamic democracy has proven illusory and a failure. Over the past seven years, the inability of the reform movement led by Khatami to overcome Iran's systematic hurdles to genuine democratization has frustrated an impatient electorate and generally sullied the Cinderella story of a changing Iran. The conventional wisdom has once more relegated Iranian politics to an intractable stalemate, and the recurrent Washington parlor game of predicting Iran's next revolution has resumed again in earnest. In this context, Khatami's repeated electoral triumphs and the takeover of the parliament and municipal councils by reformers is greeted with skepticism if not resignation. Real reform—it is said—remains as suppressed as Khatami's supporters behind bars.

The pervasive skepticism misses the gradual shifts in Iran's political bedrock that have taken place since the first reformist breakthrough seven years ago—subtle but fundamental changes in the structure of authority and the fabric of society. Although overshadowed by the reform movement's sensational setbacks and overlooked by jaded observers, these incremental enhancements of Iran's republican infrastructure have established the foundation for more progress. Despite the repressive tactics of the militant right, the reform movement has succeeded in empowering the average Iranian and making the citizenry an important arbiter of regime's legitimacy. Iran's restive youth and hard-pressed middle class simply refused to be relegated to the margins of the society by passively obeying the dictates of the clerical estate. It is this reality that has realigned Iran's politics and caused important shifts in both the reform and conservative blocs. As a result, the theocracy is once again defying expectations as important elements in its factions are moving uneasily and haltingly toward a new national governing compact. The Islamic Republic may yet prove a model for religious reformers in the Middle East.

REVOLUTION AND REFORM

The Islamic Republic of Iran is a regime of contradictions and paradoxes. After all, Khomeini, a master tactician, had joined a coalition of liberal intellectuals, traditional clerics, Marxist guerrillas, and members of the merchant class to his clerical base to successfully overthrow the Pahlavi dynasty. Indeed, the success of the 1979 revolution lay in "Khomeini's extraordinary ability to unify the various components—religious and secular—of a movement whose single point of departure was hatred of the shah and his government."[3] The original revolutionaries sought to usher in a virtuous order whereby temporal affairs would conform to divine mandates. Along this path, unelected institutions, such as the Supreme Leader (*vali-ye-faqih*), were created and invested with the power to abrogate election results and select the heads of the armed forces, the judiciary, and the Revolutionary Guards. The dominance of the clerical estate over national affairs was further strengthened by the creation of the Guardian Council (*shura-ye negahban*), yet another clerical dominated body responsive to the Spiritual Leader that was empowered to screen all candidates for public office and scrutinize parliamentary legislation to make certain that they were compatible with religious strictures. However, the Islamic Republic was not a standard authoritarian regime because the public that had overthrown the formidable monarchy could not be categorically excluded from the deliberations of the state. As such, the populace was given the right to elect important institutions such as the presidency, parliament, and local councils. Despite the impressive array of powers granted to the clerical oligarchy, Iran's revolutionaries created a governing arrangement whereby the collective will of the people would remain an important source of legitimacy. As Iran's clerics were to discover, institutional power devoid of popular legitimacy cannot be sustained over a prolonged period of time. For the theocracy to properly function, indeed survive, it had to find a balance between divine authority and popular representation.[4]

During the first two decades of the revolution, the unchallenged authority and charisma of Ayatollah Ruhollah Khomeini obscured the regime's contradictions. Iran's contending political factions readily acquiesced to Khomeini's fiat while the elections were an occasion for the public to endorse the Grand Ayatollah's choices and candidates. This system could function as long as the absolute majority of the population was reasonably devout and accepted Khomeini's interpretation of Islamic doctrine. Indeed, Khomeini believed that democracy and Islamism could be reconciled because right-thinking Muslims would embrace a common vision (*vahdet-e kalimah* or "oneness of discourse"). In essence, the traditional divisions within the clerical community and the democratic pretensions of the constitution remained largely dormant because Khomeini neither tolerated dissent nor honored the constitutional pledge of political freedom. Yet, as revolutionary excess and rigid dogma became the pillars of Iranian politics, the bond between the regime and the populace began to gradually erode.[5]

In the late 1980s, two events conspired to alter the dynamics and nature of Iran's polity. First, the long war with Iraq ended in 1988, and the ceasefire that followed revitalized public's political consciousness in anticipation of some tangible reward for its profound and protracted suffering. Then, less then a year later came the passing of Ayatollah Khomeini, who had founded the state and dominated its tumultuous factional politics and deep-seated contradictions. Khomeini's death eroded the fragile consensus underlying Iran's system and deprived the clerical establishment of both its charismatic leader and its institutional coherence. These two developments instigated a struggle for predominance among the ruling clerics along with unprecedented public pressure for government performance. Over the course of the next decade, simmering on the street and revisionism within ranks nurtured a new political movement in Iran.[6]

Revolutions must ultimately be judged by whether they translate their promises into achievements. Among other things, Iran's theocrats pledged to bring sustained economic benefits to the impoverished and an overburdened middle class. Yet, after two decades of clerical misrule, Iran's economy has been plagued by a bloated state sector, resource mismanagement, rampant corruption, and excessive dependence on a volatile petroleum market. Iran must now cope with the ramifications brought on by a 40 percent inflation rate and a 20 percent unemployment rate. All these problems are compounded by demographic pressure because the regime is unable to provide employment for a majority of the 800,000 graduates that annually enter the job market. And, despite its religious pretensions, the post-revolutionary state embraces a socialist approach to economic planning and remains devoted to the elimination of capitalist exploitation. The Islamic Republic's political system has been equally unresponsive to the demands of its constituents. Hard-line clerics have withdrawn earlier pledges to create a pluralistic order and have constructed instead an autocratic regime.[7]

Not unlike the revolution that it began to critique, the reform movement took shape in universities, seminaries, literary groups, and professional associations. An evolving group of intellectuals, thinkers, and political activists began to coalesce to discuss ways of broadening political representation within the context of Islamic governance. Their outlook was informed by history—by their participation as students in revolution and their service in the Islamic government—and by their position on the periphery of political viability under the increasingly domineering administration of then-President Akbar Hashemi Rafsanjani.[8]

Foremost among the first wave of new thinkers was Abdol Karim Soroush, a Tehran University professor whose early training in Islamic jurisprudence enabled him to fashion a compelling exegesis into the doctrinal basis for the Iranian regime. Through articles in the intellectual journal *Kian* and lectures across the country, Soroush became one of Iran's most significant public thinkers and one of the Islamic Republic's most persistent critics. Soroush contend that the Islamic regime's adherence to rigid dogma had estranged an entire generation of Iranians from both the regime and religion. The key to revitalization of Islam and the theocracy was to reinterpret the sacred texts along progressive lines. After all, for Soroush, religious interpretation was not "sacred and therefore can be criticized, modified, refined, and redefined."[9] In rejecting the sanctification of interpretation, Soroush's ideas contradicted the prevailing orthodoxy of the clerical rule.[10]

The innovative dimension of Soroush's thoughts was his use of Islam's own precepts to promote participatory rule. In the hands of Soroush, religious texts and Islamic jurisprudence were means of ensuring individual sovereignty, government accountability, and the rule of law. Through such a progressive re-conceptualization of Islam, Soroush envisioned a political order that was to reconcile religious doctrine and pluralistic precepts. As Soroush noted, "To be a religious man necessitates being a democratic man as well. An ideal religious society cannot have anything but a democratic government."[11] Although cloaked in the vocabulary of the intelligentsia, Soroush's writings represented an unmistakable challenge to the authority of the Spiritual Leader, which secured him the enthusiastic approbation of disaffected students as well as threats and attacks.

The early evolution of the reform movement transcended the musing of university professors and was shaped by the inclusion of religious thinkers alongside lay intellectuals like Soroush and other long-time political activists. From the outset, Iran's seminaries harbored a cadre of clerics who were uneasy about the direction of the revolution and the growing estrangement of the populace from the religious establishment. A younger generation of clerics—many of whom were linked to Ayatollah Ali Montazeri, who was ousted in 1987 as Khomeini's heir apparent—sought to interpret Islam in a manner that accommodated popular sovereignty and democratic representation. Hojjat-ol-eslam Mohsen Khadivar, a leading voice of Islamic reformation, captured this sentiment by stressing, "I believe democracy and Islam are compatible. But a religious state is possible only when it is elected and governed by people. And the governing of the country should not be necessarily in the hands of the clergy."[12]

The collaboration of the clerics and intellectuals fused disparate interests within a broad-based movement articulating democratic demands in a language of a familiar faith—yet another parallel with the mobilization leading up the 1979 revolution. However, contemporary developments demonstrated the increasing political sophistication of Iran's population. Thanks largely to the rhetoric of the Islamic regime and the rivalries within it, the children of the revolution had come to perceive themselves as agents of change as opposed to passive pawns in the Kingdom of God. In political terms, this translated into an insistence that the public serve as the ultimate arbiter of proper governance and that collective will provides the primary source of legitimacy. Advocacy of this imperative that—through participation in elections and public affairs, Iranians could and should shape the ideals and direction of the state—emerged as the central principle of the reform movement. The popular appetite for change served as a propitious platform for the ruminations of the reformers and ensured that—unlike previous points in Iran's long and troubled political development—the intellectual impulse toward democracy would find fertile ground to germinate.[13]

Into this charged arena stepped Hojjat-ol-eslam Seyyed Muhammad Khatami, a mid-level cleric with impeccable revolutionary credentials who was recruited to stand in the 1997 presidential elections in token opposition to the establishment candidate. Despite his inclusion in that same clerical establishment, Khatami had long distinguished himself from it, both in his politics and his intellectual enterprises. At the then-pinnacle of his political career, the future president broke with the Rafsan-jani administration over his liberal tendencies as Minister of Culture and proceeded to immerse himself in Western philosophy as a complement to his Islamic training. In his subsequent writings, Khatami dared to contra-vene the ruling consensus by declaring that "(s)tate authority cannot be attained through coercion and dictatorship. Rather, it is to be realized through governing according to the law, respecting the rights and empowering people to participate, and ensuring their involvement in decision making."[14] In his campaign speeches, Khatami challenged the absolutism of the system by prioritizing the rule of law, the pursuit of jus-tice, and the strengthening of civil society.[15] Under the rubric of religious democracy, the reformers sought to blend what they felt were the positive attributes of the Islamic Republic—a system grounded in Islamic values that provided guidelines for the operation of state and society—with a responsiveness to the popular will. In essence, they defined this blend in the following propositions:

1. The private affairs of citizens is outside the realm of government's authority and prerogative;
2. Political pluralism with diversity of parties and views should be permitted;
3. The religious basis of society is based on free acceptance of all that religion belongs in public sphere;
4. The domain of politics is not sanctified.[16]

Ali Reza Alavi Tabar, another reformer, further clarified how a religious democracy could at the same time remain faithful to basic Islamic princi-ples yet be flexible enough to tolerate different opinions and interpreta-tions. He noted,

In a religious community, if it is ruled by a democratic system, people would want religion to be present in the public domain as well and would also want it to affect the policies adopted in this domain.

It is clear, even if the majority of the community remained religious forever, we would still not have a static society because the boundary between private and public [aspects of human life] would be changing incessantly. What is considered public today might be deemed private tomorrow. The length and breadth of pri-vate and public domains are determined by custom, social norms, and tradition. On the other hand, the possibility of development in religious knowledge and scholarship provides for social laws and regulations to undergo alterations and improvement in the process of debates, dialogue, and critiques, and be replaced with other laws. . .

Obviously, the political leaders have no right to impose their own particular reading and version of religion on the community and change religious unity to mean religious single-mindedness. In a religious democracy, even the civil institutions and non-government organizations are composed of persons and trends which are to a large extent faithful to the religious beliefs of the community and try to lead a pious life in the domain of their activities. Civil institutions affiliated to non-religious and secular trends too must naturally be allowed to flourish and enjoy legal freedom and even be given the chance to vie with religious civil institutions.[17]

This expansive vision of a newly tolerant Islamic government won the hearts and minds of the Iranian public. It also won Khatami a stunning upset over the conservative candidate whose victory had been all but assured. With a whopping 69 percent of the vote, Khatami catapulted the reform movement from theory to action, from contemplation and critique to accountability and implementation. In this sense, their initial triumph generated a new trial for the reformers—and an enormous one at that—to circumnavigate the treacherous waters of Iranian politics and institutionalize their ideas. This would prove a more difficult and cumbersome task by pitting against each other the competing factions of Iran's body politic.[18]

REFORM'S REAL TRACK RECORD

Prior to 1997, theoreticians of reform had invested considerable time and energy in mapping out a strategy for slowly reclaiming their influence over the course of the Islamic Republic. However, their real challenge began only after their unexpected capture of the nation's highest elected office. Having derailed the conservative drive to fully dominate Iran's tumultuous factional politics, Khatami and his allies faced determined adversaries who rallied their considerable resources to forestall further incursions to the structure of power.

Once in power, the reformers opted for a strategy of incrementalism by seeking to gradually reform the Islamic Republic from within its own institutions. Through a binary approach, under the catchphrase of "pressure from below, negotiations from the top," they sought to respond to burgeoning public demands for greater freedom in the context of the political circumstances that had brought the possibility of meaningful change.[19]

With a short window of opportunity, the new president selectively picked his battles and sought to avoid open clashes with the conservatives. To turn up the heat "from below," hundreds of new publications were licensed, censorship guidance loosened, and permits for reformist groups and gatherings were issued. Meanwhile, under the banner of gradualism, the reformers refrained from defying the wide jurisdiction accorded to the Supreme Leader, territory that his hard-line allies guarded jealously. Instead, the reformers focused on expanding their institutional power base by taking full advantage of the opportunities accorded by provisions of limited democracy under the Islamic constitution to bring the political competition into the public arena.[20]

In its initial phase, the strategy of gradualism garnered impressive accomplishments. The reformers persisted electoral triumphs allowed them to take over key segments of Iran's body politic. Iran's democratic infrastructure was broadened in 1998 when it held elections for the local councils that were called for in the constitution but never held. Suddenly, the number of elected officials in Iran went from 400 to a massive 200,000 with the overwhelming majority of those posts being held by politicians sympathetic to the proposition that the public is the ultimate determinant of state policy. In February 2000, the reformers triumphed in the parliamentary plebiscite and reclaimed an institution that had long served as the bastion of the conservative power. At this point, reform held sway throughout the provincial administrations, newly inaugurated municipal councils, and the parliament. The reformers capitalized on their institutional gains by developing protean political parties as a means of mobilizing their mass constituency. The reformers' capacity for securing this influence is in and of itself a meaningful achievement; it demonstrates that they can overcome the sustained opposition from conservatives with overriding authority.[21]

The reformist ascendancy in the institutions of the Islamic Republic soon produced a number of tangible victories. The most important among these is the reaffirmation of the parliament's prerogatives to scrutinize organizations under the Supreme Leader's jurisdiction. This has empowered the elected representatives of the people to supervise previously unaccountable institutions such as the Ministry of Intelligence, the state broadcasting authority, semi-governmental economic foundations, and even over the armed forces—extending Iran's heretofore-limited popular sovereignty. Under its reformist majority, the parliament has taken up this investigatory license with a vengeance by probing into issues that range from the security organization's behavior to the prospect of relations with the United States. In this respect, the MPs have appropriately taken up the mantle of challenging the system first forged by the enterprising reformist newspapers.[22]

Despite its accomplishments, Khatami's strategy of incremental reforms did not lead to the anticipated democratic breakthrough. Once the reform movement sought to revise the critical demarcations of power, the hard-liners counter-reaction was not long in coming. The essential conservative strategy for retaining the upper hand soon crystallized—the targeting of individual reform leaders, the selective use of violence to intimate and create divisions, and the central role of the judiciary—along with the Guardian Council—in blocking genuine reform. Each time that the reformers' inventive circumnavigations of the system managed to gain even the most ambiguous advantage, they were more than out-gunned by the concerted hard-line response, particularly in the courts. Through cynical use of their institutional powers, the conservatives shut-tered hundreds of publications, impeached, and imprisoned many reformist intellectuals, journalists, and officials and brutally suppressed the peaceful student gatherings. At the end, a militant faction of the cleri-cal community with impressive reigns of power in its hands simply refused to countenance a challenge to its anachronistic vision of theoc-racy.[23]

Despite the concerted conservative backlash, Iran's reform movement has not ended but instead entered a new and more aggressive phase. Dur-ing the past decade, the Latin American and Eastern European demo-cratic transitions reveal that, as democratic movements evolve, they inevitably alter their strategies. Iran's reform movement is undergoing a similar trajectory, which is leading to emergence of a younger generation of leaders who are pressing for more immediate results. Among the rising starts of the more robust reform movement are parliamentarians such as the president's own brother, Mohammad Reza Khatami, dissident clerics such as Mohsen Khadivar, and student leaders led by Ali Afshari and Akbar Mohammadi. These reformers are gradually moving away from the strategy of incremental change and opting for a more assertive policy of disengagement and confrontation. Along this line, reform parliamen-tarians and politicians are threatening to leave the government, which thus in essence de-legitimizes an Islamic Republic whose survival requires a degree of popular consent. In the mean time, student organiza-tions are intensifying their defiance of the theocracy's prohibitions and are increasingly moving to active street protest. The objectives of the reform movement remain constant—namely by conceiving a polity that harmonizes religious injunctions with democratic imperatives. However, the tactic employed to achieve this aim is altering. Instead of changing the system from within, the reformers are seeking to pressure it from out-side.[24]

The new reform strategy crystallized during the parliamentary contest of February 2004, when the Council of the Guardians eliminated the vast majority of the reformist candidates. Iran's largest reformist party, the Islamic Participation Front, quickly boycotted the elections, while the reformists viewed the conservatives' latest move as a simple and brutal coup. After years of struggling within the reqime, the reformists are now plotting their strategy outside the realm of conventional politics. Ebrahim Yazdi, one of Iran's most prominent dissidents, pointedly declared, "We are approaching a turning point. Basically, down deep, there is confrontation between tradition and modernity."[25] In the mean time, Iran's universities have noticed a considerable degree of unrest with student demonstrations calling for rapid change.

In defiance of government bans, student associations such as the Office for Consolidation of Unity and Union of Islamic Students have emerged as a vanguard of the newly emboldened reform movement. A protesting student captured the spirit of the new partisans of change when declaring, "We aren't afraid. They can't frighten us."[26] Instead of the now-banned newspapers, the Internet has emerged as a potent weapon of information and organization. Many Iranian journalists are busy establishing Internet sites, as the dot.com revolution is subverting the strictures of the theocratic regime. "Technology always wins, and, therefore, the closure of reformists' newspapers is unimportant when there is the Internet," declared one of Iran's enterprising journalists.[27] The conservatives' obstruction of evolutionary change and Khatami's strategy of cohabitation has led to rise of an even more determined reform movement, whose leaders are not just impatient but capable of confronting the Islamic republic with a pronounced challenge to its legitimacy and viability.

The reform movement launched seven years ago has not realized the totality of its ambitious aims. However, to pronounce the end of the reform movement is to neglect the manner that Ian's political culture and national discourse have altered in the recent years. Through a series of stepping-stone reforms and the unshakable—if often unsuccessful—advocacy of a greater freedom for Iran's citizens and greater accountability from its government, the past five years have provided the basis that is essential to facilitating Iran's transition to genuine democracy. As the reform movement alters its tactics, it is beginning to cause a shift in the conservatives' perspective. An important segment of the conservative faction is beginning to appreciate that their long-term relevance is contingent on their reengagement of Iran's youth and commitment to creation of a tolerant society. Indeed, the potential changes within the right could finally lead Iran's fractious political wings to transcend the prevailing impasse and create a new national governing compact.

A CIVIL WAR IN THE RIGHT

The new reform movement's strategy of disengagement and confrontation is not just making an imprint on Iran's politics, but it has triggered an important debate within the conservative camp. Seldom has a political movement been as poorly understood as the Iranian right. Although often presented as an undifferentiated group of reactionaries, Iran's conservative front is in fact hardly monolithic, and its natural divisions have widened by the unexpected popular mantle of the reform movement. As the fragile compact fastening Iran's fractious ruling coalition deteriorates, an influential segment of the right is beginning to call for a pragmatic adjustment of the conservative doctrine as a means of preserving its influence and the framework of Islamic governance. Confronted with an emboldened reform movement, there will be further defections from the uncompromising position of the militant right.[28]

In the past few years, the most conspicuous faction of Iran's right has been its militant wing, whose command of powerful institutions has allowed it inordinate influence over national affairs. Although it pays ostentatious fealty to Khamenei, the true leaders of this faction are the radical clerics such as Ayatollah Ahmad Jannati (head of the Guardian Council) and Ayatollah Mohammad Yazdi (former chief of the judiciary). At the outset, these hard-liners uneasily tolerated the reform movement because it had not infringed on the fundamentals of their power and the lucrative, commercial dominance that subsidizes their belligerence. This radical cohort is categorically contemptuous of democratic rule and openly acclaims the virtues of despotism. Hamid Reza Taraqi of the Islamic Coalition Society captures their totalitarian sentiments when he proclaimed, "Legitimacy of our Islamic establishment is derived from God. This legitimacy will not wash away even if people stop supporting it."[29] In an even more defiant note, another stalwart of the right, Hojjat-ol-Islam Moslemin Ghavarian declares, "In my view, a despotism which is rationale must be accepted. Genuine despotism means obeying divine decree."[30] Despite their manifest popular defects, the radical conservatives remain committed to their interpretation of Islam and view themselves as the only legitimate heirs of Khomeini.

The shrill rhetoric of the militants cannot be discounted given their power base, which primarily comprises a vast financial network of legal and semi-legal enterprises and a dedicated group of supporters in the Revolutionary Guards and the organized vigilantes, Ansar-e Hezbollah. Ayatollah Yazdi readily provided a theological justification for an assault on the reformers by stressing, "According to Koranic interpretation, these people who claim to be reformers are true examples of corrupters on Earth."[31] This core group of militants will remain defiant and will not shrink from violence as a means of sustaining its power. In a recent statement, the Revolutionary Guard leadership warned the reformers that "they have exceeded all bounds by openly supporting subversion on the streets."[32] Ansar-e Hezbollah, the appellation for a loosely organized confederacy of thugs deployed by the hard-liners, has predictably gone further by declaring, "This will be the decade of settling scores with the seditionists by the friends of the Revolution."[33] Khomeini's militant disciples refuse to countenance a challenge to their vision of theocracy, and they have little hesitation about utilizing terror as a means of imposing their ideology.

Despite the bellicosity of this faction, its strength should not be exaggerated, as the instruments of repression at its command may not prove reliable. As with most institutions in Iran, the security services have fractured along demographic lines. While most high-ranking officers of the Revolutionary Guards remain loyal to the conservatives, the reliability of the junior officers and enlisted men remains in serious question. In the last presidential election, 70 percent of the rank and file members of the Guards voted for Khatami, and internal polling revealed that 80 percent of the Guards support the reformers while only 9 percent endorsed the conservatives.[34] Although the hard-liners have the capability to suppress occasional student demonstrations and orchestrate selective violence, they do not command the strategic depth sufficient for suppressing a defiant reform movement over a prolonged period of time. Their awareness of their limitation serves as a powerful, unspoken restrain on conservatives' militancy; they can, in fact, be defeated by a more tenacious and defiant reform movement.

The conservatives' consciousness that coercion is ultimately unsustainable has generated a subtle—but still relevant philosophical awakening—within their ranks with influential members of this faction highlighting the necessity of revamping the conservative ideology and becoming electorally relevant once more. The voices of conservative pragmatism can be heard in many right-wing newspapers, particularly *Entekhab*, which enjoys the tacit endorsement of the Ayatollah Khamenei. For the pragmatists, the modernization of the conservative thought is not only necessary for the revitalization of the right as a political force but as a means of preserving the state from degenerating into civil discord. Taha Hashemi, the editor of *Entekhab* and a close advisor of Khamenei, outlines the contours of the pragmatic right by claiming, "The new religious thinking goes beyond encounters with individuals, and we believe that fundamental and ideological outlooks must be reformed."[35] Given the right's declining electoral prospects, another conservative thinker, Amir Mohebian warned that, "If we insist on preserving our past policies and ignore popular support, our faction will become like a sect."[36] The conservative daily *Siyasset-e Ruz* argued that the task at hand is to "start fundamental reforms in order to make ourselves more attractive to the people."[37] The pragmatists are not inclined to accept the totality of the reformist agenda but instead seek areas of cooperation. Unlike their militant allies, these pragmatists are willing to countenance a relaxation of certain cultural and social restraints imposed on the youth. In essence, the pragmatists acknowledge the need for compromise as a means of fostering a consensus behind a broad national accord that would respond to the aspirations of Iran's frustrated youth while sustaining the Islamic structure of the state. For Hashemi and his fellow pragmatists, adjusting to the popular will is necessary for the "survival of the revolution."[38]

In the midst of this melodrama stands the Spiritual Leader Ayatollah Ali Khamenei, whose influence can still have a material impact on the intra-conservative dispute. Despite the impressive array of powers at his disposal, Khamenei appears to recognize that, for the Islamic Republic to sustain its legitimacy, it cannot categorically defy the collective will. Despite popular characterization of Khamenei as harsh and unyielding, he is better understood as an indecisive politician whose limited stature in Iran's religious hierarchy left him highly vulnerable to challenge as the successor to the incomparable Khomeini. Although temperamentally conservative and prone toward a rigid definition of Islam, Khamenei has episodically restrained the militants—primarily in order to defend the institutions of Iran's embattled theocracy. He has countenanced the evisceration of Iran's briefly liberalized media and the merciless crackdown on those who flout is social strictures, but he has also imposed compromise rather than risk a massive confrontation. Ultimately, Iran's supreme leader ascended to his post as a political survivor rather than an ideologue, and his recent remarks have demonstrated a degree of pragmatism. In recent months, Khamenei has tentatively signaled his approbation of the conservative pragmatists, as he confessed, "The main characteristic of the new though is its ability to regenerate itself, bring itself up-to-date with the changing needs and circumstances and provide political and social resolutions for contemporary society."[39] The reality remains that the Spiritual Leader and his cohort are now confronting a different reform movement and face the daunting task of ruling over an angry, disillusioned, organized opposition movement with popular leaders and well-delineated objectives. In a sign of times, Khamenei acknowledged this reality when noting, "When we speak of the Islamic Republic, we cannot possibly ignore the role of the people."[40]

The ongoing impasse of Iranian politics increasingly elevates violence as an arbiter of change. Even if the Spiritual Leader were to take a decisive stance for moderation—itself an improbable development given the Islamic leadership's predilection for veiling its policy shifts in ambiguity—he is unlikely to be respected by the hard-liners who maintain their own system of patronage and militias. Although the radical clerics have invested their fortune in Khamenei, they have always been skeptical of his resolution in times of crisis. Given the increasing tensions and accumulated grievances, even the Spiritual Leader may not be able to temper Iran's drift to civil disorder. Although the militants' narrow base of support and the defections from the right makes the triumph of the popular will inevitable, it still may not spare Iran a degree of disorder and even violence. The civil war within the right will inevitably be won by the pragmatic conservatives, and the Islamic Republic will evolve into a more responsive polity but only after this hapless nation undergoes further trials and tribulations.[41]

THE NEW IRAN?

Iran today is a nation in search of an identity, a state that oscillates between promises of democratic modernity and retrogressive tradition. The one enduring legacy of Khatami and his electoral triumphs is to make it impossible for Iran to return to the pre-1997 situation. The call for representation and the rule of law, accountability, and equality have transformed the average Iranian from a passive observer of clerical politics into an active agent of change. The power of the reform movement stems from the diversity of social classes pressing for a new governing template. This is a movement that encompasses clerical reformers, disillusioned youth, burdened middle class, women seeking emancipation, and intellectuals yearning for freedom of thought. Despite the ominous shadow of violence, the old order will change. The transformation of the society cannot be obstructed through coercion or appeased by cosmetic reform. As Iran's foremost jailed journalist Akbar Ganji noted, "The genies are out of the bottles. And the bottles that once contained them are cracked."

Iran's reform movement began in the late 1980s in intellectual and clerical circles by those seeking to transform the theocracy into a polity that was both politically representative and culturally sensitive. The original architects of the reform movement, men such as Abdollah Nuri, Mohsen Khadivar, and Muhammad Reza Khatami and the current cast of student leaders will eventually prevail and finally construct a state that harmonizes Islamic precepts with republican ideals. The tragedy of Iran's polarized politics is that a period of social tumult may precede the arrival of the new dawn in Iran's modern history.

NOTES

1. Muso, Dinorshoyev. Interview by B. Turekhanova. *Agenstvo Politicheskikh Issledovaniy (Almaty)*, January 10, 2001.

2. "Khatami's Programs for the Next Four Years: The Second Phase of Reform," *Hambastegi*, May 27, 2001, 1.

3. Kepel, 112.

4. "Iran: The Struggle for the Revolution's Soul," *International Crisis Group*, August 2, 2002; Stephen Fairbanks, "Theocracy versus Democracy: Iran Considers Political Parties," *Middle East Journal* (Winter 1998); Mark Gasiorowski, "The Power Struggle in Iran," *Middle East Policy* (Winter 1998); Asghar Schirazi, *The Constitution of Iran: Politics and the State in the Islamic Republic* (London: I. B. Tauris and Co., 1997); Wilfried Buchta, *Who Rules Iran?* (Washington: Washington Institute for Near East Studies, 2000).

5. Daniel Brumberg, "Dissonant Politics in Iran and Indonesia," *Political Science Quarterly* (Fall 2000) and *Reinventing Khomeini: The Struggle for Reform in Iran* (Chicago: University of Chicago Press, 2001); Hamid Dabashi, *Theology of Discontent: The Ideological Foundation of the Islamic Revolution in Iran* (New York: New

York University Press, 1993); Evrand Abrahamian, *Khomeinism: Essays on the Islamic Republic* (Berkeley: University of California Press, 1993).

6. Baqer Moin, *Khomeini: Life of the Ayatollah* (New York: St. Martin's Press, 1999); Venessa Martin, *Creating an Islamic State: Khomeini and the Making of a New Iran* (London: I.B. Tauris and Co., 2000); Olivier Roy, "The Crisis of Religious Legitimacy in Iran," *Middle East Journal* (Spring 1999); Geneive Abdo, "Re-Thinking the Islamic Republic: A Conversation with Ayatollah Hussein Ali Montazeri," *Middle East Journal* (Winter 2001); Mehran Kamrava, "The Civil Society Discourse in Iran," *British Journal of Middle Eastern Studies* (2001); David Menashri, "Shiite Leadership: In the Shadow of Conflicting Ideologies," *Iranian Studies* (1980).

7. Takeyh, "Islamism RIP," 101.

8. Mehrzad Boroujerdi, "The Paradox of Politics in Post-Revolutionary Iran," and Farideh Farhi, "Reform and Resistance in the Islamic Republic of Iran," in *Iran at the Crossroads*, eds. John Esposito and R.K. Ramazani (New York: Palgrave Macmillan, 2000); H.E Chehabi, "The Political Regime of the Islamic Republic of Iran in Comparative Perspective," *Government and Opposition* (Fall 2000); Robin Wright, "Deadline Tehran: A Revolution Implodes," *Foreign Policy* (Fall 1996).

9. Robin Wright, *The Last Great Revolution* (New York: Vintage Books, 2000), 42. See also Ali Ansari, *Iran, Islam and Democracy: The Politics of Managing Change* (London: Royal Institute of International Affairs, 2000); Elaine Sciolino, *Persian Mirrors: The Elusive Face of Iran* (New York: Touchstone Books, 2000).

10. The best sources in English for his thought include Abolkarim Soroush, *Reason, Freedom, and Democracy in Iran* (New York: Oxford University Press, 2000); Robin Wright, "Iran's Greatest Political Challenge: Abdol Karim Soroush," *World Policy Journal* (Summer 1997); Forough Jahanbkhash, *Islam, Democracy and Religious Modernism* (London: Brill Academic Publishers, 2001), 140–196; Valla Vakili, *Debating Religion and Politics in Iran: The Political Thought of Abdulkarim Soroush* (New York: The Council on Foreign Relations, 1997).

11. Wright, *The Last Great Revolution*, 40.

12. See the reporting in the *New York Times*, September 18, 2000; also Ansari, *Iran, Islam and Democracy: The Politics of Managing Change*, 110–141.

13. See especially, Shireen Hunter, "Is Iranian Perestroika Possible without Fundamental Change?" *Washington Quarterly* (Autumn 1998); Daniel Brumberg, "Is Iran Democratizing," *Journal of Democracy* (October 2000); Haleh Esfandiari, "Is Iran Democratizing: Observations on Election Day," *Journal of Democracy* (October 2000); Mohsen Milani, "Reform and Resistance in the Islamic Republic of Iran," in *Iran at the Crossroads*, eds. John Esposito and R.K. Ramazani

14. *Islamic Republic of Iran News Agency* (IRNA), May 5, 1997.

15. Shaul Bakhash, "Iran's Remarkable Election," *Journal of Democracy* (October 1998); Ansari, *Iran, Islam and Democracy,* 141–176; Fariba Adelkhah, *Being Modern in Iran* (New York: Columbia University Press, 2000), 79–139; see also Tarek Masoud, "Misreading Iran," *Current History* (January 1998).

16. "Distinctions between the two notions of religious democracy and liberalism," *Dowran-e Emruz*, December 10, 2000, 9.

17. "Distinctions between," 9.

18. See, among others, Shaul Bakhash, "Iran's Unlikely President," *New York Review of Books* (November 5, 1998); Ray Takeyh, "God's Will: Iran's Democracy

and the Islamic Context," *Middle East Policy* (October 2000); Stephen Fairbanks, "Iran's Democratic Efforts," *Middle East Policy* (October 1997).

19. Two primary sources in English include Muhammad Khatami, *Hope and Challenge: The Iranian President Speaks* (New York: Global Publications, 1997); Minoo and Milton Buffington, *Meet Mr. Khatami, The Fifth President of the Islamic Republic* (Washington, DC: Middle East Insight, 1998).

20. Patrick Smith, "The Indigenous and the Imported: Khatami's Iran," *The Washington Quarterly* (Spring 2000); Azadeh Kian-Thidbaut, "Political and Social Transformations in Post-Islamist Iran," *Middle East Report* (Fall 1999): 12–16; Geneive Abdo, *No God But God: Egypt and the Triumph of Islam* (Oxford: Oxford University Press, 2000) 187–201.

21. Suzanne Maloney, "Election in Iran: New Majlis and a Mandate for Reform," *Middle East Policy* (June 2000); Geneive Abdo, "Electoral Politics in Iran," *Middle East Policy* (June 1999) and "Days of Rage in Tehran," *Middle East Policy* (October 1999).

22. See, among others, Eric Hooglund, "Khatami's Iran," *Current History* (February 1999); Stephen Fairbanks, "A New Era for Iran?" *Middle East Policy* (September 1997) and "Iran: No Easy Answers," *Journal of International Affairs* (Spring 2001); Farhang Rajee, "A Thermidor of Islamic Yuppies," *Middle East Journal* (Spring 1999).

23. Some of the articles that discuss this include Ladan and Roya Boroumand, "Is Iran Democratizing? Reform at an Impasse," *Journal of Democracy* (October 2000); Geneive Abdo, "The Fragility of Khatami's Revolution," *The Washington Quarterly* (Fall 2000); Christopher de Ballaigue, "The Struggle for Iran," *New York Review of Books* (December 16, 1999); Jahangir Amuzegar, "Iran's Post-Revolutionary Planning: The Second Try," *Middle East Policy* (March 2001).

24. Ray Takeyh, "Iran's Emerging National Compact," *World Policy Journal* (October 2002).

25. *IRNA*, May 15, 2002.

26. *IRNA*, July 26, 2002.

27. *Reuters*, August 5, 2002.

28. See Ray Takeyh, "Re-Imagining US-Iranian Relations," *Survival* (Fall 2002) and "Iran's Emerging National Compact," *World Policy Journal* (October 2002).

29. *IRNA*, June 21, 2001.

30. *IRNA*, April 21, 2001.

31. See the reporting in the *Washington Post*, June 2, 2001.

32. *AFP*, July 21, 2002.

33. As reported in the *Financial Times*, July 10, 2001.

34. *Iran News*, November 16, 1999.

35. *Entekhab*, February 18, 2001.

36. As reported in the *New York Times*, July 21, 2001.

37. *Seyassat-e Ruz*, June 21, 2001.

38. See the report in the *Economist*, February 22, 2001.

39. *Entekhab*, March 3, 2001.

40. *IRNA*, June 5, 2001.

41. *Asr-eh Azadegan*, November 18, 1999.

Chapter 3

Islamism in Algeria: A History of Hope and Agony

THE GROWING POLITICAL AND SOCIAL GAPS

With its vast oil deposits as well as a Francophone intellectual and ruling elite devoted to reshaping the state along modern—albeit socialist—lines, decolonized North Africa was seen as one region where secular modernization had the greatest chance of success. Throughout the 1960s and 1970s, Algeria—the principal state of the region—fulfilled these expectations because its functioning socialist economy and leadership of Third World causes made a celebrated state throughout the Middle East and left-wing Western circles. It was a leader in the Group of 77 and one of the proponents of the New International Economic Order.[1] It was casually ignored that Algerians had not discovered the magic formula for making socialism function, but they relied on oil revenues to mask over the shortcomings of the command economy. In the mean time, the Algerian regime's draconian practices at home were similarly neglected in favor of the great service that the small North Africa state was performing in the cause of the world revolution. Algeria may have been a country of contradictions and precarious stability, but it was also the model of Third World revolution that had to be acclaimed as an alternative to the decadent capitalism exported by the United States.

The Algerian revolutionaries also viewed themselves as a modernizing vanguard for the entire Arab world. They were Western-educated; some were more conversant in French than in Arabic. Although they might oppose the policies of the West, especially those of France and the United

An earlier version of this chapter appeared in the *Middle East Policy* (Summer 2003).

States, they admired the progressive nature of Western culture. In essence, they were seeking to build a modern nation-state that was secular and scientific in nature within the Muslim world.[2]

By the late 1980s, the dream shattered. As the oil revenues declined, the governing regime no longer had the funds to subsidize its ideological dogmas and was compelled to launch liberalization measures that inevitably provoked political repercussions. As the imported Western models failed to fulfill their promises, an increasingly disillusioned middle class turned to the Islamists and their devastating critique of the prevailing order, especially the notion that Algerians had lost their way by abandoning their own traditions and culture to ape the West. However, for the Islamists to succeed, they had to appreciate that their mandate was not the restoration of the mythical seventh century. Instead, it was a reconciliation of demands for cultural authenticity with equally compelling calls for political empowerment. The North African state that has been the greatest laboratory of this experimentation is ironically the one state that appeared to be the foremost model of modernization.[3]

Although Algeria had long been acclaimed by the Arab salon as the paradigm of secular modernization, the Front de Liberation Nationale (FLN) coalition that managed the extraordinary feat of defeating the French empire greatly relied on religious forces and symbols to mobilize the population behind the cause of independence. For example, revolutionary fighters were referred to as *mujahideen*, which was a deliberate attempt to link their cause with the notion of fighting for the Islamic community. Despite the clerical community's contributions to independence, the secular leaders of the FLN viewed religion from a utilitarian perspective; It was sufficient for mass mobilization but inadequate as a template for governance. For the architects of the revolution, Algeria was to spearhead the emerging Third World and usher in a new epoch among the newly independent Afro-Arab states.[4]

In many ways, the story of Algeria unfolded in a manner all too familiar among developing Middle Eastern states. A series of military-led regimes managed for a long time to maintain their power initially through revolutionary legitimacy and, as time passed on, through allocation of resources. During the first two decades of the revolution, the petroleum market and its Western consumers perversely subsidized Algerian socialism. The poor planning favoring heavy industry that frequently underproduced, a neglected agricultural sector, and a bloated, corrupt bureaucracy went unnoticed as the petro-dollars continued to mask the economy's deep-seated structural flows. By the 1980s, as the oil market experienced a steep decline, the regime suddenly found itself confronted with souring foreign debt, diminished revenues, and a hard-pressed populace increasingly disenchanted with the failed promises and pledges of state socialism.[5]

Ironically, the revolution's foremost achievement was to prove its primary source of implosion. The expansion of the university system and its peculiar division between fields taught in French and those taught in Arabic provided the Islamists with a rich source of recruits. The Arab language fields of law and literature took a decisive backseat to the French-taught scientific fields in terms of funding and job opportunity. The Arab language students soon recognized that, despite their newly acquired diplomas, they were dismissed by the French-speaking elite that dominated the heights of the economy and were consigned to the margins of the society. As the demographics began to saturate the market, Algeria began to experience the explosive and troubling problem of underemployment among its graduates. In any developing society, the most difficult challenge for the state by far is not managing the poor but controlling an aggrieved intelligentsia whose aspirations remain unfulfilled. It is from this cadre that militants emerge and organize the political opposition to the state. The children of the revolution were the first to question their patrimony and the foundation upon which the socialist regime rested.[6] The clashes between Francophone Marxist students and Arabic-speaking Islamists in November 1982 were ominous signs of the violence inherent in these cleavages.

The precipitous decline of the Algerian economy in the late 1980s, beginning with the decrease in oil revenues after 1984, not only politicized the restive youth, but it accentuated the Algeria's many cultural, political, and social cleavages. The disturbing gap between elite and masses, the cultural tensions between Arabs and Berbers, the hollowness of the regime's revolutionary rhetoric, and the resentment of the traditional sector of society now suddenly came to the surface with a vengeance. Algeria was about to enter one of the most precarious stages of its modern history.[7]

The regime attempted to shore up its position, interestingly enough, by trying to co-opt the Islamist movement and to solidify its own Islamic credentials. Houari Boumediene, who replaced Ben Bella after deposing him in a coup in 1965, was especially interested in fusing the socialist principles of the regime with the precepts of Islamic law. Boumediene espoused policies that helped the Islamists, including a quiet toleration by the Ministry of Religious Affairs of radical preachers in local mosques throughout Algeria. Boumediene's successor, Colonel Chadli Bendjedid, who was sworn in as president on February 9, 1979, following Boumediene's death in December 1978, continued this approach. Under his leadership, a new Family Status Code was adopted in 1984 that represented major concessions to the Islamists, especially with regard to the status of women. Chadli also invited a leading Egyptian scholar and preacher, Muhammad al-Ghazali, to preside over a new Islamic educational institution, the Université Émir Abdelkader des Sciences Islamiques, in 1982. Al-Ghazali helped to legitimize the positions taken by the radical Islams by issuing a number of *fatwas* (judicial rulings) favorable to their positions. Al-Ghazali was also joined by a second Egyptian sheik, Yusuf al-Qaradawi. As Gilles Kepel observed, "the importation of two imams belonging to this school of thought showed the regime's desire to strengthen the religious dimension of the FLN's nationalist ideology . . . The two imported preachers gave only lip service to the government while encouraging the 'Islamic awakening' at work in society."[8]

The conventional breakdown of the authoritarian state took an innovative departure in the case of Algeria. The Algerian opposition came eventually to be dominated by the forces of tradition. The Islamists not only proved adept at mass mobilization, but they offered a vision that seemed compatible with pluralism and political representation. The reality remains that Islamic politics in Algeria differs from other Middle Eastern states and can only be properly understood within the context of Algeria's evolution as a state and its inability to fully reconcile its multiplicity of identities.

THE EVOLUTION OF POLITICAL ISLAM IN ALGERIA

The spectacular rise of Islamism in Algeria may have stunned the Western media, but, in reality, such activism has deep roots in Algerian society. The Islamic reform movement initially evolved under the shadow of French imperial rule and dedicated itself to harmonizing modernist concepts and Islamic precepts. The Islamic opposition under legendary figures such as Sheik Abd-al Hamid Ben Badis successfully responded to the intellectual challenge of colonialism by insisting that modern political institutions need not be imported and can indigenously evolve. Beyond their political contributions, Algerian Islamists devoted considerable effort to maintaining local identity and preventing the Algerian culture from being completely eclipsed by French norms and mores. This was a moderate expression of local values that made an important imprint on the emerging Algerian identity.[9]

In the post-independence period, the heady policies of socialism and Third Worldism pursued by the FLN elicited Islamist resistance and, at times, organized opposition. The most significant group to emerge in the 1960s was *Al Qiyam* (values) that called for Algeria's cultural rehabilitation to complement its national autonomy. Under the leadership of Hashemi Tidjani, Ben Badis's successor, this group successfully lobbied Ahmed Ben Bella to mandate Islamic religious education in public schools. Through its social networks and journal *Maggallot al-tadhib al-Islamiyya*, the association stood firm against the tide of secularism sweeping the Algerian society. The essential blueprint of Islamic politics emerged at this point as insistence on cultural integrity often led to political expressions inconsistent with the demand of the state.[10] This process culminated in the unveiling of a Charter for an Islamic State at Algiers University on November 12, 1982. Demonstrations on university campuses led to clashes with police and a number of arrests in the following weeks.

Qiyam's activism was complemented by other groups, notably *Al-Irshad wa al-Islah*, under the leadership of Mahfoudh Nahnah. This group similarly deprecated the leftist proclivities of the regime and the inequalities fostered under the banner of socialism. In a departure from the pattern of Islamic dissent, Nahnah focused closely on socioeconomic issues and adversities that the Arab-trained graduates experienced under a state whose leadership remained in the hands of a Francophone elite. Family law, human rights, and economic equity accompanied the traditional focus on cultural values. The important aspect of these organizations is that they pressed for evolutionary change by concentrating on incremental reform and continually propounding the notion that religion and modernity were indeed compatible.[11]

Along with such moderate expression of Islamism, a radical strand was always present that acclaimed the virtues of violence as a means of fostering social change. The foremost figure of this cohort was Moustafa Bouyali whose death in 1987 at the hands of the security services neither diminished the zeal of his followers nor the potency of his vision to some. Bouyali, an avid reader of Qutb, had led the Armed Islamic Movement (MIA) formed in 1982, and his militant members always opposed the gradualism of the moderates and dismissed democratic rule as an alien device for Muslim submission. As one of the intellectual architects of this movement, Said Mekhloufi insisted, "The majority cannot be taken into account when preparing the Islamic state." A rigid theocracy was the best means of achieving God's vision as public opinion was to be countermanded by divine revelation disclosed to a privileged few.[12]

The interplay of religion and politics in Algeria reveals the complexity of a movement that defies easy characterization. Algerian Islamism has deep roots and a long pedigree of resistance—first to French imperialism and later to the authoritarianism fostered by the military regime. Algerian Islamists tried to emphasize the fundamentally religious nature of native resistance to the French. It began with the July 5, 1830, call by the religious brotherhoods for a *jihad* to liberate Algiers and continued through the War of Independence, during which time the anti-colonial forces utilized Islamic rhetoric by terming the struggle a *jihad*, describing those who fell as martyrs, and so on. Indeed, the Islamists sought to link their program with the true fulfillment of Algerian independence. Abbas Madani, who was to emerge as one of the leaders of the Islamist movement, declared, "The Algerian state of 1962 had nothing to do with what had been projected on the first of November 1954 for which we had taken up arms—an independent State founded on Islamic principles.

The state that has risen before our eyes was founded on secular, socialist principles. This was a serious deviation."[13]

In its long years of struggle, resistance, and accommodation, different visions and diverse figures emerged and competed for power and influence. From local clergy and laymen pressing for cultural and social activism to guerilla leaders calling for armed struggle, Algerian Islamism encompassed a multiplicity of voices. The notion that Islamic expression in Algeria is necessarily violent is belied by a rich history of peaceful activism. At the same time, a violent dimension of Islamism cannot be ignored and viewed as an unavoidable result of state repression. Whatever its modalities, by the late 1980s, Islamism was to escape its narrow confines and confront the Algerian regime with its most formidable of challenges.

THE RISE AND FALL OF THE ISLAMIC SALVATION FRONT (FIS)

The year 1988 proved to be a watershed year in Algeria's modern history by marking an important turning point. The declining oil prices and the emergence of a global surge toward free markets led the regime to launch a liberalization and deregulation program that entailed elimination of many social welfare services and subsidies. The removal of state controls at a time of financial crunch particularly affected the urban working class and the poor. The socially disruptive ramifications of this policy were exacerbated by high inflation rates and the emergence of an underground economy. The gap between the rich and poor continued to grow while official corruption, an endemic feature of Algerian bureaucracy, reached alarming rates. The much eroded historic compact between the revolutionary regime and the populace ruptured with the October 1988 riots throughout Algeria's urban centers. The brutal suppression of the marches by the military further undermined the legitimacy of a regime that legitimized its power on its historic role as a force for liberation. In the aftermath of the riots, that historic pillar of the state began to finally crumble.[14]

The Chadli regime's response to the enveloping economic and political crisis was an introduction of sweeping political liberalization measures. Given the failure of its economic policies, the regime perceived that electoral triumphs would resurrect its sagging fortunes and once more refurbish its tarnished image. The aging military men still immured in a revolutionary vision in which the army was the great liberator and therefore the legitimate depository of power failed to note the arrival of a new generation. This was a generation that focused less on revolutionary élan than on the practical achievements of the failing state. The political liberalization measures came at a time when mass discon-

tent with the ruling elite reached a fevered pitch and was awaiting an avenue for its expressions.[15]

Despite the looming problems, the liberalization policy initially appeared to yield considerable advantage. For the first time in its history, Algeria witnessed a relatively free political atmosphere with a flourishing press, competitive political parties, and intense debate on the direction of the state. Hovering over this renaissance was the ominous shadow of persistent economic decline and a restive military hierarchy that was uneasy about departures from the status quo. Algeria's liberal interregnum was bound to be short-lived because the forces of radicalism would soon be plotting to reclaim the political landscape.[16]

The Islamic Salvation Front (FIS) stepped into this explosive arena and was determined to compete for political power and even displace the existing ruling system. Proclaimed on March 10, 1989, at the Ben Badis mosque in Algiers, the fifteen founders of the FIS sought, in order to challenge the nationalistic patrimony of the FLN, to include under its banner the totality of Islamist expression. The FIS gained further legitimacy when it proved more capable of rallying assistance to the victims of the October 1989 earthquake in the Tipasa region than official government agencies.

Yet, the FIS was not a unitary movement. Instead, it was a broad coalition of militants and moderates, clergy and laymen, as well as young and old. The contrary character of the FIS was best illustrated by its choice of leaders, included the tempered Abbas Madani and the firebrand radical Ali Belhaj. While Madani pressed for inclusive politics and constructive participation in a pluralistic society, Belhaj denounced a democratic order as a sinister tool of the West. The reality remains that the FIS's propensity to participate in the elections in the first place and accept the limits and restrictions of the electoral process reflected the triumph of the moderate wing. The radicals were present but, so long as the democratic process moved forward, their leadership claims were marginal and largely ignored.[17]

In line with most opposition parties, the FIS never published a detailed program and limited itself to bland assurances of implementing plans that would lead to prosperity and order. In part, this was due to the fact that the FIS had no real mechanism for adopting policies. In theory, the FIS was guided by a *Majlis al-Shura* (consultative council). Yet, no statutes or regulations for its operation were ever published, and its meetings were held in private at irregular times. It essentially brought together the different factions and groups that comprised the FIS, but there was no way to streamline or standardize its operations.

Concerning the economy, the FIS program was to advocate a vibrant private sector coexisting with enhanced social welfare provisions. Traditional Algerian themes of independence, self-sufficiency, and autonomy from Western imperialism constituted the hallmark of the FIS's rhetoric. The FIS soon declared, "Whether we proceed with production or consumption, we must proceed with investment in order to alleviate poverty and in order to find objectives for promotion of man." The great macroeconomic challenges facing Algeria in a global economy remained largely unaddressed by the FIS. Although such opacity is the prerogative of opposition parties, in the case of the FIS, it stemmed from internal contradictions and an inability to craft a consensus on detailed economic blueprint.[18]

Although the FIS's economic platform was discursive, its political proclamations seemed outright contradictory. Madani continued to assert his intention to accept the rulers of democracy and deprecated the notion that FIS sought to superimpose a theocratic ideology on Algeria. As the FIS's principal leader, Madani made his democratic commitments clear when declaring, "Pluralism is guarantee of cultural wealth and diversity needed for development. Democracy, as we understand it means pluralism, choice, and freedom."[19] A survey of Islamist publications, such as *El Forkane* and *El Mungidh*, reveals a surprising injection of democratic discourse with power rotation and pluralism being continued invoked as guiding principles.[20]

At the same time that important elements of FIS appeared to accommodate democratic norms, another segment remained defiant in its denunciation of such heretical thoughts. Belhaj led the charge against pluralism or any governing framework that detracted from the religious mission of the sate. "When we are in power, there will be no more elections because God will be ruling," professed Belhaj.[21] Democracy was seen as an insidious foreign innovation that would subvert the divine order. Belhaj and his followers were vociferous in their condemnation of democratic rule as a contrived Western instrument for subverting the cohesion of the *umma*. It was blasphemy to suggest that God's will—as revealed and interpreted—should submit to the popular will in the governance of the country. The most that the radicals would concede was that elections might prove to be the instrument by which Islamists could come to power in Algeria. The task at hand for the Algerian leaders was therefore to ensure that the ascendance of the moderates and continued marginalization of the radicals.[22]

In a sense, the unity of the FIS was always precarious because it rested on an alliance of a disparate collection of forces. The main constituents of the FIS were small merchants, civil servants, and first generation college graduates. All of these groups struggled with diminishing economic fortunes, loss of cultural identity, and rampant corruption. These elders of the FIS sought an accountable government and greater representation in the context of cultural continuity. However, this element of the FIS always had an uneasy relationship with the other wing of the party that was primarily composed of desperate young men suffering from escalating unemployment rates. As disillusioned youth, their claims were more immediate, and their patience was always more limited. The task of the authorities was to ensure that the leadership of the FIS rested with the moderates, the so-called politicians among the Islamists, such as Madani or Abdelkader Hachani, and their tempering influence on the firebrands remained intact. This was the task that the regime bitterly failed to perform.[23]

The elections of the early 1990s would prove to shift the bedrock of Algerian politics by revealing fault lines and differing dimensions of its national identity. In the municipal elections of 1990, the FIS garnered 43 million votes, which granted it a formal power base in the localities for the first time. In an even greater upset in December 1991, the FIS captured 188 out of 430 parliamentary seats in the first round of the legislative elections.[24]

The electoral triumphs of the FIS have often been dismissed as a strong reaction of the masses against the FLN's troubled tenure and not so much as an endorsement of the FIS. It is certainly true that the frustrated Algerian populace was not about to extend the FLN's hold on power and, when granted an opportunity, it flocked to the most viable alternative.[25] However, it would be remiss to disregard the electoral results as mere antagonism toward the FLN because they do indicate an affirmation of the FIS's message of moderate Islamism. The FIS proved not only capable of channeling the disenchantment with the FLN to its advantage, but its moderate leaders such as Madani and his temperate message resonated with the populace. In a sense, the FIS appropriated the essence of the original revolution by claiming modernist solutions to contemporary problems in the context of cultural authenticity.[26]

However, in one of the greatest miscalculations of modern Algerian history, on the eve of the second round of parliamentary elections, the military stepped in and nullified the election results. On January 11, 1992, Chadli resigned under heavy pressure from the military, and a state council took power. This action undertaken by the generals ended Algeria's liberal period. Parliamentary elections scheduled for January 13, 1992, were canceled, and the FIS itself outlawed on March 4. This ushered in a civil war that would consume tens of thousands of lives—estimates range from 50,000 to over 100,000 killed and more than 20,000 disappeared—[27] and institutionalize violence as a means of resolving disputes. One of the first victims of the violence was Muhammad Boudiaf, one of the heroes of the Algerian revolution who returned from exile in Morocco to head a transitional administration after Chadli Benjedid's resignation. Appointed in January 1992, he was assassinated on June 29 of that year.

The post-coup governments that have ruled Algeria since 1992 have attempted to sporadically sanction their rule through controlled and

contrived elections. A new party, the National Democratic Rally, was created while several safe parties were allowed to contest elections, including the Movement of Society for Peace, an Islamist option approved by
the generals; the Rally for Culture and Democracy; and the Party of
Algerian Renewal. Nevertheless, many Algerians believed that these
opposition parties were primarily for show. General Liamine Zéroual
won the presidency in 1995 in elections boycotted by the Islamists, and
Abdelaziz Bouteflika, the candidate of the generals, was elected in April
1999. He ran unopposed after the other five candidates withdrew from
the election campaign and claimed the election results would be rigged.
However, the larger problem remains that such measures cannot com-
pensate for the resounding lack of legitimacy that the original abrogation
of elections fostered. Not only did Algeria's lingering economic problems remain, but they were exacerbated by the ensuing civil war. A
report issued by the Council for Arab Economic Unity observed that
investment in Algeria from other Arab countries, which had amounted
to $27.3 million between 1990 and 1992, had fallen to zero by 1993 due to
the "Islamist violence that has engulfed the country."[28]

A widespread perception existed among the disenfranchised masses
that the military clique and Francophone minority that had benefited dis-
proportionately from the wealth of the nation had once more conspired to
preserve its system of privilege. For many Algerians, elections represented—not so much an opportunity to implant a theocracy—but a
chance to finally infiltrate the corridors of power and share in Algeria's
great wealth. The abrogation of the elections made violence the ultimate
arbiter of change in a polarized Algerian society.[29]

It is in this context that the radical dimension of Algerian Islamism
began to explode into the scene. Followers of Bouyali combined forces
with returning Algerian veterans of the *jihad* in Afghanistan to prepare
for open combat with the regime and scorned the politicians who sought
change through elections. On November 28, 1991, a group of militants
seized an army post at Guemmar and executed the conscripts stationed
there.

The military coup discredited the moderate wing of the FIS that had
put such trust in electoral institutions as a way to bring about change.
That, along with the fact that many of the key leaders of the FIS were now
imprisoned, more radical elements were allowed to rise to the fore, especially those who formed the Armed Islamic Group (GIA). The GIA's philosophy was as simple as it was self-defeating. The GIA not only
condemned the FIS electoral strategy, but it ominously declared, "Power
is within the range of our Kalashinkovs."[30] It professed that the failure of
the Islamic movement to reclaim power was due to a lack of resolution in
the pursuit of *jihad*. Since a number of the leaders of the GIA had been
Algerian volunteers who had fought against the Soviets in Afghanistan

during the 1980s, the argument resonated that armed force could bring down an illegitimate regime. The tactics of the GIA were equally fallacious. By using violence, it sought to challenge the notion of regime's invincibility and spark a mass uprising. The partisans of the GIA made it clear that their goal diverged from the FIS because they did not seek the resumption of the electoral process or the rehabilitation of the political order. Instead, they sought the creation of a new Islamic utopia through armed resistance. The second leader (*amir*) of the GIA, Cherif Gousmi, who was eventually killed in a skirmish with government forces in September 1994, made this clear that the GIA was not fighting to open any sort of dialogue with apostate rulers or to establish any sort of moderate Islamic democracy.[31] The human way—elections—had failed. Now, the only option was to engage in *jihad* against an illegitimate regime that claimed to be Muslim, but that was, in the eyes of the radicals, an infidel order. The challenge of the GIA was not just to the regime but to moderate Islamists who had participated in the political process and accepted its demands and limitations.[32]

The methods and rationale of the GIA were not that dissimilar from the totalitarian parties of the West who saw themselves as a vanguard force seeking to lead a nation by first shocking its sensibilities. The failure of such parties is inevitable and follows a predictable pattern of state retribution followed by defection of the party's remaining cadre. Somehow, this lesson eluded the combatants of the GIA. In its initial spat of violence, the GIA focused on the regime's officials, intellectuals, and secular activists. Beginning in March 1993, academics, intellectuals, writers, doctors, and journalists were marked for death by the death squads of the GIA, which was often composed of disaffected young men with little education and with a pronounced vendetta against "the sons of France."[33] As the violence evolved, the GIA spectacularly miscalculated by turning against small merchants, entrepreneurs, and petty bourgeoisie that had formed the backbone of the Islamic opposition. The GIA activists began to press these groups for funds and operated well-developed racketeering schemes that masqueraded as voluntary payments of the Islamic tax (*zakat*). The movement that acclaimed piety and professed to create a virtuous order had turned into a violent street gang and thus provoked an orgy of violence throughout Algeria. Moreover, the GIA adopted an apocalyptic view of the struggle. One of the GIA's leaders, Antar Zouabri, the GIA's fourth *amir*, proclaimed that "In our war, there is no neutrality. Except for those who are with us, all others are renegade."[34] As a result, the Islamists were unable to preserve the critical alliance between the young urban poor and the devout middle classes that had enabled Khomeini to take power in Iran in 1979.[35]

Despite the abrogated elections and rampant violence, in November 1994 and January 1995, the remnants of the FIS in conjunction with other

Algeria's leading parties, including the FLN, offered the beleaguered nation an avenue out of its bloody impasse. The Rome Accords that were signed by the FIS leadership was a remarkable compact between the secular and religious forces of Algeria. In a unique gesture of unity, all renounced violence and accepted democratic procedures as the only means of acquiring and retaining power. The agreement dramatically rejected "dictatorship, whatever its nature and form" while guaranteeing "fundamental individual and collective liberties such as race, sex, religion, and language." The Rome Accords were an unprecedented acknowledgement of alternative ideologies by an Islamist organization long accused of undemocratic designs. In contrast to the GIA, the FIS also pledged to refrain from "the use of violence to gain or maintain power."[36] Significantly, for an Islamist party, the Rome document also reaffirmed popular sovereignty as the only basis for legitimate authority.[37] However, the angry rejection of the accord by the military constituted an emasculation of all moderate forces and transformation of Algerian politics into a contested terrain between the military eradicators and militant Islamists.[38] The war in Algeria has essentially been a war of attrition between both sides with each side hoping that the other collapses first. The military has—with some justification—believed that it could win the war of attrition. Starting in 1995, the GIA began to break up as a coherent, unified organization with the defection of several leading Islamists, including Mohammad Said, from its ranks. These men were subsequently killed by the GIA under the leadership of Djamel Zitouni for their deviance. Zitouni himself was assassinated by followers of the executed men. Zouabri, his successor, alienated many in Algeria by proclaiming that the whole of Algerian society, including the moderate Islamists, were impious. By late 1997, the GIA had ceased to function as a single, coordinated organization and broke up into factions led by independent salafist commanders.[39] Yet, this did not mean an automatic end to the violence. In the month of Ramadan, which fell in late January–early February in 1997, and in August and September 1997, hundreds of Algerians were killed, often in clashes between village militias and bands of Islamists. This "contributed to the privatization and spread of the violence by adding the ingredients of vendetta and local dispute to the wider struggle. . ."[40] Today, small-scale clashes continue in many areas of the country, usually involving small groups of militants on the one side and government security services and official militias on the other. Attacks in the larger cities are rare. Most of the violence occurs in villages and hamlets.[41]

Algeria's tragic impasse persists and develops its own legacy. Despite contrived presidential and parliamentary elections, a military clique continues to dominate power. President Bouteflika may be the statutory leader of the state, but the real power continues to rest in the hands of the military custodians of the regime. Like civilian leaders in Turkey,

Bouteflika must operate within red lines that have been defined by the military, which remains divided between a wing urging conciliation with the Islamists and another pressing for full eradication of the Islamist presence.[42] After the death of more than 100,000 people, only one factor has been cleared—namely that radical Islamists cannot displace the regime and that the generals cannot forcefully eradicate all of their opponents. The cycle of violence can only end when all parties recognize that a stable Algeria is a democratic, inclusive state that provides for individual sovereignty while accepting moderate Islamism as part of the political landscape. Thus far, this revelation has eluded all parties in that tragic state.[43]

Florence Beauge, reporting from Algeria for the French newspaper *Le Monde*, summed up the current situation in Algeria as follows:

The announcement of each new massacre is received in Algiers with a mixture of weariness and indifference. The security forces keep the capital and other major cities under high surveillance, which spares them from large-scale massacres. The killing that takes place elsewhere almost seems to be abstractions for those people who are not directly involved. On top of it all, "we want to live." This is what people in Algiers repeat over and over again underscoring that "ten years of war is enough."[44]

WHITHER ALGERIA?

The role of Islam in post-independence Algeria cannot be minimized because it provided a foundation for an otherwise secular state. Despite the regime's modernizing pretensions, the religious functionaries continued to inculcate the ways of the tradition and provide the populace with a value system that they could not find in the secular state. Under the august shadow of the modernizing regime, the forces of religion persisted in conditioning individual consciousness and political culture of Algeria. As the first generation of Algerians passed from the scene, the notion of revolutionary élan as the basis for state legitimacy and mass mobilization declined. Increasingly, the power of the state rested on the efficiency of its security services and the availability of petro-dollars. As the legitimacy of the regime became tenuous, it became subject to a challenge from traditional forces operating at a deeper and more substantial level.

The Islamic Salvation Front must be seen as part of a larger tradition of religious activism that had always featured competing factions of moderates and hardliners. In a departure from its predecessors, the FIS focused more closely on national problems and called for political participation as a means of addressing these issues. Obviously, as a religious-based party, both the problems and solutions were expressed in a distinct religious idiom. As such, the FIS challenged the regime—not just on charges of moral decay—but also for practical shortcomings, such as corruption, managerial incompetence, and inefficiency. The abrogation of the elections ensured that those whose preferred method of protest was violence displaced the voices of moderation calling for social mobilization as a means of expressing dissent.

The Islamic Salvation Front's stunning electoral triumphs in 1990–1991 cannot be ignored or dismissed. The Algerian military has demonstrated an ability to maintain order through the most repressive of methods. However, in the long run, the possibility of imposing an authoritarian rule on a populace that poured into the street demanding representation is improbable. The irony is that Algeria stands as one state in the Middle East that possesses the important preconditions for democratic transition. The continuing cultural and educational links to France, the sophisticated nature of elite politics, and ethnic diversity that has long mandated subtle compromises and concessions make Algeria different than the typical Arab authoritarian state. By building bridges to the moderate Islamists, the military can finally ensure not only a democratic polity but also an end to a civil war that has already brutalized an entire generation of Algerians.

Steps in this direction have already been taken. When Liamine Zeroual was elected as president in 1995, some elements within the FIS were prepared to recognize his legitimacy and hoped that a dialogue to end the conflict could be initiated.[45] A number of analysts predicted that Algeria had reached the hurting stalemate that might push both sides to negotiations.[46] What was certainly clear was that one of the main bases for Islamist support in the early 1990s—the lower middle class—was increasingly alienated by the violence unleashed by the radicals. As Gilles Kepel concluded, the use of extortion and murder as tools of intimidation by radical Islamists against pious Muslim merchants, craftsmen, and businessmen as much as against secular doctors or writers provided for "a gradual return of the middle class to the government fold."[47]

In 1997, the armed organization of the FIS, under the leadership of Madani Merzag, unilaterally declared a cease-fire, and, in 1999, after negotiations with Abdelqader Hachani, who was considered to be the number-three man within the FIS, the groundwork was laid for Bouteflika's civil reconciliation program, the centerpiece of which was a general amnesty for members of the FIS and its armed wing, the Islamic Salvation Army (AIS). Many believed that Bouteflika's policies were designed to co-opt the national Islamic tendency within a government based upon unity, a government in which ministers of different political factions could work together to peacefully reconstruct Algerian society.[48] Bouteflika himself hoped that this would enable the government to concentrate on combating the GIA and another radical militant organization, the Salafist Group for Preaching and Combat (GSPC). However, the more militant Islamists have refused to abandon the armed struggle, and Hachani himself was assassinated in November 1999. Bouteflika has vowed to exterminate armed radicals who did not surrender to the state under the terms of the amnesty—the GIA and the GSPC are estimated to number between 5,000 and 7,000 militants.[49] Nevertheless, while violence still continues in Algeria, the government has had greater success since 1999 in containing and localizing the bloodshed; yet, low-level outbreaks continue. However, the war of attrition has made some gains. Antar Zouabri, the fourth *amir* of the GIA, was reportedly killed in a clash with security forces on February 8, 2002; another regional GIA commander died on February 17.[50] However, this has left the GIA without any centralized command structure and, significantly, no one with any authority capable of entering into negotiations for a cease-fire. Instead, "these groups have no links with one another."[51]

Another interesting development has been the revitalization of the FLN under the leadership of Prime Minister Ali Benflis. For the last several years, he has tried to situate the FLN as the political force best able to project healing and reconciliation in Algerian society. The FLN won 199 seats in the National Assembly in May 2002 parliamentary elections and enjoyed convincing victories in local elections in October 2002. Benflis has tried to shift attention away from ideology toward economic progress and has tapped into the desire of many Algerians for peace and reconstruction.[52] Interior Minister Nourredine Yazid Zerhouni maintains that, in contrast with the early 1990s, "People now fully reject the armed groups and no longer provide them with any support."[53]

At the same time, the official Islamists have seen their popular support erode. Collectively, Mahfoud Nanah's Movement of Society for Peace and Abdallah Djaballah's Movement for National Reform, which polled 26 percent of the vote in 1997, saw their combined total shrink to 21 percent in 2002. This is significant because it is estimated that up to 25 percent of the candidates and activists in these movements are former members of the FIS, and Nanah was viewed as a plausible alternative to the radical Islamists for leadership of the Islamist movement. Some of the decline may be attributed to the ongoing boycott of the electoral process that the FIS still asks of its followers and so true believers sought to punish the official Islamists for collaborating with the government, but it may also reflect a growing dissatisfaction among Algerians with Islamist ideology. Some of the data indicates that Algerian voters trust the FLN, the former party of state, to do a more effective job in reconstructing the economy than the Islamists.[54]

The tragedy of Algeria is that the FIS, which had won elections, was unable to reach a *modus vivendi* with the ruling establishment, particularly the military. Of course, it is not entirely clear that even the moderate wing of the FIS would have been willing to function within a system of managed pluralism defined by the secular military. The failure of the moderates to successfully establish a government encouraged the radical forces to make a bid for power using violent, revolutionary means. However, what is clear is that a majority of Algerians who were prepared to support a modest Islamist regime that promised to engage in political and economic reforms were not desirous of bringing to power utopian radicals, especially once the violence and corruption escalated.

It is too early to speculate on the future of Islamism in Algeria. The legacy of the civil war has been to create a hard core, even if numerically small, of rejectionists who have embraced the use of violence against the regime and are unprepared to negotiate or accept any sort of cease-fire. In March 2003 alone, over fifty people were killed in clashes between security forces and militants.[55] It has also produced a counter-reaction among the military of people who want to confine Islam to the mosques and envision no role whatsoever for political Islam in Algerian public life. Whether or not moderate Islamism will remain a political force remains to be seen. It is entirely possible that a revitalized FLN will be able to co-opt some of the ideas—and personnel—of the moderate Islamist movement, perhaps under the rubric of national unity and reconstruction. Moderate Islamists may also end up having a defined niche within the military-directed system of limited political pluralism. However, what is apparent is that no caliphate is likely to arise in Algeria at any point in the near future. It is significant that Bouteflika observed,

> Our problems are substantive and not simple. They need to be examined in the same way that the Europeans and Americans examine their problems. We have to learn from them. Our fate in the Maghreb in particular appears to be linked to a large degree to the European one and the EU. We must at least adopt some of the Europeans' traditions and their rationality.[56]

The basic rules of the Algerian political system will continue to be the Western norms agreed to at Rome, not a new order that hearkens to the Muslim golden age of the seventh century.

NOTES

1. Saad Eddin Ibrahim, "Crises, Elites and Democratization in the Arab World," *Middle East Journal* (Spring 1993); Mohammad Harbi, *Le FLN, Mirages et realities* (Paris: Jeune Afrique, 1980) and *L'Algerie et son Destin-Croyants et Citoyens* (Paris: Medias Associes, 1993); Abdelkader Yesfsah, *Processus de Legitimation du Pouvoir Militaire et la Construction de l'Etat en Algerie* (Paris, 1982); John Ruedy, *Modern Algeria: The Origins and Development of a Nation* (Indiana: Indiana University Press, 1992); Robert Malley, *The Call from Algeria: Third Worldism, Revolution and the Turn to Islam* (Berkeley: University of California Press, 1996); Roger Murray and Tom Weingraf, "The Algerian Revolution," *New Left Review* (December 1963).

2. Raphael Patai discusses the phenomenon of cultural dichotomy among the Francophone North Africans seeking to navigate between an Arab-Muslim and a French-Western world in *The Arab Mind*, rev. ed. (New York: Scribner, 1983), 191–195.

3. Ernest Gellner, "The Unknown Apollo of Biskra: The Social Base of Algerian Puritanism," *Government and Opposition* (Summer 1974); Lahourai Addi, *L'Algerie et la Democrite: Pouvoir et Crise du Politicque dans l' Algerie Contemporaire* (Paris: Editions Decouverte, 1994); Jean-Claude Vatin, "Religious Resistance and State Power in Algeria," in *Islam and Power*, eds. Alexander S. Cudsi and Ali Hilal Dessouki (Baltimore: Johns Hopkins University Press, 1981), 119–157.

4. Francois Burgat, *The Islamic Movement in North Africa* (Austin: University of Texas University Press, 1993), 25–63; John Entelis, *Algeria: The Revolution Institutionalized* (Boulder: University of Colorado Press, 1986); Fanon Frantz, *The Wretched of the Earth* (New York: Grove Press, 1968); William Quandt, *Between Ballots and Bullets: Algeria's Transition from Authoritarianism* (Washington, DC: The Brookings Institution, 1998), 15–42; Matthew Connelly, *A Diplomatic Revolution: Algeria's Fight for Independence and the Origins of the Post-Cold War Era* (Oxford: Oxford University Press, 2001).

5. Bradford Dillman, *State and Private Sector in Algeria: The Politics of Rent-Seeking and Failed Development* (Boulder: University of Colorado Press, 2000); John Entelis, "Sonatrach: The Political Economy of an Algerian State Institution," *Middle East Journal* (Winter 1999); Arslan Humbaraci, *Algeria: A Revolution That Failed* (New York: Frederick Praeger, 1964), p. 23–38; Mahfoud Bennoune, "The Industrialization of Algeria: An Overview," in *Contemporary North Africa*, ed. Halim Barakat (Washington, DC: Center for Contemporary Arab Studies, 1985); Marina Lazerg, *The Emergence of Class in Algeria* (Boulder: University of Colorado Press, 1976).

6. John Ruedy, *Modern Algeria: The Origins and Development of a Nation* (Indiana: Indiana University Press, 1992), 29–89; William Quandt, *Revolution and Political Leadership: Algeria, 1954–1968* (Cambridge, MA: MIT Press, 1969,) 24–65.

7. See three articles by Hugh Roberts, "Radical Islamism and the Dilemma of Algerian Nationalism," *Third World Quarterly* (April 1988); "Algerian State and the Challenge of Democracy," *Government and Opposition* (Fall 1992); and "From Radical Mission to Equivocal Ambition: The Expansion and Manipulation of Algerian Islamism, 1979–1992" in, *Accounting for Fundamentalism: The Dynamic Character of Movements*, eds. Martin Marty and Scott Appleby (Chicago: University of Chicago Press, 1994), 420–447. For more on this phenomenon, cf. David and Marina Ottaway, *Algeria: The Politics of Socialists Revolution* (Berkeley: University of California, 1970), 120–153.

8. Kepel, 165.

9. See two contributions by John Entelis, "Islam, Democracy and the State: The Reemergence of Authoritarian Politics in Algeria," in *Islamism and Secularism in North Africa*, ed. John Ruedy (New York: St. Martin's Press, 1996) and "Political Islam in Algeria: The Nonviolent Dimension," *Current History* (January 1995). See also Michael Willis, "Algeria's Other Islamists: Abdallah Djaballah and the Ennahda Movement," *Journal of North African Studies* (Fall 1998); Robert Mortimer, "Islamist, Soldiers and Democrats: The Second Algerian War," *Middle East Journal* (Winter 1996); David Gordon, *The Passing of French Algeria* (New York: Oxford University Press, 1987), 65–93.

10. Ricardo Rene Laremont, *Islam and the Politics of Resistance in Algeria, 1782–1992* (Trenton: Africa World Press, 2000), 10–103; Michael Willis, *The Islamists' Challenge in Algeria: A Political History* (New York: NYI Press, 1996), 1–69; Martin Stone, *The Agony of Algeria* (New York: Columbia University Press, 1997), 25–37.

11. John Entelis, ed., *Islam, Democracy and the State in North Africa* (Indiana: Indiana University Press, 1997), 63.

12. *Jeune Afrique*, March 16, 1993; *Jeune Afrique*, November 6, 1985; *Jeune Afrique*, December 11, 1985; Willis, *The Islamists' Challenge in Algeria*, 71–88.

13. Slimane Zeghidour, "Entretien avec Abbasi Madani," *Politique Etrangere*, 49 (1990): 180.

14. Lynette Rummel, "Privatization and Democratization in Algeria," in, *State and Society in Algeria*, eds. John Entelis and Philip Naylor (Boulder: University of Colorado Press, 1995), 50–63; Abed Charif, *Octobre* (Algiers, 1990); and reporting in *Le Monde*, especially in the October 8, 1988; October 13, 1988; October 15, 1988; and October 24, 1988, issues; see also *Le Monde Diplomatique*, November 1988.

15. Consult Lahouari Addi, *L'Algerie et la democratie*, and "Algeria's Army, Algeria's Agony," *Foreign Affairs* (July/August 1998).

16. *El Watan*, June 20, 1991; *Le Monde*, March 28, 1991; Quandt, *Between Ballots and Bullets*, 42–62; Stone, *The Agony of Algeria*, 64–81; Robert Mortimer, "Algeria: The Dialectic of Elections and Violence," *Current History* (May 1997); Anthony Pazzanita, "From Boumedienne to Benjedid: The Algerian Regime in Transition," *Journal of South Asia and Middle Eastern Studies* (Summer 1992); John Entelis, "Islam, Democracy and the State: The Reemergence of Authoritarian Politics in Algeria," in *Islamism and Secularism in North Africa*, ed. John Ruedy (New York: St. Martin's Press, 1994), 219–251; Robert Mortimer, "Islam and Multiparty Politics in Algeria," *Middle East Journal* (Fall 1991), 574–593. For general discussion of democratic transitions, see Juan Linz and Alfred Stephan, *Problems of Democratic Transition and Consolidation* (Baltimore: Johns Hopkins University Press, 1999); Gullermo O'Donnell and Phillipe Schmiter, *Transitions from Authoritarian Rule: Tentative Conclusions About Uncertain Democracies* (Baltimore: Johns Hopkins University Press, 1986); Adam Pezeworski, *Democracy and the Market: Political and Economic Reforms in Eastern Europe and Latin America* (Cambridge: Cambridge University Press, 1991).

17. Abassi Madani, *Azmat al-fiar al-hadith wa mubarryrat al-hal al-islami* (Algiers, 1989); readers should also consult the interview with Abbas Madani, *Horizons*, January 14, 1990; Ahmed Rouadjia, "Doctrine et discours du Cheikh Abassi," *Peuples Mediterraneens* (52–53*); Algerie: Vers l'Etat Islamique* (July–September 1990); the interview with Ali Beljaj, *Horizons*, January 23, 1989; Ahmed Rouadjia, "Discourse and Strategy of the Algerian Islamist Movement," in *Islamist Dilemma: The Political Role of Islamist Movements in Contemporary Arab World*, ed. Laura Guzaaone (London: Ithica Press, 1995), 69–103; Yahia Zoubir, "The Painful Transition from Authoritarianism in Algeria," *Arab Studies Quarterly* (Summer 1993), 88–97; Anwar Haddam, "The Political Experiment of the Algerian Islamic Movement," in *Power-Sharing Islam?*, ed. Azzam Tamimi (London: Liberty Press, 1993), 122–137.

18. Hugh Roberts, "Doctrinaire Economic and Political Opportunism in the Strategy of Algerian Islamism," in Ruedy, *Islamism and Secularism*, 123–147; Bradford Dillman, *State and Private Sector in Algeria*; readers may also wish to consult

the precursor document *Projet de la Front Islamique du Salute*, released March 7, 1989.

19. Ray Takeyh, "The Lineaments of Islamic Democracy," *World Policy Journal* (Winter 2001/2002).

20. See especially Yahia Zoubir, "Algerian Islamists' Conception of Democracy," *Arab Studies Quarterly* (Summer 1996); Kate Zebiri, "Islamic Revival in Algeria: An Overview," *The Muslim World* (October 1993): Burgat, *The Islamic Movement in North Africa*, 247–306; Henri Sanson, *Laicite islamique en Algerie* (Paris: CNRS, 1983), 34–76; Mustapha Al-Ahnaf, *L'Algerie par ses islamistes* (Paris: Karthala, 1991); Augustus Richard Norton, "The Future of Civil Society in the Middle East," *Middle East Journal* (Spring 1993).

21. Ray Takeyh, "Islamism RIP," *The National Interest*, 130.

22. Ali Belhaj, *Fasl al-kalam fi muwajhat al-hukkam* (Algiers, 1989) and "Qui est responsible de la violence?" *El –Mousqid* (November 1990); *Algerie Actualite,* April 26, 1990.

23. Dirk Vandewalle, "Islam in Algeria: Religion, Culture and Opposition in a Rentier State," in *Political Islam: Revolution, Radicalism or Reform*, ed. John Esposito (Boulder: University of Colorado Press, 1997), 20–35; Andrew Pierre and William Quandt, "Algeria's War on Itself," *Foreign Policy* (Fall 1995); Lahouari Addi, "Algeria's Tragic Contradictions," *Journal of Democracy* (Spring 1996).

24. Jacques Fontaine, "Les elections locales Algerinnes du 12 juin 1990, *Maghreb-Machrek* (July/September 1990); Keith Sutton, Ahmed Aghrout and Salah Zamiche, "Political changes in Algeria: An Emerging Electoral Geography," *Maghreb Review* (1992).

25. Pierre and Quandt, 135.

26. Willis, *The Islamist Challenge in Algeria*, 107–259; Quandt, *Between Ballots and Bullets*, 124–165; Stone, *The Agony of Algeria*, 1145–1174.

27. Paul A. Silverstein, "No Pardon: Rage and Revolt in Algeria," *Middle East Insight* (September/October 2001), 61.

28. *AFP,* June 7, 1995.

29. See especially Hugh Roberts, "The Struggle for Constitutional Rule In Algeria," *The Journal of Algerian Studies* (1998) and "Algeria's Ruinous Impasse: An Honorable Way Out," *International Affairs* (Summer 1995); Yahia Zoubir, "Stalled Democratization of an Authoritarian Regime: The Case of Algeria," *Democratization* (Summer 1995); Constance Stadler, "Democratization Reconsidered: The Transformation of Political Culture in Algeria," *Journal of North African Studies* (Fall 1998); Dirk Vandewalle, "At the Brink," *World Policy Journal* (Fall 1992).

30. Takeyh, "Islamism RIP," 130.

31. Kepel, 266.

32. For more information, consult Luis Martinez, *La Guerre civile en Algerie* (Paris: Karthala, 1998); Severine Labat, *Les Islamistes algeriens entre les urnes et le maquis* (Paris: Seuil, 1995); Willis, *The Islamists' Challenge*, 307–385; Mohammad Hafez, "Armed Islamist Movements and Political Violence in Algeria," *Middle East Journal* (Fall 2000).

33. Kepel, 262.

34. Larmont, *Islam and the Politics of Resistance in Algeria*, 197–230; Stone, *The Agony of Algeria,* 180–196; Hamou Amirouche, "Algeria's Islamist Revolution: The

People Versus Democracy?" *Middle East Policy* (January 1998); Marc Yared, "Qui Derriere le GIA," *Jeune Afrique* (January/February 1994).

35. Kepel, 175.

36. Of course, there are lingering suspicions as to whether the FIS "truly" has renounced violence and the armed struggle. These once again began a matter of public debate when reports surfaced that the FIS had held its third congress in Europe, reportedly in the outskirts of Liege or Maastricht. The Belgian Ministry of the Interior announced that it had no plans to shut down the assembly of a party that "has renounced the violent struggle" while members of the legislature demanded hearings to investigate whether the FIS continues to act as a front for radical movements who are still engaged in violence. See the reporting in *Le Monde Diplomatique*, August 8, 2002, 4.

37. An English text of The Rome Accords is available at http://www.ub.es/solidaritat/observatori/english/algeria/documents/plataform.htm.

38. See the comment in *Le Monde Diplomatique* (March 1995): 7.

39. For a discussion of this process, see Kepel, 265–274.

40. Kepel, 272–273.

41. See, for example, *AFP* press reports on the violence for October 2, 2002, and February 18, 2002. The attacks are mainly raids, and deaths occur in the exchange of fire between militants and soldiers.

42. See "Diminishing Returns: Algeria's 2002 Legislative Elections," *Middle East Briefing* (Brussels: International Crisis Group, 2002): 2–3.

43. Mortimer, "Islamists, Soldiers, and Democrats: The Second Algerian War" and Omar Bellhouchet, "Pourquoi Alger voit rouge," *Le Nouvel Observateur* (February 9–15, 1995); Matthew Connelly, "Déjà vu All Over Again: Algeria, France and Us," *The National Interest* (Winter 1995–96); Benjamin Stora, *La gangrene et Poubli: La memoire de la guerre d' Algerie* (Paris: Decouverte, 1992).

44. See her article in *Le Monde*, October 31, 2002.

45. Paul M. Lubeck, "Islamist Responses to Globalization: Cultural Conflict in Egypt, Algeria, and Malaysia," in *The Myth of Ethnic Conflict: Politics, Economics and Cultural Violence*, eds. Beverly Crawford and Ronnie D. Lipschutz (Santa Cruz, CA: University of California Press, 1998), 309–310.

46. Pierre and Quandt, 137.

47. Kepel, 263.

48. See his interview in *Al-Sharq al-Aswat*, September 12, 2000, 5.

49. Boubker Belkadi, "Reconciliation threatened by FIS leader murder," *AFP*, November 23, 1999.

50. *AFP*, February 18, 2002.

51. *Le Monde*, October 31, 2002. The interior minister also claims that the radicals are not recruiting younger fighters to their cause—most fighters are between the ages of 35 and 45. In other words, the remnants of the original cadres recruited in the early 1990s.

52. "Algerian PM's Party Scores Convincing Win in Local Vote," *AFP*, October 11, 2002.

53. *Le Monde*, October 31, 2002.

54. "Diminishing Returns," 10.

55. *AFP*, March 24, 2003.

56. See Bouteflika's interview in *Al-Sharq al-Aswat*, September 12, 2000.

Chapter 4

Egypt: The Struggle for a Nation's Soul

Egypt, the most populous nation in the Arab world, is its intellectual center. It is home to the leading Arab intellectuals, filmmakers, and writers as well as the most authoritative interpreters of Sunni Islam at al-Azhar University. Egypt, in essence, helps to set the tone and the agenda for the entire Arab world.[1] It is therefore not surprising that Islamists hoped to construct a new order in Egypt for it would serve as a model for the rest of the Arab world. This desire did not lessen after the 1979 Iranian revolution for, while that event represented a major advance for the Islamist movement, it took place in a country that was on the periphery of the Arab world—Persian-speaking and Shi'ite in orientation.

Islamists had their sights set on Egypt for a second reason. Egypt was the vanguard of the Arab world. It was the first part to experience sustained modernization and Westernization, beginning with Muhammad Ali in the early nineteenth century. Indeed, it was Muhammad Ali's efforts "to consolidate control over Egypt and gain military parity with Europe" that motivated his policies of Westernization.[2] It was in Egypt that attempts were made to shift the basis of the political community away from the Muslim *umma* toward the concept of the nation-state, which, in the words of Lord Cromer, "will enable all the dwellers in cosmopolitan Egypt, be they Muslim or Christian, European, Asiatic, or African, to be fused into one self-governing body."[3] Once the British took effective control of Egyptian affairs in 1882, it was secular, middle-class nationalists who took the lead in formulating opposition to colonial control.[4] It was in reaction to the secular modernizers that Islamism was born in an attempt to provide an alternate path to modernization and development that did not require Westernization.[5]

NASSER AND THE MUSLIM BROTHERHOOD

The first chapter has already covered in great detail the origins of Islamist ideology; although, it bears repeating that the first major attempt to form an Islamist-based movement took place in Egypt with the creation of the Muslim Brotherhood (*Jamiat al-Ikhwan al-Muslimeen*) in 1928.[6] Like its secular competitors, such as the Wafd, the Brotherhood emulated modern, European political movements, and possessed its own media, schools, and youth groups in addition to the main party organization. Like the nationalists, it opposed British control over Egyptian affairs. However, the Brotherhood also opposed the existing Islamic establishment and believed that it was increasingly out of touch with the needs and concerns of Muslims living in the modern world.[7] The Brotherhood engaged in what the British termed as terrorist activities, but the violence that was engendered also affected the Brotherhood itself when its founder, al-Banna, was assassinated in 1949.[8]

The Muslim Brotherhood was an uneasy partner in the coalition that overthrew the monarchy of King Farouk on July 23, 1952. However, it soon became clear that a republican Egypt would not become a stepping-stone to a restored Islamic caliphate. Colonel Gamal Abdul Nasser, who had consolidated his position as head of the Egyptian state by March 1954, moved to establish his ideological vision of pan-Arabism/Arab Socialism as paramount for Egypt, which brought him into conflict both with the Communists and the Muslim Brotherhood.[9] The Brotherhood was officially outlawed as an organization in October 1954, a ban that has remained in place to this day. Qutb and other Islamist thinkers were rounded up and imprisoned in that year; a second mass wave of arrests of Muslim Brothers took place in 1965. Eventually, Qutb, after being released for a short while in 1964, would be brought to trial in 1966 on charges of treason. He and two other Muslim Brotherhood leaders, Muhammad Yusuf Awash and Abd al-Fattah Ismail, were executed on August 29, 1966.

This does not mean that Nasser was anti-Islamic. On the contrary, he tried to bid for the support of pious Muslims by incorporating Islamic precepts into his governing ideology. In 1954, Nasser had proclaimed,

> We are endowed with a spiritual force and a faith in God and a sense of brotherhood, which fit us to open a chapter in the history of mankind like that chapter which our forefathers opened 1,300 years ago. Why should we not once again give the world a message of peace and mercy, of brotherhood and equality . . .[10]

Nevertheless, for Nasser, Islam was but one pillar in his pan-Arabist ideology. Islam existed to buttress the Egyptian state and strengthen Egyptian-Arab nationalism. This was made clear in the Draft Charter promulgated in 1962,

In the history of Islam, the Egyptian people, guided by the message of Mohamed, assumed the main role in defense of civilization and mankind . . . the Egyptian people had assumed—with unequalled courage—grave responsibilities in the interest of the whole region . . . The Egyptian people had also borne the literary responsibility of preserving the heritage and wealth of Arab civilization.[11]

This brought Nasser into direct conflict with the Islamists. As Raphael Patai noted,

This feeling of Arab unity as primary brought some opposition from the Pan-Islamists. For them, religion was the strongest, holiest bond. For the Pan-Arabists, it was merely a historical, or divine, instrument, which played a role in shaping Arab unity.[12]

This was unacceptable for the Islamists. One of the reasons that Qutb and other Muslim Brotherhood leaders posed such a threat to Nasser and his regime was the formulation of a Muslim right to rebellion, even against a government constituted by fellow Muslims. Qutb linked the status quo in Egypt and other parts of the Arab world to *jahiliyya*—the pre-Islamic pagan order—against which all Muslims were bound by duty to oppose. Thus, Qutb created a compelling theological justification of the right of revolt against any existing regime in the Arab world.

KILLING PHARAOH

After Nasser's death on September 28, 1970, his successor, Anwar Sadat, reversed several of his predecessor's policies, notably his close links with the Soviet Union. To solidify his hold on power, Sadat reached out to Islamists, released many from prison, and offered a Faustian bargain. The Muslim Brotherhood, as an organization, would remain illegal, but individual members, provided that they renounced the violent overthrow of the regime, would be permitted some access to the public square, including the ability to form Islamic Societies and the right to run for election to parliament.[13] However, for some Islamists, this was unacceptable. Thinkers such as Salih Sirrya, founder of *Shabab Muhammad*, believed that such "incrementalism doomed the Brothers to irrelevance. Real change could only come through coup d'etat."[14] Therefore, during the 1970s, more radical organizations, notably Islamic Jihad and *al-Takfir wal-Hijra*, emerged. Rejecting the idea of working within the system, these militants opted for the formation of a vanguard party, which was to destabilize the state through sporadic acts of violence. The radicals gained in strength due to growing dissatisfaction with the Sadat regime. Despite the rhetoric, its failures were apparent to all. The devastating defeat at the hands of Israel in 1967 exposed the weaknesses of the regime, and the 1973 Yom Kippur war could not be considered in any way a decisive victory—no matter how the propagandists depicted the crossing of the Canal. Economic stagnation, corruption, and the lack of true democracy complicated matters. Finally, Sadat's peace treaty with Israel was widely resented. In the eyes of many pious Muslims, Sadat was now a Khajirite, a secessionist from the community of the faithful.

The end of the 1970s was marked by renewed ferment. In 1978, the Egyptian government executed Shuqri Mustafa, a disciple of Qutb and the leader of a militant organization that had increasingly shifted to terror tactics, including the kidnapping and murder of Egypt's minister of religious foundations. While he and his group were apprehended, the subsequent trial helped to discredit the status and authority of the *ulama*. It also paved the way for other groups to take up the argument that the Egyptian regime was anti-Muslim. The Iranian revolution and the proclamation of an Islamic Republic in Iran offered inspiration to other radicals that the existing regimes of the Middle East could be successfully overthrown, despite American support. The siege of the Great Mosque in Mecca by Islamist militants highlighted the fragility of another key American ally, the House of Saud. In Egypt, militants quietly infiltrated different key institutions, including Sadat's own bodyguard, and, on October 6, 1981, during a military parade, Sadat was assassinated by Lieutenant Khaled Islambuli, who shouted: "I have killed Pharaoh!" as he pumped bullets into the Egyptian president.[15]

However, there was no revolutionary wave to accompany the assassination of the president. The militants' uprisings, especially in Asyut, were contained in Egypt, and the following year, in February 1982, the Syrian president Hafez al-Asad launched a major military operation to wipe out the Muslim Brotherhood in its stronghold within the city of Hama.

Hosni Mubarak, Sadat's vice president and his successor, initiated mass arrests of the Islamists, including Ayman al-Zawahiri, who would go on to become Osama bin Laden's deputy. A purge of the army and security services took place. The blind sheikh Omar Abdel Rahman, the spiritual leader of many militants, was brought to trial in 1982. Although acquitted based on narrow interpretations of the charges, he would eventually seek asylum in the United States. Many other Egyptian Islamists found it prudent to leave the country and join the *jihad* in Afghanistan against the Soviet Union.

During the 1980s, Mubarak pursued a carrot-and-stick approach with the Islamists. Under the state of emergency instituted after Sadat's death, his government had wide-ranging powers to arrest and detain; thousands were imprisoned, and hundreds brought to trial. Yet, a number of those arrested were eventually acquitted and released. In fact, many of the core cadres of what was to become the Islamic Group were activists amnestied in 1984. Thousands of Muslim Brothers detained by Sadat prior to his assassination were released. There is also evidence that, between 1983 and 1987, police officials were in contact with radicals and extended a tacit form of toleration for their organizational activities provided their activities were limited to preaching.[16]

The Egyptian government also sought, like its counterpart in Algeria, to co-opt the Islamists by acceding to several of their demands. In 1985, the National Assembly agreed to revise Egypt's secular legal code to bring it into closer conformity with Islamic law, impose Islamic censorship on the media, and expand religious education in the nation's schools.[17] Increasingly, state television also gave more coverage to sermons and lectures by figures associated with the Islamists, include Al-Ghazali, who was working in Algeria at that time. In 1987, the Islamic Alliance among the Muslim Brotherhood, the Labour Party, and the Liberal Party was formed to contest elections. All of this contributed to a growing Islamicization of political dialogue within Egypt. The leader of the Labour Party, Ibrahim Shukri, promoted the shift within his party from secular socialism to Islamism, and observed that,

> Our programme included Islamic precepts, even before we adopted our current position. It laid a stress on the fear of God and the importance of holding on to religion without necessarily mentioning the word Islam. Our programme also stated that Islamic shari'a should be the main source of legislation—a provision which Sadat included in the constitution.[18]

Two factors helped to restart Islamist operations in Egypt. The first was the perceived success of the Arab Islamist fighters in Afghanistan in defeating Soviet forces and driving them out of Afghanistan. In other words, the departure of the Soviets in 1989 was a "victory . . . not only for Islam but for the reformed Islam of the jihadists."[19] It reaffirmed the position of those who maintained that the armed struggle could produce results. The second was the perceived weakness of the Mubarak regime in Egypt. Mubarak's attempts to continue the Faustian bargain with the Muslim Brotherhood and accommodate other Islamist demands were interpreted as weakness. Indeed, the electoral success of the Muslim Brotherhood in the 1987 elections and the compromises offered by the regime convinced the radical Islamists that power was within their grasp. In that year, the Islamist radicals began to develop a military capability to challenge the regime.[20] The radicals also assumed that the Mubarak government had no real base of support within the Egyptian populace and was propped up mainly by copious amounts of American aid. When Mubarak dispatched Egyptian forces to take part in the coalition against Iraq during the first Gulf War in 1991, this "confirmed the Islamist portrait of the regime as a corrupt, subservient vassal of the United States and thus allowed the Islamists to seize the banner of nationalism and populism."[21] Thus, the radical elements concluded that, with sufficient pressure, Mubarak could be toppled. After all, he had been widely condemned for siding with the West against a fellow Muslim and Arab leader. One jingle proclaimed, "Mubarak, you beggar, you have sold Mecca and the Nile."[22]

The Islamists also hoped to play on rising economic discontent and frustration with corruption, particularly with the so-called Gang of Sons, the offspring of Mubarak and other leaders. In the aftermath of the Gulf War, the average Egyptian's living standard was eroded by a 20 percent inflation rate while the budget deficit hovered at approximately 18 percent of GDP. Egypt's external debt doubled between 1980 and 1991 to over two-thirds of the country's GNP ($40.6 billion). The state's inability and unwillingness to address problems of chronic unemployment offered an opening to extremist groups.[23] As in Algeria, many of those who joined the radical Islamists were "would-be members of the overstaffed technical and administrative classes" who were negatively affected by "the scarcity of economic and political opportunity."[24] The radicals, by intimating that they held feasible solutions to Egypt's economic crisis, enjoyed an initial wave of popularity by deriving from the fact that they offered Egypt's disenfranchised youth an idiom of dissent and a sense of community. This grew out of the reality that, by the 1990s, Islamic charities, rather than the government, had become the primary delivers of social services to the Egyptian population.[25]

Under the inspiration of the blind sheikh, new armed organizations emerged alongside Islamic Jihad—al-Gamaat al-Islamiyya (Islamic Group) and Gihad al-Gihad (New Jihad)—the latter comprised mainly of Afghan returnees. Their purpose was to destabilize Egyptian society and pave the way for an Islamist takeover of the state. In the fall of 1988, the security police clashed with the Islamic Group in the slums of Heliopolis in Cairo. In 1989, an attempt was made on the life of then-Interior Minister Zaki Badr, and, in 1990, the speaker of Egypt's parliament, Rifaat al-Mahgoub, was assassinated. Armed radicals began to attack the police and other officials of the regime. Low-level clashes had begun in 1987 when police began to launch crackdowns on meetings and seminars in mosques, particularly in Upper Egypt. The radicals also targeted Egypt's economy by launching attacks against the Islamists' financial institutions and production facilities but especially against tourists and tourist sites by hoping to dry up an important stream of revenue. Before the Gulf War, tourism generated some $2 billion in foreign exchange for the regime. Between 1990 and 1992 alone, more than 800 people were killed in violence instigated by the radicals.

By 1992, Egypt faced one of its most serious crises as it confronted the twin plagues of economic stagnation and armed insurrection. In that year, the radicals formally declared war on the regime, and the nightmare of the Iranian revolution loomed. A 1993 U.S. National Intelligence Estimate predicted, "Islamic fundamentalist terrorists will continue to make gains across Egypt, leading to the eventual collapse of the Mubarak government."

However, the state did not collapse. In part, this is because, as in Algeria, the government decided that the policy of co-optation had failed. This was especially confirmed after the Islamic Group assassinated the author and intellectual Farag Foda in June 1992. Foda had been one of the main voices opposing the implementation of Islamic law in Egypt. At his trial, Sheikh Al-Ghazali was called as a witness for the defense. He testified that Foda was indeed an apostate and that, if the state did not follow Islamic law in sentencing him, individual believers could justifiably take the law into their own hands and carry out the sentence of death. This convinced some within the Egyptian security establishment that any further attempts at conciliation would be interpreted as yet another sign of the regime's weakness.[26]

Between 1992 and 1997, an additional 1,200 people were killed in clashes between Islamist insurgents and government forces. In Cairo, the Islamists resorted to occasional bomb and gun attacks, but, in the villages of Upper Egypt, the conflict at times was best described as a low-intensity civil war in which the military chose to follow an Algerian-style eradication policy. The radical forces also tried to assassinate leading figures within the Egyptian government with attempts to kill the prime minister, the minister of the interior, the information minister in 1993, and Mubarak himself during a visit to Ethiopia in June 1995. Egypt's Coptic Christian community also faced the wrath of the Islamist fighters, who viewed them as a Western fifth column.

The state responded with force. Alaa Mohieddin, a spokesman for the Islamic Group, was murdered in 1989, reportedly by government agents. In Upper Egypt, as well as in poorer areas of Middle Egypt and Cairo itself, it dispatched policed units who were "given a green light to root out armed Islamic groups and do to it without the kinds of protections and restraints a society of laws honors and expects . . . Massive searches and arrests have been routine there."[27] The Egyptian state tolerated no quasi–Islamic republics in any part of Egypt. When militants boasted that the Embaba neighborhood in Cairo was being run along Islamist lines, the government launched an operation in December 1992 that cleared the neighborhood of Islamist elements and led to the arrests and deportations of some 5,000 individuals. This was followed by active social reconstruction. Mosques in the neighborhood were closely supervised by the Ministry of Religious Affairs, and the provision of social services was taken under state supervision. This was part of a concentrated effort by the Egyptian regime to forestall any close alliance between the militants and the urban poor.[28] Military courts handed down dozens of death sentences for arrested fighters, and some 10,000 remain imprisoned or detained. Some are under special orders that limit their contact with the outside world. Some have estimated that at the height of the anti-terrorism campaign, up to 20,000 people connected with the Islamists were in prison.[29]

However, after five years of struggle, the militants came to the conclusion that the Egyptian state could not be overthrown by force. Moreover, by 1996, many of the original fighting cadres, men with combat experience from Afghanistan, had been killed or captured and could "not be replaced by men of similar fighting skill."[30] Torture and ill-treatment at the hands of the security forces further eroded the will to resist. On July 5, 1997, from their prison cells, several leaders of the armed radicals issued a statement calling for an end to the uprising. Some Islamists did not honor the cease-fire. In November 1997, a machine-gun attack at the Temples at Luxor killed over 100 foreign and Egyptian tourists and guides. Nor was the cease-fire immediately honored by a number of Egyptian Islamists in exile, particularly in London, who continued to call for struggle against the government.[31]

Yet, the Mubarak government not only survived, but it has, through concerted economic and security measures, largely succeeded in crushing the Islamist challenge. Not only did the regime possess an excellent domestic intelligence service (GDSSI), it deployed a 300,000-strong special police force. Many of whom were themselves drawn from lower- and middle-class origins in Upper Egypt and thus able to do battle with radical forces on their home turf.[32] The radicals discovered that, while many Egyptians may have had no deep love for the existing regime, they were not prepared to embrace the violence of the Islamists. Attacks such as the one at Luxor in 1997 prompted widespread public revulsion. An editorial in the influential daily, *Al-Ahram*, captured the public mood by declaring, "If this is what they will do to get into power, then what are they going to do to us once they are in power?"[33] Indeed, Islamist violence succeeded mostly in mobilizing the Egyptian populace behind the government's anti-Islamist platform. As in Algeria, many of the Islamic militants turned to robbery and extortion as a way to fund their operations. These acts of rapacity, along with the killing of average policemen, "alienated otherwise neutral or sympathetic elements of the population from the radical militants and their works."[34] Islamic vigilantism, as practiced by the Islamic Group, such as raiding homes, disrupting services at mosques led by clergymen who disagreed with the Islamists, and harassing couples on the streets, also eroded popular support.[35] As one Egyptian student observed,

Café bombings and assassination attempts like the one against Gen. al-Alfi [the Minister of the Interior] cause a great deal of collateral damage. Much of this damage affects fellow Muslims and their property. The state-controlled news agencies, in another tactical maneuver, tend to focus on this damage in order to alienate the perpetrators. In this, they are eminently successful. There have been numerous reports of terrorists being chased and attacked after an act of violence. In one instance, a terrorist was caught and beaten nearly to death by an angry mob as he tried to flee after tossing a bomb into a drugstore in Cairo. The use of indiscriminate violence is counterproductive and is responsible for the distinct lack of success of the militants' attempts to sway the populace into open revolt.[36]

More importantly, it led the military to conclude that the radicals could not be negotiated with and therefore, under no circumstances, could Islamists be allowed to come to power in Egypt.[37] The government therefore rejected a 1993 tentative offer transmitted through several clerics that the Islamic Group would end its armed campaign in return for full freedom to propagate its message. The failure of these talks led to the resignation of the then-Interior Minister, Abdel Halim Moussa.[38]

However, the radicals also found it difficult to win popular support for their call to revolution. Beyond their self-defeating campaign of terror, Islamic Jihad and *al-Gamaat al-Islamiyya* were unable to offer specific solutions to Egypt's seemingly intractable economic problems. The Islamist economic program was limited to slogans such as "God will provide" and the equally vague "Quran will feed the hungry." As with Islamists elsewhere, the whole emphasis was on achieving political power. Yet, their conception of politics was similarly muddled. Muhammad al-Ghazali, a leading Egyptian Islamist intellectual, who, during his tenure as head of Algeria's Islamic university had helped to bring Islamists into official structures during the 1980s, proclaimed, "Democracy is objectionable because it treats equally the virtuous and the debauched, the strong and the weak, the believer and the infidel."[39] Islamist discourse calling for the implementation of Islamic law offered powerful symbols, but it never addressed issues such as political empowerment, corruption, and one-party rule. Despite their efficiency in providing social welfare services, the inability of the Islamists to proffer a coherent economic agenda and a palatable political program prevented them from emerging as an alternative to the established order. More importantly, targeting the tourism industry proved to be a major strategic blunder because this directly imperiled the livelihoods of millions of ordinary Egyptians. Ironically, even the Islamic Group branch in Aswan, a city hard-hit economically by the collapse of the tourist trade, was one of the first organizations to argue for a cease-fire with the government.[40] Even a number of the militants in exile recognized that attacks on tourists had not only failed to advance the cause of Islamic revolution, but it had, in fact, harmed the Islamists.[41] In fact, this was a renunciation of an earlier ruling that had declared tourism to be *haram* because tourism was "an enterprise of debauchery," in the proclamation by Sheikh Omar Abdel Rahman.[42] The fact that most of those killed by the radicals were themselves Muslims also delegitimized the Islamists in the eyes of the general public, who could "not understand how acts of murder could be committed in the name of Islam."[43] Following the execution of five returnees from Afghanistan for a spate of 1993 terrorist attacks, including ones on tour buses at the pyramids at Giza and the Egyptian Museum, an Egyptian newspaper editorialized,

> They conspired in killing and sabotage. They shed the blood of the innocent. They corrupted and spoiled the very earth that God has promised as a safe haven. They wanted to frighten and alarm society and the national economy by trying to strike at tourism. They allowed what God forbade, and the court applied to them the Divine Ordinance of God and the ruling of the law.[44]

A popular television preacher also took to the airwaves to denounce the radicals and accused them of distorting Islamic truth. In 1995, Muhammad Metwali el-Sharawi declared that the tactics of the radicals were inconsistent with the axioms and tenets of Islam. He observed that "killing innocent people, sabotage, destruction, and frightening innocent people" were all crimes against Islam and called upon Islamic scholars "to intensify their efforts to show that these actions are completely remote from our true religion's values, principles, and tenets."[45] The anti-terrorist campaign also pushed the more moderate Muslim Brotherhood to explicitly renounce the use of force or violence. In May 1995, the Brotherhood released a statement after Mubarak proclaimed that "violence is always an integral part" of its methods. In it, the Brotherhood insisted that it "is in no way involved in violence and denounces all forms of terrorism, calling on those who commit this sin to return to the correct path of Islam."[46]

THE EGYPTIAN STALEMATE

By 1997, it was becoming clear that the Egyptian government could not be overthrown by internal insurrection. Despite the enormous economic damage wrought by the campaign, the state was holding its own. Ironically, the Luxor killings of that year, the single most devastating Islamist attack in Egypt, also proved to be the last major act of armed resistance.[47] Yet, unlike in Algeria, the Mubarak government had no new solutions to the intractable economic problems faced by ordinary Egyptians. Nor could it initiate political reforms designed to encourage greater pluralism and public participation in government. This led Muntasir al-Zayyat, a lawyer who has often acted as a spokesman for the radical Islamists, to complain: "The blocked channels of understanding and the absence of an opportunity for an objective and serious dialogue are the major problem that encourages the climate of violence in Egypt."[48]

This is why many Egyptians believe that, over time, the Mubarak regime must begin to lay the conditions for a peaceful transition to a moderate Islamist regime that is capable of launching economic and political reforms.[49] Indeed, moderate Islamists are ideologically more in line with neo-liberal economic thinking than the Egyptian status quo that remains largely in thrall to notions of state control over the economy. In fact,

A privatized economy is consistent with classical Islamic economic theory and its well-established protection of market and commerce. The Islamist parties have been among the most persistent critics of state restrictions on trade and measures that obstruct opportunities for middle-class entrepreneurs.[50]

Moderate forces have also risen to the fore within the ranks of the Islamists because the moderates have capitalized on the failure of the radicals to seize power. Moderates believe that peaceful means and acceptance of democratic principles are more likely to lead to greater Islamist influence in Egypt. Indeed, Egyptian society has become more Islamically flavored during the 1990s, even as the crackdown against the militants intensified.[51]

The moderates could also claim real successes in creating conditions for greater religiosity and adoption of Islamic norms within Egyptian society, which helped to undercut the radicals' position that an Islamic state could only come about by armed revolution. Through its social, business, and educational networks, the Muslim Brotherhood has had much more of an impact on daily life in Egypt than small groups of radicals engaged in pitched battles with the security forces. As Gregory Starrett observed, the thousands of professionals who are connected with the Muslim Brotherhood "volunteer their time providing social, educational, and health services for the poor through private voluntary organizations operating in centers associated with private mosques."[52] Since the late 1980s, the Brotherhood has emerged as a leading force in Egyptian civil society, especially within the professional organizations, both in technical fields, such as engineering and dentistry, and in traditional liberal strongholds, such as law and academia.[53] In turn, exposure to the give-and-take of democratic procedures within such institutions has given Islamists direct experience with building coalitions and reaching out to moderate forces. In 1995, some of them attempted to create a moderate political party, *Hizb al-Wasat* (Center Party) that included an Egyptian Coptic Christian as one of its leaders and would concentrate on pursuing political and economic reform rather than implementing a religious agenda. Although this party was not recognized by the state, it does reflect that, among some of the Islamists, there is a growing trend toward political moderation.[54] Interestingly, the Brotherhood in that year also proclaimed that Christians in Egypt "have the same rights and responsibilities as Muslims as well as the same civil and political rights"[55] This proclamation, by a group that views itself as Islamist, is a remarkable development because the traditional view has always been that Christians are a community that enjoys protection in return for payment of the poll tax but in no way enjoys equal rights with Muslims.

What the Mubarak government has been trying to do over the last decade is control and channel, rather than repress, the Islamic trend. It has supported the Brotherhood to the extent that undercuts the radical forces but not to the point that the Brotherhood could supplant the ruling establishment. Thus, the regime has taken some contradictory steps. On the one hand, it has permitted the growing Islamicization of the country's legal and educational systems and increased censorship of the media per Islamic guidelines. The furor surrounding the Nasr Abu Zayd affair demonstrated the extent to which Egypt was moving away from secular norms. Abu Zayd, a professor at Cairo University, had written a controversial literary analysis of the Quran and was denounced by many Muslim leaders. Suit was filed in a court of law to have him declared an apostate from Islam who, in consequence, could not remain married to his wife because Egypt's family law, which is based on Islamic models, forbids marriage between a Muslim woman and a non-Muslim man. In 1995, he was found to be an apostate by the appeals court. On the other hand, the state, using its powers of appointment, has sought to remove radical imams and teachers from their positions and replace them with more moderate figures. It also initiated crackdowns against the Muslim Brotherhood in 1995 and prior to the 2000 parliamentary elections.[56] The state also tried to supplant independent sources as the primary publisher of Islamic material. Thus, the ruling National Democratic Party has issued a number of publications and magazines such as *al-Liwa al-Islami* (*The Islamic Standard*) as "part of a concentrated effort to adopt the language and tactics of the Islamist movement so as better to compete with them on their own ground." Moreover, in 1993, Muhammad al-Ghazali, the scholar and preacher whose own views on the compatibility between Islam and democracy were cited previously, was appointed to a commission to supervise the production of religious textbooks for use in public schools.[57]

Egypt today presents a paradoxical face. The Muslim Brotherhood continues to be outlawed while Islamist interpretations of law increasingly guide policy. Terrorism is denounced; yet, the state-controlled media publishes material that appears indistinguishable from the diatribes of the radicals. Liberal intellectual Hazem Saghiya called attention to this duality when he wrote,

> Egypt's Islamists operate between two poles: executing people on the one hand and controlling the cultural and even social space on the other hand. Egypt's intellectuals swing between Emmanuel Kant on the one hand, and Saladin on the back of a horse in the battle of Hittin on the other.[58]

Yet, it is also important not to overstate the influence of the Islamists. Sociologist Saad Eddin Ibrahim estimates that, in truly free and fair elections, Islamists would poll approximately 15 percent of the votes. The current wave of support for the Brotherhood reflects not simply ideological agreement with its agenda but also reflects dissatisfaction with the status quo, which is akin to the number of Russian voters who cast ballots for nationalists and communists in parliamentary elections during the 1990s, and gratitude for the alternative social service network the Brotherhood maintains.[59] All of the evidence suggests that Islamism, in its more moderate forms, remains an influential part of the Egyptian social and political landscape, but most Egyptians have rejected the utopian revolution offered by the radicals. Indeed, the lasting impact of the revolutionary campaign of the 1990s has been the production of "a generation that seeks to avoid any confrontation with the state."[60] Indeed, a number of Islamist fighters found it prudent to leave Egypt during the 1990s to migrate to fight elsewhere, notably in Bosnia. Others came to the conclusion that battling the Egyptian state was a lost cause that diverted attention from other pressing matters, such as the fate of the Palestinians. A number of the members of Islamic Jihad apparently believed that the cessation of the violent campaign inside of Egypt "would unify the Muslims' ranks, bring about good, and direct the *jihad* toward the liberation of the Aqsa mosque from the hands of the enemies of the religion."[61]

ISLAMISM AND MODERATION IN EGYPT

The Egyptian government believed that a harsh policy of repression against the militants combined with selected economic reforms might engender conditions that could lead to more moderate elements rising to the fore in Egypt. So far, their calculations appear to be correct. As Gilles Kepel concluded,

The policy of privatizing and modernizing the economy led to the emergence of a new class of entrepreneurs . . . The regime gambled that the growth of wealth would allow the social interest of the devout middle class to prevail over their ideological inclinations and that it would join the bandwagon of prosperity while at the same time deploying and funding a species that would acknowledge political consensus, instead of encouraging the kind of confrontational Islamism embodied by the Brothers and the Gamaa.[62]

The year 2002 marked a watershed year in the development of the Islamist movement in Egypt. First, a number of the jailed leaders of the Islamic Group who had issued the 1997 cease-fire were permitted to tour Egypt's prisons to explain its rationale to the imprisoned rank-and-file, especially those on the verge of being released. This was followed by a series of interviews conducted by the editor-in-chief of *Al-Mussawar*, Makram Mohammad Ahmad, who considered himself to be a close confidant of President

Mubarak, with the leaders of the Islamic Group's Consultative Council, including Osama Ibrahim Hafez, Hamdi Abdel-Azim Abdel-Rahman, Karam M. Zohdi, and Assem Abdel-Maged Mohammed. Finally, a series of four books by the Islamic Groups leaders explaining why the armed struggle violated Islamic law and why peaceful action was the only acceptable method to strive for change were published and widely distributed.[63] The four works are (giving their English titles): *The Initiative for the Cessation of Violence; Shedding Light on Errors Committed in the Jihad; The Ban on Narrow Positions in Religion and on the Excommunication of Muslims;* and *Advice and Clarification to Rectify Concepts of Those Who Assume Responsibility for Society.*

These public actions brought to light what for several years had been "an unpublicized rift within the Islamists' ranks with some willing to be part of the system and others determined to shun the current political order."[64] Predictably, exile elements within the Islamic Group, as well as the more radical Islamic Jihad, have rejected the cease-fire initiative. Al-Zawahiri denounced it from Afghanistan in 2002. However, the cease-fire and change of tactics seem to have found broad agreement among radicals in Egypt.

What makes the four books of interest is the way in which the radical leaders moved away from their initial utopian and hard-line views in the wake of their actual experiences. The first book, which lays out the initiative itself, made the case that any *jihad* that has little chance of success should be abandoned, especially if it causes dissension among Muslims or aids the enemies of Islam. The second book, which deals with the errors committed during the *jihad*, notes that the views of past Islamic scholars must be interpreted and adapted to modern conditions, not accepted uncritically. Furthermore, it argues that foreign tourists who legally visited Egypt were in fact under Muslim protection and should not have been targeted for attacks. The third and fourth volumes call for an end to narrow interpretations of Islam and the practice of excommunicating Muslims who disagree with the viewpoints of the radicals, as well as enjoin Islamists "not to impose their values upon those who do not adhere to their interpretations."[65]

Mustapha Kemal Al-Sayyid, a professor of political science at Cairo University and director of its Center for Developing Countries Studies, has offered an optimistic appraisal of the initiative by seeing in it the intellectual renunciation of violence and *jihad* as a means of achieving political change in favor of dialogue. The repudiation of much of the ideology upon which the Egyptian Islamists grounded their revolutionary activity holds open the possibility that radical Islamists are prepared to forego violence. It also serves to legitimate the stances taken by more moderate groups that seek to marry Islamic principles with liberal values and institutions. However, there remains a lingering suspicion that these developments are merely tactical, efforts undertaken by imprisoned men to facilitate their early release. There is also a risk that members of the rank-and-file will be radicalized by their experiences in prison. Al-Zayyat warns that earlier violent movements were a result of the "torture and long imprisonment. It was the direct outcome of this state, and this affected the country for many years during which it suffered from acts of violence."[66] Only time will tell whether this ideological change of signposts represents a genuine conversion to the values of tolerance and compromise.

In the end, the transformation of a formerly utopian-revolutionary movement into a moderate political force may have ramifications far beyond Egypt because the Egyptian example is closely watched—and to some degree emulated—by Islamists from all over the Muslim world, from sub-Saharan Africa to the Far East.[67]

NOTES

1. Ray Takeyh, *The Origins of the Eisenhower Doctrine: The US, Britain and Nasser's Egypt, 1953–57* (New York: St. Martin's, 2000), 14.

2. Gregory Starrett, *Putting Islam to Work: Education, Politics, and Religious Transformation in Egypt* (Berkeley: University of California Press, 1998), 26.

3. George E. Kirk, *A Short History of the Middle East*, 7th rev. ed. (New York: Frederick A. Praeger, 1964), 117.

4. This is discussed by Kirk in chapters V and VI of his history.

5. It is interesting to note that a number of the early and mid-twentieth century Islamist thinkers lived in Muslim countries under strong British influence—Egypt and the British Raj on the Indian subcontinent—and in countries where there were very strong secular nationalist movements leading the anti-colonial struggle.

6. Two of the leading academic works on the Brotherhood are Richard Mitchell, *The Society of the Muslim Brothers* (Oxford: Oxford University Press, 1969) and Gilles Kepel, *Muslim Extremism in Egypt: The Prophet and Pharaoh* (Berkeley: University of California Press, 1986).

7. Starrett, 63.

8. There are some indications that he was killed by agents of King Farouk. Robin Wright, *Sacred Rage* (New York: Simon and Schuster, 1985, 2001), 179.

9. Takeyh, *Origins*, 28.

10. Quoted in Kirk, 290–291.

11. Quoted in Kirk, 291.

12. Raphael Patai, *The Arab Mind*. Revised edition (New York: Scribner, 1983), 207–208.

13. Of course, this bargain has been unevenly enforced. At various points, when the regime perceives that the Brotherhood has become too active, arrests break up the organization and thin the ranks of the leadership. Cf. Mona Makram-Ebeid, "Egypt's 2000 Parliamentary Elections," *Middle East Policy* VIII, no. 2 (June 2001): 35–36.

14. Daniel Benjamin and Steven Simon, *The Age of Sacred Terror* (New York: Random House, 2002), 69.

15. "Pharaoh," of course, represented the wicked pre-Islamic order in keeping with Qutb's conception of regimes like Sadat's as being fundamentally pagan in nature. This also draws upon a long-standing Islamic understanding of despotic leaders as *taghyia* (the tyrant), who consider themselves to be above even God. Fatema Mernissi, *Islam and Democracy*, trans. Mary Joe Lakeland (Cambridge, MA: Perseus Publishing, 2002), 105.

16. Mustapha Kamel Al-Sayyid, *The Other Face of the Islamist Movement* (Washington, DC: Carnegie Endowment for International Peace, 2003), 16.

17. Wright, 189.

18. See his interview with *Al-Ahram Weekly*, no. 244. (26 October–1 November 1994).

19. Benjamin and Simon, 103.

20. Al-Sayyid, 16.

21. Paul M. Lubeck, "Islamist Responses to Globalization: Cultural Conflict in Egypt, Algeria, and Malaysia," in *The Myth of Ethnic Conflict: Politics, Ecnomics and Cultural Violence*, eds. Beverly Crawford and Ronnie D. Lipschutz (Santa Cruz, CA: University of California Press, 1998), 302.

22. Mernissi, 107.

23. Ray Takeyh. "Islamism: R.I.P." *The National Interest*, no. 63 (Spring 2001), 99.

24. Starrett, 199.

25. Paul Lubeck observes that, in Egypt, "social services such as education, health, and charity are increasingly provided by Islamic agencies." 305.

26. Kepel, 287.

27. Fouad Ajami, "The Sorrows of Egypt," *Foreign Affairs* 74, no. 5 (September/October 1995): 77.

28. For a description of the state's strategy, see Kepel, 289–292.

29. *AFP*, March 1, 1995.

30. Kepel, 294.

31. See, for example, the comments of Abu-Hamzah al-Masri, the leader of the *Ansar al-Shari'ah* organization in London, who maintained that the jailed leaders had no authorization to order a cease-fire. As reported in *Al-Sharq al-Awsat*, December 2, 1998, 5.

32. This also meant that the clashes between militants and police have been amplified by local traditions of blood vengeance. See Mamoun Fandy, "Egypt's Islamic Group: Regional Revenge?" *Middle East Journal* 48, no. 4 (1994), 609.

33. As quoted in Takeyh, "Islamism: R.I.P.," 99.

34. Kepel, 295.

35. Al-Sayyid, 18.

36. Wassim Absood, "The Militant Islamist Threat to Egypt," at http://info-manage.com/nonproliferation/najournal/militantislamegypt.html <accessed February 14, 2003>.

37. Lubeck, 306.

38. Al-Sayyid, 15.

39. Takeyh, "Islamism: R.I.P.," 99.

40. Al-Sayyid, 23.

41. Exiles associated with Islamic Jihad and the Islamic Group announced in 1998 that they too were preparing to endorse a ban on attacks on tourists. *AFP*, August 5, 1998.

42. Kepel, 288.

43. Al-Sayyid, 17.

44. *Al-Akhbar*, July 18, 1993, 3.

45. As reported in *MENA*, February 1, 1995.

46. *AFP*, May 1, 1995.

47. Al-Sayyid, 18.

48. See his interview in *Al-Sharq al-Awsat*, August 13, 1999, 3.

49. Mary Ann Weaver, "The Novelist and the Sheikh," the *New Yorker* LXX, no. 47 (January 30, 1995): 52–69.

50. Ray Takeyh, "Faith-Based Initiatives," *Foreign Policy*, November/December 2001, 70

51. Absood.

52. Starrett, 212.

53. Al-Sayyid, 12. The Brotherhood successfully took control of the executive committee of the Egyptian Lawyers' Syndicate in 1992. The Brotherhood had earlier won majorities on the boards of the Cairo University Faculty Club and the Pharmacists', Physicians', and Engineers' Syndicates. Starrett, 212.

54. Kepel, 359.

55. *AFP*, May 1, 1995.

56. Andrew Hammond, "Between the Ballot and the Bullet: Egypt's War Against Terrorism," *World Press Review Online* (November 14, 2001) http://www.worldpress.org/Mideast/329.cfm; Starrett, 207–209; Makram-Ebeid, 35–36.

57. Starrett, 209, 210. Muhammad al-Ghazali (1917–1996) is considered one of the most influential Islamic scholars of the twentieth century. He was a leading member of the Muslim Brotherhood and considered to be an exceptional preacher. One of his essential concerns was combating Western influence and moral degradation, but he was considered a moderate because of his rejection of violence and insurrection as a solution. Al-Ghazali was also approached by the government to act as a mediator with the militants, along with the popular television preacher Muhammad Metwali el-Sharawi and another veteran preacher with a great deal of popular influence, Sheikh Abd al-Hamid Kishk. However, these efforts were ended by the regime in 1993 after Al-Ghazali's testimony at the trial of Farag Foda's killers.

58. *Al-Hayat*, July 29, 2001.

59. Makram-Ebeid, 42.

60. Ibid., 37.

61. See the interview with Osama Ayub, in *Al-Sharq al-Awsat*, February 15, 2000, 6.

62. Kepel, 298.

63. Al-Sayyid, 16–19.

64. Makram-Ebeid, 37.

65. Al-Sayyid, 20.

66. *Al-Sharq al-Awsat*, 3.

67. Kepel, 88.

Chapter 5

Islamism in the Former Yugoslavia

In September 1992, Yossef Bodansky and Vaughn S. Forrest co-authored a policy paper for the House Republic Research Committee's Task Force on Terrorism and Unconventional Warfare entitled, "Iran's European Springboard?" The thesis of this paper was that a growing radicalization of Yugoslavias Muslim population, especially in Bosnia-Herzegovina and Kosovo, would lay the basis for Islamists to come to power in several regions of former Yugoslavia and thus provide the basis for the radicalization of Muslim populations living in the rest of Europe.[1] This was the specter of the Green Crescent of Islam that would span the axis Istanbul-Tirana-Sarajevo and provide the springboard for an Islamic assault on Europe.[2]

Notwithstanding the presence of indigenous Islamists and foreign activists among the *mujahedin* who came to Yugoslavia to fight in Bosnia and Kosovo, have Islamist movements been successful in gaining ground in the region? More importantly, is there now a base within the population at large—and not simply among a small group—upon which Islamist movements in Europe can build?

As in the former Soviet Union, the identification of Islam with particular ethnic groups has helped to cloud the situation. This has been particularly true in Yugoslavia. As Michael Sells aptly noted, many in the region embrace a religious identity that "is not dependent on personal piety, self-conscious beliefs, or sincerity." Most people, even those purporting to act on religious grounds, are not "religious in the sense of having a committed sense of theological beliefs and a faithful religious practice based on them. It is also true that the vast majority of Yugoslavs in 1989 were largely secular, and many of them are still committed atheists."[3] Despite the ravages of civil wars, ethnic conflicts, and external intervention, there is still no indication that a majority of Muslim Slav-Bosnians or Kosovar Albanians are predisposed to embrace Islamist movements.

ISLAM AND NATIONALITY IN YUGOSLAVIA:
A GENERAL OVERVIEW

Islam arrived in the Balkans in the wake of the Ottoman conquest. With the exception of Turkomans and Tatars deliberately settled in the region by the Ottomans to serve as colonists, most Muslims in the region are the descendants of Slav or Albanian converts.[4] Islamization in the Balkans was most successful in those regions that were border zones between Orthodox Christianity and Roman Catholicism, such as the Shkumba valley in Albania or in Bosnia, or in lowland areas such as Kosovo where a combination of out-migration by Christians and deliberate policies of settling Muslims was undertaken by the Ottoman regime.[5] For the most part, Balkan converts embraced Sunni Islam of the Hanafite school; although, especially in Albania, followers of the Bektashi Sufi sect were numerous.

Within the Ottoman Empire, populations were classified and ruled "not along ethno-linguistic lines but by religious affiliation—the millet system."[6] In the modern period, this has led to "a confusion of the concepts of citizenship, religion, and ethnicity."[7] This process was further muddled by the tendency after the eighteenth century to identify religious identity with a specific national/ethnic one—indissolubly linking all people of Orthodox faith with Serbian ethnicity and all Catholics with Croatian ethnicity.[8] Because all Muslims, regardless of ethnicity, were grouped together in the same millet, there was a tendency for some Albanian and Slav Muslims to identify themselves as Turks,[9] and even to speak Turkish as a sign of status;[10] although, for the most part, there was less pressure on the Muslim groups to seek a definite national identity because they "shared their faith with that of the Ottoman rulers and hence were initially less receptive to the new ideology of nationalism."[11]

Because of their identification with the Turks due to a shared membership in the Muslim millet as well as the ability of Slav and Albanian Muslims to rise into the ranks of the Ottoman elite, over thirty grand viziers of the Empire were of Albanian origin alone.[12] As the Ottoman Empire began to contract in the nineteenth century, some Muslims chose to relocate to Anatolia in order to remain a part of a Muslim empire. This tendency was not limited to the Balkans. In the wake of Russian expansion into the Caucasus during the same period, tens of thousands of Circassians and other Muslim groups chose to emigrate to Anatolia and other core Ottoman lands. As the ascendant Kingdom of Serbia began to take control of more territories in the Balkans, some Albanians chose to emigrate rather than remain under Christian rule, and many relocated to Anatolia, the homeland of the Turks.[13] After Bosnia-Herzegovina came under Austrian supervision in 1878, the Muslim population, which was already decimated by wars, was further reduced by the departure of Slav

Muslims from the region. Some estimate that the Muslim population of Bosnia declined by one-third after 1878. When Austria formally annexed Bosnia in 1908, there was a subsequent out-migration of the Muslim population to Anatolia.[14] Bosnia's Muslims, in particular, had been characterized by what nineteenth century observers termed a fanatical devotion to Islam, and the community found itself increasingly dislocated by the end of Ottoman rule over the region.[15]

The collapse of the Ottoman Empire also ended experiments in creating a new, non-ethnic, imperial identity for all residents of the Empire as Ottomans. The failure of *osmanlilik* was understandable. An Ottoman state whose initial *raison d'être* was the advance and defense of Islam could not easily reinvent itself as a state based on the concept of the citizen. Moreover, the Muslim elites of the Balkans had no desire to give up the privileges that went along with membership in the Muslim millet or accept the social and political equality of Balkan Christians.[16]

As a result of the disintegration of the Ottoman and Hapsburg Empires, combined with the territorial settlements after the Balkan Wars (1912–1913) and the decision after World War I to unite a number of South Slavic territories with the Kingdom of Serbia to create Yugoslavia, Muslims now found themselves in changed circumstances. Albanian-speaking Muslims in Kosovo and Vardar Macedonia and Slav-speaking Muslims in Bosnia and the Sanjak were no longer privileged members of the Muslim millet in the Ottoman Empire, but they were instead citizens of a Christian-dominated, South Slav federation in which identities were nationally defined.[17]

One post-war option was to adopt Turkish nationality, that is, continue the process of Turkification. Although some Albanian and Slav Muslims chose this path, it was not embraced by a majority of Yugoslavia's Muslims. For one thing, it proved difficult to claim a literary, political, and cultural heritage that was largely adopted and not indigenous to the region.[18] Even when Slav and Albanian Muslims described themselves as Turks, they were aware that they were linguistically different from the Turks of Anatolia.[19] More importantly, there were political risks in assuming a Turkish identity. If the homeland of Turks was Turkey, then, by definition, Turks living in Yugoslavia were aliens. In keeping with this idea, Yugoslavia actually concluded agreements with Turkey in the 1930s to provide for the repatriation of Albanian Muslims to Turkey from Kosovo, and there were further out-migrations of Slav Muslims to Turkey in 1918 and 1945.[20] Assuming a Turkish identity also carried with it the risk that the populations so identified as Turks would be seen as occupiers who had no indigenous connection to the land.[21]

However, for the Albanian population, there was another alternative—secular Albanian nationalism. The Albanian national awakening, which began in the nineteenth century was led and influenced largely by

Christian and Bektashi Albanians. Aware of the divisive power of religion, they focused upon elements of common language and culture that could unite Albanians of diverse faiths. The Albanian Catholic poet Pashko Vasa, in his epic work *O moj Shqypni* ("My Poor Albania") written in 1879–1880, declaimed,

> Albanians, you are killing each other/You are divided into a hundred factions...But you are all brothers, you miserable people! . . . Awake, Albanians, wake from your slumber/Let us all, as brothers, swear an oath/Not to mind church or mosque/The faith of the Albanians is Albanianism![22]

Naim Frasheri, the intellectual, poet, and Bektashi leader, likewise promoted an all-inclusive Albanian identity by calling on his countrymen to "Come close, Albanians! We are all of the same seed, we are not divided, we are all brothers, and have one soul and one heart." In fact, Frasheri hoped that the Bektashi Sufi order would provide a bridge between Muslims and Christians to provide for joint action.[23] The League of Prizren, which was formed in 1878, called for the creation of a state in the Balkans that would unify all Albanians—defined as such on the basis of native language.[24]

The perceived lack of religious consciousness among Albanians,[25] which was enshrined in the famous dictum that "the religion of Albanians is Albania," was important in the formation of national identity because it enabled Albanians to transcend their religious differences.[26] Even though religious tensions persisted between Albanians of different faith communities,[27] it became the official position of Albanian nationalists that religion is a private matter and that Albanians should tolerate the faith choices of other Albanians.[28] This was not simply a position adopted by a few intellectuals; nineteenth- century travelers in the region were struck by the mass sentiment among Albanian Muslims that they were Albanians first and Muslims second—in stark contrast to the situation in Bosnia.[29] Thus, over time, Albanian Christians have joined with their Albanian Muslim brethren, even to the point of standing in opposition to their co-religionists among the Slavic peoples.[30] This was aided by the pledge taken by the members of the League of Prizren to foreswear blood feuds in order to concentrate on the national struggle.[31]

Aware that they differed from the Serbs of Kosovo and the emerging nationality labeled Macedonian by virtue of language and culture (and largely by religion as well because most Kosovar and Macedonian Albanians are Muslim), most of the Albanian population of the region embraced the Albanian national identity. The role of Islam thus shifted from being a faith community uniting Albanians with their co-religionists elsewhere in the Balkans and the Middle East to a marker of ethnic identity differentiating Kosovar Albanians from Orthodox Slavs.[32] Over time, not only did the appeal of claiming a Turkish identity diminish among

Albanians living in Yugoslavia,[33] but, in a reversal of the millet system, other minority Muslim groups living in Albanian-dominated areas of Kosovo and Macedonia were now facing increased pressure to fully assimilate into the Albanian community.[34] At the same time, the Albanians have de-emphasized Islam and been willing to play up the Christian roots and heritage of Albanians. In this respect, the role of the *laramans*, the Albanian crypto-Catholics of Kosovo, and the wave of interest shown in Catholicism by Kosovar Albanians "helped the Albanians to present themselves as an originally 'Christian' and 'European' nation in spite of their present-day Muslim appearances."[35]

However, in contrast to the Albanians, the Slavic-speaking/ethnically Slav Muslim populations of what was to become Yugoslavia faced a major problem that the Albanians had largely overcome by de-emphasizing religion as a component of national identity in favor of language. For the Slav Muslims, especially those living in Bosnia and the Sandjak, the only basis for group and community identity *was* Islam, on the foundation of belonging to that particular millet within the Ottoman Empire.[36] This identity was reinforced, particularly by the late nineteenth century, as Muslim refugees from other parts of the Balkans, particularly from Serbia, sought refuge in Bosnia among their co-religionists.[37]

Like their counterparts in Bulgaria and Georgia, the indigenous Muslims in what was to become Yugoslavia had been zealous defenders of the Ottoman state, usually taking the lead in putting down the rebellions launched by their Christian neighbors.[38] However, once the Ottoman Empire contracted, the Slavic Muslims had no other state or local institutions upon which to construct a national identity,[39] especially since previous Bosnian states had been Christian. The Slav Muslims of the area were also faced with an existential question. Could they continue to exist as a community within the framework of a state dominated by Christians?[40] This was compounded by their clear unwillingness in the nineteenth century to contemplate any meaningful association in national terms with any of their Christian-Slavic neighbors.[41] In turn, the phenomenon of Christoslavism, that is to say, the ideological notion that Slavic peoples must by definition be either Orthodox or Roman Catholic Christian in order to be *true* Slavs precluded the formation, either among Croats or Serbs, of a sense of national identity that could encompass Muslims as equal co-nationals, as the Albanians were doing.[42]

Ottoman nationalism never attracted much interest among Muslims in Bosnia and other parts of the Balkans. This was especially true as Ottomanism became linked to imperial reforms that the Muslims of the region thought might challenge their political and economic hegemony. Slav Muslims living within the territory of Bosnia did have a sense of territorial identity as Bosnians, to the extent of sometimes referring to themselves as Bosnians and referring to their South Slavic dialect as Bosnian, writing it either in Arabic letters or the Croatian recension of Cyrillic script.[43] This tendency accelerated especially after the 1850 revolt against Omar Latas Pasha, the Ottoman official and Serb convert charged with breaking the power of the local Muslim lords. However, the Bosnian identity was problematic. First, it could not encompass Slav Muslims outside of Bosnia itself. Second, Bosnian identity was also put forward in the second half of the nineteenth century by the Austrian authorities as a way to create a sense of unity among Orthodox, Catholic, and Muslim populations living in Bosnia and also to weaken the lure of Serbia as a independent South Slav state.[44] However, most Serbs and Croats living in Bosnia were neither willing to subordinate their own sense of national identity to any sense of Bosnian-ness. On the other hand, neither were Serbs nor Croats willing to abandon their claims to Bosnia and make any recognition of the Muslim population as alone constituting a Bosnian nation.[45]

Drawing upon their defined status as members of the Muslim millet, Bosnian Muslims formed the Movement for Cultural and Religious Autonomy and, in 1903, petitioned the Austrian authorities for the establishment of an autonomous national-political unity among the Muslim populace. However, this step was rejected by Vienna on the grounds that it would form a Muslim-based para-state within the provinces of Bosnia and Herzegovina.[46]

When Yugoslavia was created in 1918, the three main nations comprising the South Slavs were said to be the Serbs, the Croats, and the Slovenes. In the inter-war period, the prevailing sense was that the Muslims of Yugoslavia were, by nationality, either Serbs or Croats, whose ancestors had gone over to Islam. Thus, census forms contained provisions for Muslim Serbs, Muslim Croats, and Muslims of indeterminate nationality. The Muslims had to face the prospect of Serbianization during the inter-war period or of being Croatianized during the Second World War. In turn, the principal Muslim political organization, the Yugoslav Muslim Organization (JNO), sought to steer a middle course and obtain autonomy for Bosnia within Yugoslavia.[47]

As a result of World War II and with the coming of Josip Broz Tito and the Communists to power in Yugoslavia, new solutions had to be found. Tito coined the slogan that a "weak Serbia means a strong Yugoslavia"[48] and thus found ways needed to be found to balance Serbian aspirations with the other nationalities comprising the multinational state. Three principal methods were employed by Tito: one was to increase the number of constituent nations comprising Yugoslavia through the separation of Macedonia and Montenegro from Serbia; the second was to create autonomous provinces within Serbia, Vojvoidina, and Kosovo; and the third was to use Bosnia as a balancing force between Serbia and Croatia. Thus, the two main concentrations of Muslim population in Yugoslavia became key factors in the Titoist balancing act in post-war Yugoslavia—a largely autonomous, Albanian-dominated Kosovo and a Bosnia that could be dominated neither by Serb nor Croat, which thus requires a new constituent nation.

Therefore, beginning in World War II, the Yugoslav Communist Party began to promote the idea that Yugoslav Muslims formed a separate and distinctive ethnic-national group. At first, the Party concentrated on the idea that Muslims were "a separate, but, for the most part, still nationally undeclared-Slavic ethnic group, equal to Serbs and Croats."[49] After the war, Bosnian Muslim leaders began to develop and promote the thesis that Bosnian Muslims were the lineal descendants of the medieval Bogomil heretics, who were identified with the Bosnian Church of medieval historic records and then converted *en masse* to Islam after the Ottoman conquest; which thus proves the existence of a separate, historic Bosnian nationality distinct from Serbs and Croats.[50] By the mid-1960s, Tito saw in the Muslims of Bosnia and their reliable Communist leadership a way to keep in check rising nationalist sentiment in both Croatia and Serbia. Under his guidance, the Muslims of Bosnia-Herzegovina and the Sandjak were raised to the status of a constituent nation of Yugoslavia.[51] The process evolved in the following way. In 1948, the population was classed as indeterminate Muslims. In 1953, it was classed as indeterminate Yugoslavs. In 1961, it was classed as "Muslims in an ethnic sense." In 1971, it was classed as "Muslims in the sense of nationality." In 1981, it was unambiguously recognized as a separate nation within Yugoslavia.[52]

Muslim nationality was not conferred by religious practice of Islam, but, like the earlier millet system, it was based upon one's birth into a community. As Julie A. Mertus noted,

The term Muslim did not refer only to religion; the practicing of Islam was neither necessary nor sufficient for inclusion in this group. (For example, Muslim Albanians were not considered to be part of this national grouping of Muslims.) Rather, Muslim referred to a group defined by a bundle of markers of distinctiveness: language, culture, economic life, real and imagined history, and a sense of territoriality.[53]

Most importantly, this new nationality was defined in secular terms. Muslim-ness was predicated not on faith but on a "shared environment, cultural practices, a shared sentiment, and common experiences."[54] Muslims in Yugoslavia could be agnostic, atheist, or even members of the Jehovah's Witnesses![55] Like the survivals of the millet system found in Syria or Lebanon, one's public, confessional-national identity, which was conferred by birth, did not have to have any relation to a person's personal religious commitment.

The secularized nature of society in Bosnia-Herzegovina also led to a growing number of intermarriages between national groups and a greater willingness among residents of Bosnia to embrace the Yugoslav/South Slav identity in place of narrower national designations. This was especially true of the offspring of mixed Serb-Muslim marriages. It is estimated that some 16 percent of the people living in Bosnia qualified as being of mixed ancestry, and, according to the 1981 census, some 8 percent of the population declared themselves to be Yugoslavs by nationality.[56] The assumption of a Yugoslav identity was most pronounced among those who had been educated in the 1950s and the 1960s.[57]

Thus, by the 1970s, the main focal point of identity, organization, and mobilization for most of the historically Islamic populations of Yugoslavia was the nation, rather than the *umma*. Kosovar Albanians defined their position in Yugoslavia from the basis of Albanian national, rather than Islamic religious identity. Similarly, the newly coined Slavic-Muslim nationality defined itself as one of the constituent nations of the South Slav Federation alongside Serbs, Croats, Slovenes, Macedonians, and Montenegrins. National differences were reflected in the fact that Slav Muslims were more apt to intermarry with Catholic Croats and Orthodox Serbs than to seek spouses from among their Albanian co-religionists. Increasingly, the very unity of the Muslim religious establishment in Yugoslavia was also threatened, as Muslim Albanians, increasingly frustrated with the dominance in the Sunni establishment (*Islamska Zajednica*, the Islamic Community, or IZ) of Sarajevo Bosnians turned to an alternative religious establishment known as the Community of Dervish Orders based in Prizren.[58] Attempts to forge a single pan-Islamic party or political movement also foundered.[59] Therefore, the situation that existed in the days of Ottoman rule, when ostensibly Muslim Slavs and Albanians formed a single nation and shared a common identity as members of the same millet, had been replaced by the adoption of modern, secular national identities.

MUSLIMS, ISLAM, AND THE WAR IN BOSNIA, 1990–2002

The creation of a Muslim nationality represented a dual compromise. The first was between Serbs and Croats. Both had alternatively claimed the Muslims as strayed sheep from their respective national folds and were unwilling to allow the other group to claim the Muslims for fear of upsetting the demographic balances between Serbs and Croats, both in Bosnia and Yugoslavia as a whole. The second was a compromise in that the Muslims living in Bosnia could formally establish and maintain their distinctiveness as a group, but they were not to claim the designation Bosnian, which might then legitimate them as the sole national group entitled to claim the territory of Bosnia. The new nationality was officially secular, but its roots in religious differences could not be denied or hidden.[60]

Religious observance in Bosnia among tended to be low-. A 1985 survey indicated that only about 17 percent of Muslims in Bosnia were actively religious. Thus, the Muslim identity was transmitted less by religious faith and was based much more on "customs and culture and the millet legacy."[61] Bosnian Muslims prided themselves on their European orientation and secular attitudes, especially in contrast to their nominal co-religionists in the Middle East.[62] Women did not wear the veil, and the headscarf was worn generally by old women only or other women only during religious ceremonies.[63] Generally, it was only in rural areas that "the expression of a religious (Islamic) identity was an integrated part of the expression of a Muslim secular (cultural) identity."[64] In fact, during the 1970s, surveys indicated that, among Bosnian Muslims,

> Religion did provide the initial basis for which the Muslims constituted themselves as a nation, but religious factors were losing their former significance in giving way to other spiritual and material factors, not unlike the process characteristic of other Yugoslav peoples.[65]

However, the secularizing trend was resisted by the Muslim clergy and some in the intelligentsia, who maintained that one could not be termed a Muslim without believing in the tenets of Islam. In other words, the faith was the central component in the national identity.[66] This was the approach taken by one of the intellectuals, Alija Izetbegovic, who, in the summer of 1983, along with twelve other Muslim activists, was placed on trial for "hostile and counter-revolutionary activities."[67] Despite these actions, a modest Islamic revival began in Bosnia during the 1980s, due in part to the elevation of the Muslims to national status in Yugoslavia, which sparked a new sense of consciousness.[68] By the end of the 1980s, new surveys were suggesting that religiosity was on the rise among Bosnian Muslims with some 34 percent being characterized as religious.[69] Pan-Islamic nationalism was also "evident among certain quarters of Bosnia's Muslim intelligentsia," but most Slav Muslims in Bosnia continued to be supporters of a united Yugoslavia.[70]

After serving six years in prison, Izetbegovic was released and resumed his political and educational activities. Izetbegovic maintained that the Slav Muslims of Bosnia and the Sandjak "have not sufficiently affirmed themselves as a nationality. They have not been sufficiently aware, and their interests have not been articulated in any manner whatsoever."[71] As the Yugoslav League of Communists began to lose authority and support, new parties began to emerge. Izetbegovic was one of the organizers of a new, non-Communist political movement, the Party of Democratic Action (SDA). The SDA was formally organized on May 26, 1990. It was the first party in Bosnia to be set up on strictly ethnic-national and confessional lines.[72] The party described itself explicitly as a "political alliance of Yugoslav citizens belonging to Muslim cultural and historical traditions."[73] Almost immediately, the party was labeled by some as Islamist because most of its forty-some founding members were representatives of Bosnia's pan-Islamic group of intellectuals.[74]

Alija Izetbegovic was named as the head of this party. Izetbegovic (1925–2003)was and has remained a controversial figure. He has often been described by some as a religious conservative or a religious nation-alist.[75] In the 1940s, Izetbegovic was part of the group Young Muslims (*Mladi Muslimani*), which itself drew inspiration from Islamist groups in the Middle East, such as the Muslim Brotherhood. This group also had links with the grand mufti of Jersualem, Amin el-Huseyni, and some of its members joined with the Germans in the SS Handzar division set up for quisling Muslims by the Nazis. After World War II, Izetbegovic was arrested for his role in founding the journal *Mudzahid* and was jailed from 1946 to 1949.[76]

Izetbegovic's main ideological work, *The Islamic Declaration*, which was written in 1970 and served as the ultimate cause of his second arrest and incarceration, is likewise the focus of controversy. Is it "nothing but a summary of the main principles of the Muslim religion" or is it a "Mus-lim version of *Mein Kampf*?"[77] Perhaps the single most cited section of this work was Izetbegovic's statement that,

> There is no peace or coexistence between the Islamic faith and other, non-Islamic social and political systems . . . Islam clearly denies the right and opportu-nity in its own domain to any alien ideology.[78]

The *Declaration* sounds many classic Islamist themes—the stress upon the essential unity of all Muslim peoples, the need to unify faith and law, and the creation of a political, social, and economic order based upon Muslim principles.[79] As with other Islamist thinkers, Izetbegovic called for "the creation of a united Islamic community from Morocco to Indone-sia,"[80] and asserted that "A weakening in the influence of Islam on the practical life of the people has always been accompanied by their degra-dation and that of social and political institutions."[81]

What has remained under debate is whether or not Izetbegovic believed this to be a realistic course of action for Bosnia or whether he was speaking hypothetically.[82] Zlatko Dzidarevic, a Sarajevo journalist, concluded,

> I have always encountered numerous proofs for the claim that, in Izetbegovic's case, there is a consistent political and philosophical concept...that faith and nation should together be the sole axes of everything else . . . I think that, from the start, Izetbegovic started from the belief that we are part of that Islamic world and that we should consistently realize exclusively that lifestyle, that type of political organization, that type of social organization in this region and as an absolute majority.[83]

Like Izetbegovic, from its inception, the SDA found also itself in an ambiguous position by moving back and forth between two poles. On the one hand, the SDA proclaimed as its mission the establishment in Bosnia of a civic state predicated upon an inclusive Bosnian nationalism encompassing all three nations. On the other hand, it promoted itself as an ethnic-religious party that stood for the interests of the Muslims.[84] Bosnia was likewise an undefined concept. At times, it was a secular-geographic construct, a federal unit of Yugoslavia. At other times, it was defined as the state comprised of the Muslim nation.[85] After its founding congress, the SDA seemed to operate with two wings: one that was a moderate and secular faction led by Adil Zulfilkarpasic and another that was committed to religious nationalism and led by Alija Izetbegovic along with a number of his associates—some of whom had been his comrades in the Young Muslims during the 1940s. However, prior to the legislative elections in Bosnia in 1990, Zulfilkarpasic and his supporters broke off from the SDA and formed a new party, the Muslim Bosniak Organization (MBO)[86] After the departure of these moderates, the SDA adopted a more explicitly Muslim and Islamic orientation. Omer Behmen, one of Izetbegovic's Young Muslim associates and one of his fellow defendants in the 1983 trials, became president of the cadres' commission of the party. The SDA stressed the need "for suitable recognition of its ethnic group's relative majority status in Bosnia-Herzegovina and of [Muslim] religious values."[87] Izetbegovic was asked in a September 1990 interview whether the SDA was a political party or a religious movement, and he responded,

...neither the one nor the other . . . It is a Muslim party, which resembles the nation from which it recruits its partisans. It is a religious nation. In its scale of values, faith represents the summit. It is impossible for these features not to leave their mark on the general atmosphere which prevails at SDA rallies.[88]

The SDA began to display explicitly Islamic insignia and symbols and moved away from its commitment to a multiethnic, multicultural Bosnia. Instead, it promoted the notion that Islam was a necessary pillar for Bosnian identity.[89] Izetbegovic himself made official visits to Pakistan, Turkey, and Saudi Arabia and began to send Muslim envoys to Islamic states to establish relations and seek support.[90] Izetbegovic, in a number of speeches, seemed to indicate that an Islamic state could not be established in Bosnia only because Muslims did not, as of yet, make up the absolute majority in the population. One Bonsian commentator, Esad Cimic, pointed out, as a result of Izetbegovic's unclear positions, "It isn't difficult to conclude that the creation of some kind of Islamic, Muslim state . . . is not rejected but simply postponed."[91] Izetbegovic himself has insisted that statements about the creation of an Islamic state were hypothetical in nature and were not to be applied to the situation in Bosnia.[92] Yet, Bosnia's non-Muslim population were unsettled by several of the statements in Izetbegovic's writings. "An Islamic society without an Islamic authority is incomplete and without power; Islamic governance without an Islamic society is either utopia or violence . . . The non-Muslim minorities within an Islamic state, on condition they are loyal, enjoy religious freedom and all protection."[93]

In the elections of 1990, the nationalist parties in Bosnia swept the elections. The Party of Democratic Action, the Croatian Democratic Alliance, and the Serbian Democratic Party won 84 percent of the seats in the legislature. Bosnian voters decisively rejected political parties espousing reform communism or a continuation of a neutral Yugoslav identity. The SDA itself won seventy-one seats out of 240. Izetbegovic decided to establish a coalition government with the two other nationalist parties and was elected as president of the seven-member collective executive of the Bosnian state.[94]

However, this coalition broke down after Croat and Muslim deputies approved legislation in October 1991 that provided for Bosnia's secession from Yugoslavia. A referendum held in February 1992 on the future of Bosnia was split along ethnic lines. Serbs almost completely boycotted the election; most Croats and Muslims voted for independence. To head off the impending civil war, an international conference held in Lisbon recommended the division of Bosnia into three territorial entities corresponding largely to ethnicity with a decentralized central government coordinating inter-canton relations. Under pressure from Muslims not to give away territory to the Serbs and Croats, Izetbegovic, at the last minute, rejected the Lisbon arrangements.[95]

The outbreak of civil war along ethnic and religious lines in Bosnia strengthened the position of those within the Muslim establishment that sought a greater role for Islam in Bosnia. The Chief of Staff of the Army of Bosnia-Herzegovina, Rasim Delic, stated, "In time of war, religion always attracts more followers . . . It is very important for us to motivate the people in this way."[96] After 1992, there was a noticeable Islamicization of life in Bosnia. In that year, a document, "The Declaration of Independence of the Islamic Republic of Bosnia and Herzegovina," was promulgated that called for Bosnia to adopt *shari'a* law and have one house of parliament composed exclusively of Islamic leaders.[97] It was perhaps meant to be similar to the "Assembly of Experts" in the Islamic Republic of Iran. Several military units in the Bosnian military, among them the elite Black Swans unit and the Seventh Muslim Brigade defined themselves in Muslim terms, adopted *shariat* principles as a code of conduct, and instituted daily prayer and religious instruction. As ethnic cleansing and forced migration changed the demographic balances in villages and regions, some Muslim areas tried to emulate the example of an Islamic republic. The *imam* of Sarejevo and the head of the IZ, the *reis ul-ulema*, Mustafa Ceric, became much more outspoken in his calls for the reconstruction of Bosnia along Islamic lines, including restrictions on the rights of non-Muslims, limitations on intermarriage with non-Muslims, censorship of art and the media, and limitations on the sale of pork and alcohol.[98] The army became overwhelmingly Muslim in its officer corps, and Muslim religious leaders began to occupy key posts in the army and civilian administration.[99]

Moreover, as the war progressed, Bosnian Muslim leaders increasingly turned to Islamic states for assistance. Iran, in particular, increased its efforts by sending humanitarian aid and weaponry and announcing its readiness to dispatch troops to Bosnia as part of any international peace-keeping force. Iran also insisted that the war in Bosnia constituted a "crisis that relates to the entire [Islamic] world."[100] Hasan Cengic, a former cleric who had been imprisoned with Izetbegovic and was appointed deputy minister of defense, played a critical role in securing financing and weaponry for the Bosnian Muslim military forces and acted as liaison between Iran and Bosnia. Under his supervision, training centers for Bosnian Muslims were set up in the central regions of the country utilizing Iranian instructors. It was also Cengic who was responsible for ensuring the "religious and ideological fitness" of the Bosnian army along Islamist lines. [101]

Islamic fighters (*mujahedin*) arrived, particularly from Libya, Iran, and Algeria, and numbered between some 1,500 to 2,000 by 1995; although, some sources indicated that up to 8,000 fighters were smuggled in.[102] Islamist organizations began to set up branches in Bosnia, including one Egyptian charity in Zenica whose members were wanted for acts of terrorism committed in Egypt. Zenica was also the site of what was described as a terrorist-training center where large quantities of weapons were discovered in 1995. An incident several months later, when Croatian militiamen detained a group of Islamists—three Algerians, one Iranian, and three Egyptians—near Kiseljak, heightened fears that "the world would soon come to know the strength of the Islamic Jihad in Bosnia." There were also concerns that U. S. soldiers being sent to Bosnia as part of the Dayton Accords would be targeted for attack.[103] This created the specter of the Islamicization of Bosnia.[104] One observer commented, "All of this warns us of the huge and serious danger that Islamic extremism, for which terror and violence are the only form of political action, is establishing roots in the immediate neighborhood...This does not contribute to an atmosphere of tolerance, understanding, and security for the non-Islamic population of Bosnia-Herzegovina."[105] Under the patronage of Islamist elements within the government and the Agency for Investigation and Documentation (AID), radical Islamists from other parts of the world, including from Sudan's Islamist regime, were able to set up training camps and other support facilities on Bosnian territory. Bosnian passports were also issued to a number of Islamist radicals.[106]

Indeed, a core of support has remained within the Muslim establishment in Bosnia for Islamist solutions. One of the leading Islamic figures in Bosnia has described the Iranian revolution as a blessing from God because it enabled Muslims to become "acquainted with an Islamic form of education and economy."[107] Some Bosnian Muslims have traveled to Pakistan to study Islamabad's application of Islamic law and the feasibility of such models for Bosnia.[108]

In 1997, allegations were made that the SDA was pursuing a policy of silent ethnic cleansing in the territories under its jurisdiction.[109] A Zagreb newspaper concluded,

> . . . When all these facts are supported by others about certain forms of Islamization of public life (in schools, public services, media), one is not surprised to find that the number of non-Muslims in the territories under the control of the Muslim army is constantly diminishing. Therefore, what has recently been going on in Bosnia-Herzegovina is the last and the most rigid form of preparation by Muslim politicians for the creation of an ethnically pure Muslim state in a certain territory of Bosnia-Herzegovina. So, we are not talking about isolated incidents but about a systematic campaign whose objective is to eliminate from Bosnia the last non-Muslim institution still there—the Catholic Church. The evidence for this is the fact that the Orthodox Church is no longer active in an organized manner in Sarajevo, nor is the Jewish community, there are neither political nor cultural institutions of other nations.[110]

There were also charges proffered that Izetbegovic and the SDA were seeking to create a monoethnic/monoreligious state on all or part of Bosnia's territory and were uninterested in a true federation with non-Muslim Bosnians. Sefer Halilovic, who was commander of the Army of Bosnia-Herzegovina at one point but later fell out of favor with Izetbegovic, charges that Izetbegovic and the SDA leadership were more interested in creating a purely Muslim entity to the point of considering negotiations for land swaps with Serbia or reaching a settlement for a reduced Bosnia that would be entirely Muslim in population.[111] These charges were particularly potent when dealing with the tragedy surrounding the fall of Srebrenica. The Bosnian government had intentionally allowed the safe area to fall to Bosnian Serb forces, which resulted in the ethnic cleansing of the region on the understanding that the Serbian suburbs of Sarajevo would be exchanged in any subsequent peace deal.[112]

However, secular Muslims—as well as those who remained committed to a multi-ethnic and unified Bosnia—moved to challenge the reconstruction of Bosnia along Islamist lines.[113] There were also practical considerations. Some Bosnian Muslims were afraid of alienating potential supporters in the West by moving too closely to Iran. While some have alleged that Izetbegovic believed that Bosnia could survive without American assistance as long as Iranian support remained firm,[114] the United States issued a clear ultimatum in 1996. The Bosnian leadership was to sever its close military ties with Iran and Islamist groups, and foreign Islamists were to leave the country. Washington also demanded that Cengic, in particular, be removed from his position as deputy minister of defense and other pro-Iranian members of the defense establishment be purged. The United States withheld some $100 million in military assistance and delayed the implementation of its Train and Equip program until Cengic was removed. As a result, he took up the portfolio dealing with refugee and resettlement affairs.[115]

While Izetbegovic continued to champion the idea that it was vital to construct a strong Muslim identity in Bosnia, his Prime Minister, Haris Silajdzic, echoed the arguments of the moderates within the SDA that the Bosnian government had to remain committed to the vision of a multi-communal, secular Bosnia. If the Muslims could not forge some working relationship with non-Muslims in Bosnia, Bosnia itself would not survive.[116] As a result, attempts to Islamify Bosnia have had mixed success. In some Muslim-dominated areas of Bosnia, primary schools offer Islamic religious education as part of the curriculum, but this is not universal. Secular tendencies remain strong. A 1999 report noted that the "*Reis-ul-ulema*, head of the Islamic community in the country, sent a public letter to the management of Federation State Television (RTV BiH) criticizing its 'excessive' Christmas coverage and its 'inadequate' coverage of Ramadan. The *Reis-ul-ulema's* chief of staff also noted that the Islamic community (IZ) was dissatisfied with RTV BiH's treatment of Islam and the Islamic community, culture, and tradition in the country."[117]

As in many parts of the former Soviet Union, there is also a division between Muslim traditionalists in Bosnia—those who want to preserve particularly Bosnian customs and practices, even when they have been borrowed from the surrounding Christian populations, versus those who want a purified Islam.[118] Moreover, despite the fighting, the war did not significantly erode the progressive or modernist bloc within Bosnian Islam.[119] Speaking at the dedication of the King Fahd mosque and cultural center in the Sarajevo suburb of Mojmilo, then Prime Minister Edhem Bicakcic reiterated his commitment to a Muslim ideology that was inclusive and tolerant, "The return of Bosniaks [Muslims], Croats, and Serbs to where they had lived before is the cornerstone of our policy. It is the policy of tolerance, globalization, a policy no one can possibly object to."[120]

Another factor that has inhibited the spread of Islamist movements within Bosnia is the strong streak of regionalism and particularism that runs in Bosnian Islam, which, at times, maintains that the Bosnian Muslims are superior in their understanding of the true essence of Islam than Muslims from the Middle East.[121] As a result, there is a reluctance to look abroad, beyond Bosnia, for leadership or advice.[122] The war has also not fundamentally reoriented Bosnian Muslims towards the Middle East and Iran. Many continue to view themselves as European in orientation and culture.[123]

Like other Islamist or quasi-Islamist movements, the SDA offered a vision of justice as the foundation of a new Bosnia.[124] Izetbegovic himself had written that "the struggle for an Islamic order and a thorough recon-struction of Muslim society can be led only by tried and true individuals at the head of a resolute and homogenous organization. This need not be any kind of political party from the arsenals of Western democracy but rather a movement founded on Islamic ideology requiring unmistakable moral and ideological criteria from its membership."[125] The educated believers would rule within the Muslim community by enforcing virtue and justice.[126] Some within the SDA wanted to construct a Muslim com-munity in which the party would unite within itself religion, state, and politics so that the SDA would become synonymous with the Muslim community.[127] In those localities where the SDA held power, it tended to engage in politics of ethnic preferentialism by filling posts in government administration and law enforcement with party members and sympathiz-ers.[128] It also tried, in some cases, to cast political opposition to the SDA as a form of treason to the Muslim community.[129]

However, because the SDA was a governing party, it developed a record and left a legacy in government. As in Iran, Islamic-based theories were put to the test. Obviously, the war helped to legitimize the SDA's hold on power and to excuse its failings, but, over time, as corruption set in, the notion that a Muslim vanguard party would prove to be more effective in governance dissipated. The widespread corruption and inept administration of the country eroded support for the SDA.[130] The grow-ing perception that Bosnian government officials—at all levels—were profiting from bribes, diversion of aid funds into private hands, and vir-tual privatization (that is, utilizing or diverting state assets into private hands) clashed with public assertions about justice and morality.[131] Izet-begovic's prestige—and that of the Bosnian government—was also severely damaged as allegations were levied that he and members of his family were involved in embezzling funds earmarked for charity and reconstruction efforts in Bosnia. Mohammed Sacirbey, Bosnia's telegenic UN ambassador and foreign minister briefly, was also accused of embez-zlement of funds and, in 2002, a warrant for his arrest was issued through Interpol.[132] Izetbegovic resigned from the Bosnian Presidency in October 2000 as support for the SDA continued to fall prior to national elections.[133]

In November 2000, the SDA as well as the other nationalist parties in Bosnia were edged out from power by the victory of opposition parties that came together in January 2001 as the Alliance for Change. The Social Democratic Party (SDP), which was led by Zlatko Lagumdzija, stressed a non-nationalist agenda committed to economic reconstruction and the restoration of prosperity. Significantly, the Alliance was bolstered by the participant of Silajdzic and his Party for Bosnia-Herzegovina (SBiH), which was created in 1996 following his decisive break with Izetbegovic. A large number of Muslim voters in the elections deserted the SDA and cast their support either to the SDP or the SBiH, which indicated their "dissatisfaction with a system that delivered wealth to the well-connected few, poverty to the many, and no cause for expecting anything better."[134] The SBiH also benefited from the defection of moderate SDA leaders, but, in return, the SBiH, which held the interior ministry portfolio, was able to "influence or restrain the investigation of past cases of official corruption, Islamist infiltration, dodgy arms deals, and organized crime networks . . ."[135] However, in the aftermath of 9/11, Lagumdzija, as prime minister of the coalition government, intensified Bosnian cooperation with the United States, including turning over six Algerian Islamists and opening investigations of Arab charities that had operated in Bosnia and were alleged to be fronts for terrorist activities.

Unfortunately, the Alliance remained an unwieldy coalition of parties and was unable to push through significant economic reform or attract foreign investment. Lagumdzija also faced increasing criticism—both from the SDA and from the official Muslim religious establishment—that close cooperation with the United States in the anti-terrorist campaign could harm Bosnia's good relations with the rest of the Muslim world.[136] The SDA also tried to rehabilitate its image by acknowledging that it had fallen into corruption, but that "such deviations were the result not of malice but of the lack of infrastructure and cadres following the war."[137]

In the October 2002 elections, the Alliance disintegrated, and the SDP and the SBiH ran their own campaigns. Voters repudiated the SDP, which saw its vote totals shrink by 10 percent. In a narrow victory, the SDA beat out the SBiH to reclaim control of the Bosniak/Muslim seat in the collective presidency, Sulejman Tihic. Having gone through a period of repentance and having capitalized on the failure of the Alliance, particularly the SDP, to deliver change, the SDA succeeded in convincing a slight majority of the Muslim electorate that it could best represent Muslim interests. Elvir Hadziahmetovic, the SDA's leading spokesman, has also insisted that the party has moved to adopt more centrist positions. One of the key trends leading toward moderation has also been the clear desire of Bosnians, including Bosnian Muslims, to pursue closer integration with the European Union, a step favored by nearly two-thirds of the population. The 2002 election platform of the SDA tried to strike a balance between promoting ties with the Islamic world and speedily fulfilling the conditions needed to ensure Bosnia's entry into the European Union. In many ways, the platform is similar to the Rome Accords signed by the Algerian FIS in its commitment to religious freedom and ideological pluralism.[138]

Yet, it is not entirely clear that the leadership of the SDA has abandoned its vision of an Islamist future for Bosnia. One of the pieces of legislation that the SDA-led government is pushing for is an amendment to the citizenship law that would allow for dual citizenship and thus protect the foreign Islamists who reside in Bosnia from being expelled from the country.[139] One possibility is that the SDA will attempt to present itself as a Muslim version of Christian Democracy in an attempt to become more palatable as a governing party to its European neighbors. At any rate, the SDA remains constrained—both by its narrow parliamentary majority and the continuing need to cooperate, both with the more moderate SBiH as well as with the non-Muslim nationalities in Bosnia.

ALBANIANS, ISLAM, AND KOSOVO, 1974–1999

Despite the ferocity of the fighting in Kosovo and the apparent clash of civilizations between Orthodox Christianity and Islam, there are no indications that Kosovar Albanians are leaning towards Islamism as the basis for their state and society. In a telling essay, Blerim Shala, editor-in-chief of the Pristina weekly *Zeri* and a member of the Kosovar Albanian delegation at Rambouillet, declares that "Kosovars are Western" and the attainment of statehood can only be achieved via the West. "The Western presence in Kosova is not the only fundamental element toward the realization of this ideal. It is the Albanian ability to embrace genuine Western values that is even more significant."[140]

Just as in Bosnia, most Muslims in Kosovo were not active believers.[141] National rather than Islamic sentiments animated the Albanian community. In 1978, the centennial of the League of Prizren celebrations focused on Albanian literature, song, and history in Kosovo with little or no reference to Islam as a key marker in Kosovo Albanian identity.[142] Similarly, the attacks on Orthodox Christian churches, monasteries, and personnel were national rather than religious in nature. These places were targeted not because of Christianity but because they were perceived as being linked to Serbs and Montenegrins.[143]

The 1981 spring protests, which advocated full and separate republican status for Kosovo, were secular in nature. The leadership of the movement was generally comprised of nationalists within the Communist Party establishment; indeed, the official Islamic clergy registered their disapproval of protests against the status quo.[144] Observers of protests during this time noted that the heroes exalted by the crowds were Kosovo's Albanian Communist leader Azen Vlasi and Albanian dictator Enver Hoxha, not any religious figure. The goals of the Albanian movement were to achieve republican status within Yugoslavia, or unification with Albania. There was no Islamist component.[145] Inasmuch as there was an anti-Orthodox Christian focus to the movement, it was based on the fact that Orthodoxy was the national faith of the Serbs and other Slavs in the area.[146] Indeed, the small Albanian Catholic community in Kosovo firmly supported the same goals and worked with their Muslim colleagues.[147] As Risa Sapunxhiu, a Kosovar leader observed, "Albanians have always been defined by language, history, and a common way of life—not by religion."[148] This lack of religious identity has been reinforced by the fact that other non-Albanian Muslims in Kosovo also faced hostility from the Albanian majority. Since 1999, non-Albanian Muslims have in fact been driven from or fled from Kosovo, including groups such as the Circassians (Adygei), or Egyptians (Muslims of Gypsy extraction who look to Egypt, rather than India, as their homeland).[149]

In 1989, Kosovo's status as an autonomous province within the Serbian Republic was revoked. This measure catalyzed the separatist movement. However, it was defined in secular terms and coalesced around a literature professor who had been expelled from the League of Communists—Dr. Ibrahim Rugova. Rugova founded the Democratic League of Kosova (LDK). In 1992, in an underground election, Rugova was elected president of a Republic of Kosova and proceeded to create a parallel, shadow administration for the province that was complete with its own parliament, schools, and health care system. Taxes levied on the Albanian diaspora helped to fund the alternate government. Yet, the LDK was in no way an Islamist organization. In fact, Rugova has in the past declined to identify himself as a Muslim believer.

However, Rugova's passive approach alienated some Albanian radicals who wanted to force an armed confrontation and fight for independence. In 1993, a more radical movement, the Popular Movement for the Republic of Kosovo (LPRK), split and a more activist group emerged, the Popular Movement for Kosovo, which set about creating an armed organization, the *Ushtria Climitare e Kosoves* or the Kosovo Liberation Army (KLA).[150] From its inception, the KLA had two ideological wings—one drawing inspiration from the World War II-era Albanian fascist movement and the other grounded in a leftist-Marxist approach.[151]

If this is the case, then why were concerns raised about the possible Islamist factor in the Kosovo conflict? The first has to do with events in Albania itself. After the fall of the Communist regime and the restoration of religious liberty, a number of Saudi and Gulf organizations targeted Albania as a candidate for re-Islamicization. Albania, the poorest country in Europe, was particularly susceptible to the aid provided by radical Islamist groups in return for acceptance of their social and political program. Scholarships for Albanians to study in Saudi Arabia also helped to recruit Islamist cadres in Albania. A recent estimate concludes that some 200 mosques in Albania are funded or supported by Wahhabite organizations. Indeed, one Albanian commentator has warned that "we are going now into a stage in which the propagators of such a religious fanaticism or Islamic internationalism are no longer ordinary Arab missionaries but Albanian citizens.[152]

While not espousing Islamism, the KLA was more than willing to accept support from radical Islamic movements, including financial aid and personnel. Along with Chechnya, Kosovo become a new battle-ground attracting *mujahideen* to fight on behalf of fellow Muslims.[153] Exact numbers are difficult to estimate, but some have cited figures of several hundred Islamic mercenaries who aided the KLA. Moreover, the battle for Kosovo was recast into a struggle between the *Dar-al Islam* and the Christian world.[154] Yet, the cooperation between the KLA and Islamist elements always appeared to be tactical rather than ideological. Nevertheless, by inserting themselves into the conflict, the Islamists have hoped to win converts to their message and have engaged in propaganda efforts that continue to this day by trying to convince Albanians in Albania, Kosovo, and Macedonia to abandon their hopes of Western integration and to turn to the Islamic world.[155] Indeed, the presence of radical Islamists is troubling to the local Islamic establishment in Kosovo, which sees the radicals as undermining Albanian Muslim traditions.[156] Yet, Qemail Morina, head of the Islamic Community, maintains that Islamists have gained little ground in Kosovo. Citing statistics that only 10 percent or so of the population practices the faith, he maintains that most believers embrace a tolerant form of Islam and that the blandishments of radical groups have enticed few Kosovo Albanians.[157] More like Bosnian Muslims, Albanians have a strong sense of regional and cultural identity that has helped to retard the spread of Islamism. "Albanians have been Muslim for more than 500 years, and they do not need outsiders [Arabs] to tell them what is the proper way to practice Islam," observed Rexhep Boja, the Mufti of Kosovo.[158]

Given the devastated conditions in Kosovo and the lack of a functioning economy or political system,[159] it is possible that, at some point in the future, an Islamist movement, particularly if coupled with copious amounts of humanitarian aid, might gain ground in Kosovo or in Albania proper. Yet, at the present time, the rhetoric of politics in Kosovo remains defined by Western values, not by Islamic models. The principal Albanian political movements in Kosovo affirm their desire to construct a liberal democracy, not an Islamic state.[160]

DID THE BALKANS BECOME AN ISLAMIST BEACHHEAD? CONCLUDING THOUGHTS

When one observes the Balkans in 2003, a decade after the wars of secession, several conclusions can be drawn. The first is that, unlike in many parts of the Arab world, radical Islamism had to compete with a number of other ideologies in relatively open political systems following the breakdown of the Communist system. In Bosnia, the Muslim community was not monolithic, and the SDA was never able to claim a complete monopoly of ideas, but it was instead forced to compete for support for its message with other, more moderate Muslim political forces. Among Albanians, a very strong sense of national identity and tradition helped to diminish the attraction of an ideology that elevated pan-Islamic sentiment over devotion to national tradition and placed a greater priority on a trans-national community rather than achieving specific national goals. The second was the attraction of Europe as a model. It is an axiom of faith among all Balkan nationalities—whether Muslim or Christian—that they properly belong to the West and therefore expect eventual integration into Western institutions such as NATO and the European Union. With few exceptions, it is the West, not the Islamic world, that holds the most attraction for the populations of the region. For many, Islamism seemed to widen rather than narrow the gap between the region and the rest of Europe.

However, this is not to say that radical Islamists gained no ground at all in the region. In Bosnia, Albania, and Kosovo, radicals were successful in carving out niches for themselves by making arrangements to have their own institutions and safe areas free from interference from outside authority. The international Islamist movement was able to develop safe havens and camps in certain parts of the Balkans by counting on either the ideological sympathy of the leadership (as in Bosnia) or through tactical bargains (as among the Albanians) to receive *carte blanche* for their activities.[161] However, in a post–September 11 environment, governments have to rethink these arrangements. Particularly in Bosnia, there has been a great deal of ambivalence becayuse the foreign Islamists are respected for their assistance during the Balkan wars of the 1990s. Nevertheless, there is a growing sense among some that the presence of foreign Islamists might prove detrimental. Moderate leaders in Bosnia worry about the Saudi presence by noting that "They are spreading around huge amounts of money to help rebuild Bosnia. But, they are also building mosques and spreading a version of Islam that is alien to our Bosnian Islam."[162] A similar process has been occurring in Kosovo where Saudi charities have replaced local traditions with Wahhabite interpretations of Islam in the institutions they support, including schools, mosques, and libraries.[163] Some Balkan observers warn that these radical groups may "exploit the poverty and fragmented social conditions . . . in order to gain an influential foothold in largely rural communities."[164]

However, to what extent these efforts will bear fruit remains to be seen. The fear of a pan-Islamic network spreading terror throughout the region has been buttressed by the revelations of the presence of Al-Qaeda operatives and the existence of some arms smuggling networks linking Bosnian Muslims and Kosovar Albanians.[165] Generally, we can speak of pockets of radicalism—some villages in Bosnia, some members of the intelligentsia, and a largely Saudi-funded network of charities and schools in Bosnia, Albania proper, and Kosovo—but these pockets have nowhere near the critical mass needed to become the dominant sociopolitical force in these societies. Moreover, as the Balkan countries move further into the European orbit, including becoming recipients of greater amounts of European aid, the value and necessity of the Saudi and Gulf contributions may diminish. However, at the present time, the Muslims of the Balkans remain committed to finding a synthesis between their Islamic heritage and membership in the political and economic institutions of the Western world. Despite the harsh experiences of war, most Bosnian Muslims and Kosovar Albanians continue to see themselves as Europeans who practice Islam, not as the advance wave of the *Dar-al Islam* against the Christian West.

NOTES

1. This point of view was also echoed in Fran Visnar, "Susak's Efficient Visit to the United States," *Vjesnik*, February 2, 1998, 4.

2. Mitja Velikonka, "Liberation Mythology: The Role of Mythology in Fanning War in the Balkans," *Religion and the War in Bosnia*, ed. Paul Mojzes (Atlanta: GA: Scholars Press, 1998), 39.

3. Michael A. Sells, "Vuk's Knife: Kosovo, the Serbian Golgotha, and the Radicalization of Serbian Society," in *Kosovo: Contending Voices on Balkan Interventions*, ed. William Joseph Buckley (Grand Rapids, MI: William B. Eerdmans, 2000), 140.

4. Zachary T. Irwin, "The Fate of Islam in the Balkans: A Comparison of Four State Policies," *Religion and Nationalism in Soviet and East European Politics*. Ed. Pedro Ramet. (Durham, NC: Duke Press Policy Studies, 1984), 208, 210.

5. Marija Taseva, "Islamisation and Its Contemporary Consequences," *The Balkans: A Religious Backyard of Europe*, ed. Mient Jan Faber (Ravenna: Longo Press, 1995), 120, 122; Irwin, 209.

6. Hugh Poulton, "Muslim Identity and Ethnicity in the Balkans," *Contending Voices*, 120.

7. Ibid., 121.

8. Robert M. Hayden, "The Use of National Stereotypes in the Wars in Yugoslavia," *The Balkans*, 85.

9. Poulton, 121.

10. Ibid., 122.

11. Ibid., 123.

12. Taseva, 121–122; Misha Glenny, *The Balkans: Nationalism, War and the Great Powers, 1804–1999* (New York: Viking, 2000), 152.

13. Fatos Lubonja, "Reinventing Skanderbeg: Albanian Nationalism and NATO Neocolonialism," *Contending Voices*, 103.

14. Justin McCarthy, "Ottoman Bosnia, 1800–1878," in *The Muslims of Bosnia-Herzegovina: Their Historic Development from the Middle Ages to the Dissolution of Yugoslavia*, ed. Mark Pinson (Cambridge, MA: Harvard University Press, 1994), 81; Mark Pinson, "The Muslims of Bosnia-Herzegovina under Austro-Hungarian Rule, 1878–1918," ibid., 94.

15. Ferdinand Schevill, *A History of the Balkans from the Earliest Times to the Present Day* (New York: Barnes and Noble, 1995), 394; Glenny, *Balkans*, 269.

16. Glenny, *Balkans*, 93.

17. Misha Glenny, *The Fall of Yugoslavia: The Third Balkan War*, revised edition (New York: Penguin Books, 1993), 139–140.

18. Pinson, 90.

19. Colin Heywood, "Bosnia Under Ottoman Rule, 1463–1800," *Muslims of Bosnia-Herzegovina*, 34.

20. Lubonja, 103–104; and Ivo Banac, "Bosnian Muslims: From Religious Community to Socialist Nationhood and Postcommunist Statehood, 1918–1992," in *The Muslims of Bosnia-Herzegovina*, 132.

21. This is reflected in the idea of Turkification via profession of Islam. See Sells, 136.

22. Cited in Ger Duijzinas, *Religion and the Politics of Identity in Kosovo* (New York: Columbia University Press, 2000), 160.

23. Ibid., 173, 168–169.

24. Poulton, 123–125; Julie A. Mertus, *Kosovo: How Myths and Truths Started A War* (Berkeley: University of California Press, 1999), 19–20; Branka Magas, *The Destruction of Yugoslavia: Tracing the Break-Up, 1980–1992* (London: Verso, 1993), 21.

25. Taseva, 124.

26. Hakan Wiberg, "Divided Nations and Divided States," *The Balkans*, 37.

27. Duijzinas, 161–163.

28. See the comments of Behar Bejko, head of the State Cults Committee of the Albanian Council of Ministers, in Nikolas K. Gvosdev, "Tolerance versus Pluralism," 8, 9–10.

29. Schevill, 464.

30. Duijzinas, 163.

31. Glenny, *Balkans*, 153.

32. Taseva, 122.

33. As witnessed by the decline in Albanian families using and speaking Turkish in favor of Albanian. Cf. Poulton, 122.

34. Taseva, 124.

35. Duijzinas, 104–105.

36. Taseva, 122.

37. Glenny, *Balkans*, 76–77.

38. Taseva, 125.

39. Pinson, 90.

40. Ibid., 91.

41. Ibid., 89.

42. Sells, 136.

43. Banac, 133.

44. Peter Palmer, "Religions and Nationalism in Yugoslavia: A Tentative Comparison Between the Catholic Church and the Other Communities," *The Balkans*, 159; Pinson, 103.

45. Wiberg, 37–39; see also Daniel Cordes, "The Communitarian Case for Bosnia's Partition," *The Transformations of 1989–1999: Triumph or Tragedy?*, ed. John S. Micgiel (New York: East Central European Center, Columbia University, 2000), 8–10.

46. Glenny, *Balkans*, 271.

47. Banac, 134–142.

48. Wiberg, 36.

49. Speech of the Serb Communist leader Rodoljub Colakovic in January 1946, cited in Banac, 144.

50. Wiberg, 38; Banac, 144–45. For a discussion about the historical accuracy of the Bogomil-Bosnian Muslim connection, see John V. A. Fine, "The Medieval and Ottoman Roots of Modern Bosnian Society," *Muslims of Bosnia-Herzegovina*, 5–15.

51. Banac, 145.

52. Poulton, 126.

53. Mertus, 18.

54. Tone Bringa, *Being Muslim the Bosnian Way: Identity and Community in a Central Bosnian Village* (Princeton, NJ: Princeton University Press, 1995), 30.

55. Banac, 134, 146.

56. Hayden, 89–90; Magas, 18.

57. Bringa, 4.

58. Duijzinas, 128, 130; see also 105–132 for greater detailed on the split in the religious establishment. However, Duijzinas correctly cautions the reader to not neglect the theological implications of the split between the Sunni establishment and the Sufi orders and so to not reduce this simply to a Slav Muslim versus Albanian dispute. In an effort to bridge the gap, in 1989, the IZ elected a Muslim leader from Macedonia, Jakup Selimovski, neither a Bosnian Slav Muslim nor Albanian, to be its head. Poulton, 126.

59. The Party of Democratic Action (SDA), which emerged as one of the leading parties in Bosnia among Slav Muslims, was initially envisioned as a pan-Islamic movement in Yugoslavia that brought together Slav Muslims, Albanians, and Turks. However, the party rapidly jettisoned this approach because of its very limited success in attracting Albanian members. See Xavier Bougarel, "Bosniaks under the Control of Panislamists (Part I)," *Dani* (June 18, 1999), http://www.cdsp.neu.edu/info/students/marko/dani/dani9.html.

60. Glenny, *Fall*, 142.

61. Poulton, 126.

62. Hayden, 96–97.

63. Bringa, 63.

64. Ibid., 9.

65. Lenard J. Cohen, "Bosnia's 'Tribal Gods': The Role of Religion in Nationalist Politics," *Religion and the War in Bosnia*, 48.

66. Palmer, 160.

67. Lenard J. Cohen, *Broken Bonds: The Disintegration of Yugoslavia* (Boulder, CO: Westview Press, 1993), 161.

68. Francine Friedman, "The Bosnian Muslim National Question," *Religion and the War in Bosnia*, 5–6.

69. Cohen, "Tribal Gods," 52.

70. Ibid., 54.

71. Friedman, 3.

72. Glenny, *Fall*, 149.

73. Radha Kumar, *Divide and Fall? Bosnia in the Annals of Partition* (London: Verso, 1997), 41.

74. Cohen, "Tribal Gods," 58.

75. Ibid., 59.

76. See materials provided by Bougarel and in a briefing paper prepared for members of the 1992–1993 Australian parliament, which is available at http://www.kosovo.net.kla/07.html.

77. Bougarel (see note 59).

78. Quoted in Palmer, 160.

79. Alija Izetbegovic, *Islamska Deklaracija* (Sarejevo: BOSNA, 1990). The publishing house BOSNA and *Mala Muslimanska Biblioteka* also issued an English-language version in that same year. Significant excerpts were reprinted in the August 26, 1992, issue of the French magazine *Figaro*.

80. Izetbegovic, 5.

81. Ibid., 16.

82. Palmer, 160.

83. Senad Pecanin, "We Are Living the Islamic Declaration," *Dani* (October 15, 1999), http://www.cdsp.neu.edu/info/students/marko/dani/dani23.html.

84. Srdjan Vrcan, "The Religious Factor and the War in Bosnia and Herzegovina," *Religion and the War in Bosnia*, 124; Kumar, 82.

85. Susan L. Woodward, *Balkan Tragedy: Chaos and Dissolution After the Cold War* (Washington, DC: The Brookings Institution, 1995), 301.

86. Cohen, *Broken Bonds*, 144.

87. Ibid.

88. Quoted in Cohen, "Tribal Gods," 60.

89. Poulton, 127.

90. Woodward, 176.

91. Quoted in Cohen, "Tribal Gods," 59.

92. Palmer, 160.

93. Izetbegovic, 26, 50.

94. Cohen, *Broken Bonds*, 145–47.

95. Ibid, 235–237.

96. Quoted in Cohen, "Tribal Gods," 43.

97. David Steele, "Religion as a Fount of Ethnic Hostility or an Agent of Reconciliation?" *Religion and War* (Belgrade: European Movement in Serbia, 1994), 171.

98. Paul Mojzes, "The Camouflaged Role of Religion in the War in Bosnia and Herzegovina," *Religion and the War in Bosnia*, 94–95; see also Kumar, 87; Cohen, "Tribal Gods," 68–69; Vrcan, 123.

99. Aleksandar Milosevic, "Terrorism Without (State) Borders," *Vjesnik*, July 1, 1996, 3.

100. "Bosnia-Herzegovina Minister Gives 'Exclusive' Interview," *Xinhua*, August 27, 1994; cited in *World News Connection: China*, FBIS-CHI-94-167 (August 27, 1994).

101. Adrian Brown, "Izetbegovic Aide: Deputy Minister Cengic To Be Replaced," *AFP*, November 2, 1996; Alenko Zornija, "Train and Equip Program Is Getting Stuck," *Vjesnik*, September 26, 1996, 1.

102. Milenko Predragovic, "Muslims Write `Graffiti,'" *Vecernje Novosti*, April 23, 1996, 6.

103. Milosevic, 3.

104. Kumar, 87, 108.

105. Milosevic, 3.

106. Damjan de Krnjevic-Miskovic, "Assessing the Militant Islamist Threats in the Balkans," *Strategic Regional Report*, 7:6, 1. A full documentation of the links between the Bosnian government, leading figures within the SDA and the international Islamist movement was provided by John Pomfret, "How Bosnia's Muslims Dodged Arms Embargo," *Washington Post*, September 22, 1996.

107. "Bosnian Figure Comments on Impact of Islamic Revolution," *IRNA*, February 10, 2001.

108. "Bosnian Islamist Plans to Promote 'True' Islamic Values in His Country," *Rawalpindi Nawa-I-Waqt*, November 8, 2000, 6, 8.

109. "Despite promises President Izetbegovic made— after pressure by the Americans— that housing laws, which prevent tens of thousands of Croats, Jews, and Serbs from returning into the region controlled by the SDA (Party of Democratic Action), would be changed, there are few indications that the Bosniaks are really ready to allow for the return." Alenko Zomija, "Everyday Life Proves That Stories About Equality of Croats Are False," *Vjesnik*, August 27, 1997, 7.

110. Marko Barisic, "Muslims—Destroyers of Bosnia?" *Vjesnik*, March 5, 1997, 4.

111. R. Gutic, "Arafat–Alija's Adviser," *Vecernje Novosti*, June 24, 1997.

112. David Rohde, *A Safe Area* (London: Pocket Books, 1997), 355–358.

113. Cohen, "Tribal Gods," 69; Kumar, 87.

114. Predragovic, 6.

115. Brown (see note 101); Zornija, "Train and Equip," 1.

116. Kumar, 82, 87.

117. U.S. Department of State, *Annual Report on International Religious Freedom for 1999: Bosnia and Herzegovina* (Washington, DC: Bureau for Democracy, Human Rights, and Labor, 1999), http://www.state.gov/www/global/human_rights/irf/irf_rpt/1999/irf_bosniahe99.html.

118. Bringa, 224–225.

119. Banac, 149.

120. "Saudi Prince Opens Largest Mosque in Balkans in Sarajevo," *Radio Bosnia-Herzegovina*, September 15, 2000; cited in *World News Connection: East Europe*, FBIS-EEU-2000-0915 (September 15, 2000).

121. Taseva, 122.

122. Bringa, 61.

123. Hayden, 96–97.

124. Pecanin, (see note 83). Indeed, Izetbegovic sometimes seemed to elevate "justice" to something beyond the rule of law. Cf. Zlatko Dizdarevic's interview to *Dani*, October 15, 1999.

125. Izetbegovic, 59.

126. "Virtuous Spoesperson and Immoral Political Party," *Dani*, May 28, 1999.

127. Pecanin, (see note 83).

128. Cohen, *Broken Bonds*, 161.

129. Jolyon Naegele, "Cazin Struggles Against Reputation of Political Violence," *Radio Free Europe/Radio Liberty*, September 3, 1996.

130. "Outgoing President Izetbegovic Satisfied Bosnia Has Taken Right Course," *Hina*, October 14, 2000.

131. Mario Marusic, "Warnings About 'Tolerance of Corruption' in Bosnia-Herzegovina Were Issued Long Time Ago," *Vjesnik,* December 3, 1998, 8.

132. "Izetbegovic to Press Charges Against *New York Times,*" *Agence-France Press,* August 26, 1999; "Government to Seek Arrest of Former Envoy to UN," *UNWire,* January 7, 2002. The initial charges, as relayed by the *New York Times* on August 17, 1999, maintained that nearly one billion dollars were missing from public funds and international aid projects in Bosnia.

133. "Outgoing President."

134. *Bosnia's Alliance for (Smallish) Change* (Brussels: International Crisis Group, 2002), 2.

135. Ibid., 4.

136. Ibid., 5.

137. Ibid., 4.

138. An English version of the platform is available at the Web site of the SDA at http://www.sda.ba/izbori.htm.

139. ONASA, December 13, 2002.

140. Blerim Shala, "Because Kosovars Are Western, There Can Be No Homeland without a State," *Contending Voices,* 187.

141. Duijzinas, 129.

142. Mertus, 19–20.

143. Ibid., 22.

144. Ibid., 33–34.

145. Robert D. Kaplan, *Balkan Ghosts: A Journey Through History* (New York: Vintage, 1993), 47–48; Mertus, 34–35.

146. Mertus, 114–115.

147. Duijzinas, 30.

148. Mertus, 52.

149. Duijzinas, 25, 139.

150. For a short history of the KLA, see Tim Judah, "A History of the Kosovo Liberation Army," *Contending Voices,* 108–115.

151. Krinka Vidakovic-Petrov, "Breaking the Balkans: Yugoslavia '99," *Kosovo-Serbia: A Just War?* ed. Frank Columbus (Commack, NY: Nova Publishers, 1999), 17.

152. Pirro Misha, "Religious Tolerance or Irresponsibility?" *Shekulli,* January 10, 2003, 1, 18.

153. Lambros Kalarritis: "The Covert US-UCK-Bin Ladin Triangle," *Ependhitis,* September 22, 2001, 32; Vidakovic-Petrov, 16.

154. Misha, 18.

155. Ibid.

156. See the comments of Islamic Community chairman Rexhep Boja in *Koha Ditore,* January 4, 2003.

157. Alexandre Peyrille, "Ethnic Albanians in Kosovo Ignore Calls to Embrace Radical Islam," *Middle East Times,* September 21, 2001.

158. Cited in Isa Blumi, "Competing for the Albanian Soul," *EES News,* January–February 2003, 1.

159. See, for instance, Damjan de Krnjevic-Miskovic, "The Conflict in Kosovo," *Society,* September/October 2002, 82.

160. See, for example, the comments of Hashim Thaci (Thaqi), in *Contending Voices,* 191.

161. See Ray Takeyh and Nikolas K. Gvosdev, "Do Terrorist Networks Need a Home?" *The Washington Quarterly*, 25:3, 97–108, for a discussion of this phenomenon.

162. Brian Whitmore, "Saudi Charity Troubles Bosniaks," *Bosnia Report* 29–31 (June–November 2002).

163. Peter Ford, "Mosques Face New Danger," *Bosnia Report* 23–25 (June–October 2001).

164. Blumi, 1.

165. In September 2001, NATO peacekeepers arrested seven Bosnian Muslims, including a former army general, Hamid Bahto, for smuggling weapons from Bosnia into Kosovo. They were ultimately sentenced to prison terms by the Supreme Court of the Croat-Muslim Federation in Bosnia to prison terms. *Reuters*, January 17, 2003.

Chapter 6

From the Red Star to the Green Crescent? Islamism in the Former Soviet Union

David K. Willis, former Moscow correspondent for the *Christian Science Monitor*, recalls that during his stay in the late 1970s, Western journalists and diplomats were intrigued by the thought of the Soviet Union collapsing as a result of massive uprisings among the non-Russian populations. Inevitably, the focus turned to the Muslim nationalities, seen as posing "the largest potential threat to Russian hegemony."[1] During the Cold War, speculation was rife about the supposed Islamic threat to the integrity of the Soviet Union. Ironically, when the Soviet Union finally did implode, the Muslim republics of Central Asia proved to be the most loyal to the idea and institutions of the Soviet state.[2] M. Nazif Shahrani is extremely critical of those who created the image of militant Islam within the former Soviet space and calls for a reexamination of the role that Islam plays in the region:

> Continued reliance on Soviet and Russian accounts and on worn-out approaches of Western Sovietology will not do if we are to comprehend the full meaning and significance of these transformations . . . This is particularly necessary in view of the track record of the studies of Islam and Muslims in Central Asia under the Soviet system by both Soviet scholars and Western Sovietologists, which has been seriously wanting, to say the least. We can all recall how some Soviet and Western scholars repeatedly asserted that Islam and Soviet Muslims posed the most serious threat to the integrity of the Moscow regime. Now other voices . . . are joining the Russian- and Western-oriented chorus saying that (largely nonexistent) fundamentalist Islam and radical Muslim political movements in the region threaten the post-Soviet "New World Order." With perfect hindsight, we now know that Islam and Muslims, at least within the borders of the former Soviet Empire, played no role whatsoever in the collapse of the Soviet state.[3]

The notion that there exists a hostile, fundamentalist Islamic crescent along Russia's southern borders retains a certain degree of currency to this day, having evolved from certain assumptions about the supposed radicalization and mobilization of the Islamic populations of the former Soviet Union. Among contemporary Russians, Islamic fundamentalism is consistently cited as the most pressing threat to Russia's national security.[4] It is therefore helpful to revisit some of the sources of this idea that there was an Islamic threat brewing in the ex-USSR and from there proceed to analyze the depths of the Islamic revival in Eurasia, as well as the actual strengths of Islamist movements.

THE SHADOW OF THE CRESCENT? ASSUMPTIONS ABOUT ISLAM IN THE SOVIET UNION

During its existence, the Soviet Union found itself in the curious position of being the fourth largest Muslim power in the world.[5] At the time of the Revolution, there had been an extensive Muslim establishment on the territory of the Russian Empire, with some 26,000 mosques served by over 45,000 mullahs. In the region of Turkestan (Central Asia) alone, there were some 8,000 Islamic primary and secondary schools (*mekteps* and *madrasssahs*); another 5,000 establishments of Islamic learning were found in the regions of Kazan, the Crimea, and the Caucasus.[6] Over time, because of the higher birthrates exhibited by the Muslim nationalities vis-a-vis the Slavic population of the USSR,[7] some scholars began to speculate that there would be an inevitable clash as the Muslim population sought a greater degree of status and self-determination. Michael Rywkin phrased it as such:

By the year 2000 the sheer numerical strength and the continuing unassimilability of the Soviet Muslim masses will present the Soviet state with its greatest internal challenge: the survival of the empire inherited from the tsars.[8]

The growing number of Muslim recruits in the Soviet armed forces and incidents such as the assassinations of the Minister of the Interior of the Azerbaijani SSR in 1978 and the prime minister of the Khirghiz (Kyrgyz) SSR in 1980 fueled speculation that a successful Muslim rebellion against Soviet rule was plausible, especially in the wake of the Iranian revolution of 1979 and the subsequent Soviet intervention in Afghanistan. The so-called Islamic threat that was popularized in the West rested on two prime assumptions, including:

1. The idea that Muslim peoples of the USSR believed themselves to form a single, supranational community of shared interests and faith

2. The belief that antireligious, secularization, and Sovietization policies pursued by the regime had little or no impact upon the Muslim nationalities; in other words, that Muslims in the USSR shared the same outlook as their co-religionists in Iran, Afghanistan, or the Arab world.

Unfortunately, neither of these propositions have proven to be entirely accurate. Although the concept of the *umma*—the belief that all Muslims form a single community without regard to national or ethnic affiliations—is an integral part of the Islamic worldview, the sheer diversity of Islam within the territory of the USSR precluded any meaningful joint action. Instead, the unity of the Muslim peoples of Eurasia has often existed only as an ideal.[9] Indeed, to speak of the Muslims of the former USSR as any sort of monolithic community is patently ridiculous. Although most Muslims in the USSR are Sunni of the Hanafite school (and Central Asians were considered the most moderate of the Hanafites),[10] there are also strong concentrations of Shiites (in Azerbaijan in particular), and Sufi brotherhoods (the *tariquat*) have been influential in a number of regions of Central Asia and the Caucasus. The Muslim experience in Eurasia is vastly different, depending on when a particular group converted to Islam, what type of Islam was embraced, the socio-economic status of the group, whether Islamic law or tribal customary law took precedence, and, not the least unimportant, the degree and extent of contact with Russia.[11]

Also of importance has been the degree to which Eurasian Muslims have been isolated from trends in the Arab world in the last several centuries, particularly those that have abetted the rise of extremist and radical elements. In many parts of Eurasia, Islam has been colored by Turkic culture. Folk tales and native idioms, for example, played a much greater role in transmitting Islamic values than Arab literature, since Arabic was not easily accessible to most nomads and peasants. The partial use of Turkic vernaculars, the embrace of Sufi mysticism, as well as the importance, in some communities, of the role of women in Islamic education and community development[12] have also meant that Wahhabite and other Arab puritanical movements were not able to gain major footholds among Eurasian Muslims. The Mongol influence on the Eurasian steppes—including traditions of tolerance and syncretism—also played a key role. Writing of the medieval conqueror Tamerlane, Ibn 'Arabshah castigated him as a bad Muslim for having "preferred Jenghiz Khan's law to the law of Islam."[13] Finally, the out-migration of some of the more hardened Islamic elements from territories acquired by the Russian Empire allowed more moderate elements to rise to the fore.[14]

In fact, the Russian Empire was able to play upon intra-Muslim rivalries in a number of areas in establishing its authority in largely Muslim regions.[15] The first All-Muslim Congress in the Russian Empire, called in 1905, in coping with the great differences among Muslims of the Empire, tried to play down differences in order to seek common ground, with only some success.[16] At the time of the Revolution of 1917, some Muslim Communists held forth the vision of the creation of a "Muslim Republic of Turan, thus embracing all the Turkic nations and ethnic ethnicities of Asiatic Russia," based on the hope that the "Islamic unity of the Muslim peoples of Idel-Ural [the Middle Volga region] and Central Asia, along with the Caucasus, will bring about the socialist unity of the same,"[17] yet this dream proved to be unrealizable. By the end of 1917 ethnolinguistic considerations "were dividing this supraethnic community into its constituent ethnic groups, fragmenting the Muslims of the former Russian Empire into distinct Central Asian, Caucasian, and Volga groupings."[18]

Instead, based upon historical, cultural, and geographic factors, it is more logical to speak of three main Islamic groupings in Eurasia: the Middle Volga communities of the Tatars and Bashkirs, those of the Caucasus and Transcaucasia, and Central Asia, each having its own distinct Islamic experience and background.[19]

Not only did the Muslims of the former USSR not form a single monolithic community, it was and remains incorrect to assume that Islam was unaffected by or even unsupportive of the Soviet experience. Most Westerners have focused upon the Islamic resistance to the Soviet state, especially the revolt of the Sufi brotherhoods in Dagestan and Chechnya that was not fully suppressed until 1936; the *basmachi* revolt in Central Asia, which went on until 1924 and continued in the Fergana Valley until 1928; and the reality of a significant number of Muslim defections to the Germans during World War II, either from among frontline soldiers or in areas occupied in the Caucasus.[20]

Anti-Soviet resistance should neither be discounted nor seen as the norm. Although the Chechens have come to symbolize the Islamic resistance to the Soviet Union (and to the post-Soviet Russian Federation), initially, the Chechen religious leadership allied itself with the Bolsheviks. In August 1917, a congress of Muslim leaders elected Sheikh Nadzhimuddin (Najimudin) Gotsinskii as the *imam* of Chechnya and Dagestan. Along with his associate, Sheikh Uzun Hadji, Gotsinskii worked with the Soviets to defeat the White Army of General Denikin.[21] Muslim support for the revolution was seen in other areas as well; in 1923, for example, the Muslim leadership in Ufa issued a *fatwa* welcoming the revolution: "By the great grace of Allah, the Revolution which has taken place in Russia has destroyed a brutal, despotic autocracy which persecuted the religion of Islam."[22]

Even before the revolution, a major cleavage was developing in Eurasian Islam, based upon the experience of Tatars and other nationalities living under Orthodox Christian rule in a Westernizing, modernizing state. The *jadid* movement, spearheaded by the Muslim Tatar intellectual Ismail Gaspraly (Gasprinskii) (1851–1914), maintained that Islam and modernity were compatible and, moreover, that Russia, although a European Christian state, was the closest in feeling to the Muslim world and that a Muslim–Christian symbiosis could take place within the framework of the Eurasian Russian Empire. The *jadids* placed a high degree of emphasis upon education and ridding Islam of what were termed archaic practices and attitudes. Not surprisingly, the *jadid* movement was opposed by conservative clergy and believers in the Caucasus and Central Asia (the *kadim*); the government of the Russian Empire was also concerned about the pan-Turkic and revolutionary tendencies of the *jadid* movement and tended to back conservative movements as well. Many of the *jadids*, therefore, were supporters of the Revolution, believing that the fall of the Russian Empire would pave the way for full social and political equality for Eurasian Muslims and that socialism, as the harbinger of modernity and development, could be reconciled with Islamic values and practices.[23] *Jadids* thus initially formed an important part of the cadres of the Communist Party in Muslim areas, especially in Central Asia.[24]

One of the more interesting projects put forth were the proposals by Mirsaid Sultan Galiev, himself a former *jadid*, on how to transform Muslims into good Communists. In addition to the skillful use of atheistic propaganda, Sultan Galiev insisted on

> giving non-Russians full and equal rights within the young Soviet state. He believed that Muslims were culturally backward because of tsarist oppression, and still refrained from participating in the party and government because they distrusted its Russian base. Only demonstrating to Muslims their new status as equal partners in the state, in deeds as well as words, would convince them of the correctness of Marxism-Leninism.[25]

In other words, modernization and full and equal opportunities to participate in the new system would undermine the traditional influence of Islam upon the masses. Although Sultan Galiev was arrested in 1923 because of the increasingly anti-Russian and pan-Turkic elements in his revolutionary musings, certain elements of his program were enacted by the Soviet state, especially the policies on producing indigenous cadres (*korennizatsia*).

Initially, the Soviet state focused on the Russian Orthodox Church as its main target in the antireligious struggle, but once Central Asia and the Caucasus were largely pacified, the Soviet regime unleashed a formidable persecution of Islam, aimed at destroying its educational and social base. The number of open mosques was dramatically curtailed; by 1942, only 1312 remained opened throughout the USSR.[26] Large-scale confiscation of clerical property (*waqf*) began in 1925, and by 1927, all usage of Islamic (*shariat*) or tribal (*adat*) laws was abolished, which ended a process that had begun in 1923 to break the influence of traditional courts upon matters such as marriage, divorce, adoption, and inheritance issues.[27] During the 1920s, the Soviet regime also began to convert Islamic schools into secular ones, so that by 1927 only 250 Islamic schools remained in operation in Central Asia.[28] With the acceleration of the antireligious campaign after 1929 under Josef Stalin, the clergy increasingly were singled out for persecution, harassment, arrest, and execution. In Uzbekistan alone, estimates are that over 10,000 members of the clergy were arrested and/or executed during the 1930s.[29] By 1942, their numbers in Soviet territory had been reduced sixfold, to 8,872.[30]

Soviet economic and nationality policies also had an impact. Whenever possible, the Soviet state concentrated on separating Muslim groups into distinct nationalities (the policy of national delimitation or *natsional'noe razmezhevaniie*),[31] aimed at "forestalling any attempt to create either pan-Islamic or pan-Turkic unity."[32] Central Asia was divided into five Union Republics; the Caucasus was fragmented into a series of small political units that sometimes divided speakers of common languages into separate administrative entities, and in other cases threw together disparate groups into a single republic; and separate Tatar and Baskhir republics were created within the Russian Federation with the aim of reducing the threat of a unified Muslim entity arising along the banks of the Volga.[33] As a result, the "Soviets have encouraged ethnic identification based on language and have systematically combatted ethnic identification based on religion."[34] Language dictates also played a key role, with Arabic being banned as a language of common communication among Muslims and with alphabet changes designed to "cut off future generations from the past cultures of their own peoples."[35] Industrialization had a dual impact of bringing in large numbers of Slavic migrants while also pulling in locals from the hinterland into urban areas where traditional institutions and practices were more likely to be eroded.[36]

Unquestionably, Soviet policies did a great deal of damage to Islam. Certainly, the antireligious campaigns of Stalin and of Nikita Khrushchev (1959–1962) led to a significant disruption of Muslim religious life. The institutional framework of schools and courts that had held together Muslim communities was swept away, and antireligious violence eliminated thousands of teachers and leaders.[37] For many, Islam shifted from being a faith able to shape a person's worldview and guide everyday action into a series of rituals and customs that often were used, not to denote belief, but to indicate ethnicity.[38] Soviet policies and modernization also contributed to a growing secularization of the Muslim population of the USSR; already by 1937 some 15 percent of adult Muslims in Soviet territory described themselves as nonbelievers.[39] Islam never lost its hold on the population; religious belief was never eliminated, and many people continued to observe some religious rites, such as having sons circumcised or having a *mullah* present at a funeral.[40] At the same time, however, it is clear that in many areas of the USSR, Islam ceased to be the lodestone of people's daily existence, except in some rural areas of

Central Asia or in areas of the North Caucasus where tight-knit family and clan structures persisted (and also in those areas of Central Asia to which people from the North Caucasus had been deported). Not surprisingly, it was largely in areas where Sufi brotherhoods had been influential, or where circuit-riding Sufi preachers, the so-called horseback *ishans*, that a higher degree of underground Muslim organizational, educational, and spiritual life, survived.[41]

Gauging the actual levels of religiosity among Soviet Muslims proved to be difficult. Nevertheless, the vast majority of nonbelievers tended to be the "urban educated class of technocrats who had been sufficiently modernized and Westernized through extra-cultural contact,"[42] whereas the highest percentage of believers tended to be rural.[43] In other words, Islamic areas of the USSR, like many areas in Western Europe, are characterized by a strong secularizing trend—levels of religiosity began to decline as the population become more educated and more urbanized. Soviet research undertaken in northwestern Uzbekistan at the beginning of the 1970s indicated that some 21 percent of the population was actively atheist, with approximately 25 percent active believers (either on account of faith or because of Islam being traditional). Most of the population, however, fell into a median gray zone, people who might observe some rites and traditions of Islam and express religious sentiments, but who were neither committed atheists nor committed Muslim believers.[44] Other, non-Soviet estimates indicated that about 20 to 40 percent of the population of Central Asia engaged in daily prayer and that up to half made some effort to observe the Ramadan fast.[45] However, it is also critical to point out that the understanding of Islam began to shift during the Soviet period. Alexandre Bennigsen and Marie Broxup noted that there was a

. . . growing confusion between the notions of 'national' and 'religious' . . . An atheist intellectual or a Party member will nevertheless comply with certain religious rules and customs for 'national' reasons, since to spurn the religious traditions of the nation would be tantamount to betrayal of the nation.[46]

As Pedro Ramet observed in 1987, "Even nonbelievers in Central Asia are apt to identify themselves as Muslims and to view any assault on Islamic religious traditions as a threat to their ethnic and cultural identity."[47]

For many people, being Muslim also began to be confused with being moral.[48] Thus, in many areas of the USSR, one could observe the phenomenon of the Muslim Communist, a person who could simultaneously move and be comfortable in a Soviet world defined by atheism, scientific progress, and modern values, and retain an allegiance to certain basic Muslim beliefs and observance of rituals and traditions that over time became inextricably linked to national identity.[49] Thus, Rafiq Nishanov,

Mikhail Gorbachev's appointee as first secretary of the Uzbek Communist Party, complained,

> Withdrawn from struggle with Islam . . . with attempts to pass off religious-patriarchal customs as national traditions, . . . for many Communists, the Muslim "science of life" is more authoritative than the Party rules and norms of socialist morality.[50]

This phenomenon resulted from the fact, as Rywkin observed, that

> It is impossible to remain totally unaffected by Soviet Russian reality, and this results in multiple social identities. Thus, for example, an Uzbek may view himself as Uzbek, as Turkestani, as Muslim, and as Soviet depending on circumstances and the person (or persons) with whom he deals or converses.[51]

One cannot also discount the influence that official Soviet Islam has had in shaping behavior and identity. During the Second World War, the Soviet regime reached out to religion in order to shore up its legitimacy. Josef Stalin was able to reach a *modus vivendi* with some Muslim clerics, notably Abdul Rahman Rasulayev (of Ufa, in Bashkiria). Four Spiritual Directorates were set up for Soviet Muslims in 1941, covering Central Asia and Kazakhstan, European Russia and Siberia, the northern Caucasus, and Transcaucasia. These directorates were, of course, closely regulated by the state. Clerical appointments and policies were carefully scrutinized. Nevertheless, within strict limits, some Islamic literature could be published and the training of clerics resumed. From the Soviet side, toleration of an official Islamic establishment was preferable to dealing with the potential rise of a more anti-Soviet Islamic underground.[52] However, official Islam within the Soviet Union, much like the official Orthodox Christian Church, had to extol the legitimacy of the Soviet regime, publicly support socialism and Soviet propaganda efforts, and deny that any persecution of religion was being undertaken within the USSR.[53]

The restoration of Islamic education, even if on a limited scale, in the USSR has produced several generations of clerics who might be termed progressive or modernist, who have placed a greater stress on independent reasoning and judgment as opposed to strict adherence to past precedents. Most of them, as Alexandre Bennigsen and Marie Broxup observed, "Like their great predecessors, they reject the *taqlid* and advocate the restoration of the *ijtihad*. They are endeavouring to reconcile Islam with science and progress."[54]

Indeed, the Soviet regime became very worried about the rise of Islamic modernism, especially in Central Asia, for its ability to adapt and cope with modern Soviet society. Islamic modernism was characterized by a portrayal of the Prophet as a "democrat, reformer, revolutionary, even as a socialist"; affirmed Islam as a bulwark of progress and as a system of ideas capable of supporting social and political change; and accepted the need to modernize Islamic values vis-a-vis women, the family, and daily life.[55]

Where, then, did this notion of the militancy and fundamentalism of Soviet Islam come from? As Geoffrey Hosking pointed out, there was never any hard evidence to suggest that an Islamic crisis was brewing in the USSR.[56] Part of the problem lies in the captive-nations mentality prevalent in Western academic circles, which suggested that Soviet minorities were implacably anti-Soviet and anti-Russian and only waiting for the opportunity to overthrow Soviet rule.[57] Another source was a popular misunderstanding of works such as Michael Rywkin's *Moscow's Muslim Challenge: Soviet Central Asia* and other books that discussed the status of Muslim nationalities in the USSR. Rywkin and other scholars pointed to the fact that Muslim nationalities in the USSR could not be easily Russianized, in part because of the awareness of Islam in forming national awareness among the ethnic groups of Central Asia and the Caucasus and the role that this awareness played in maintaining a distinction from ethnic Russians. By the 1960s, it was clear that there was a net emigration of Russians and other Slav nationalities from Central Asia, diminishing the prospects that large Slavic populations in Central Asia could bind the regions closer to Moscow.[58] At the same time, "the Slav-dominated political system has naturally given many non-Russians a sense of having their destinies controlled from outside, by foreigners."[59] Thus, the Muslim challenge that Rywkin anticipated was to what extent the Russian nature of the USSR would have to be modified to accommodate a growing Muslim population.[60]

To some extent, Westerners were also guilty of extrapolating certain facts or details that pertained to specific groups and applying them to all Muslims in the USSR. For example, it is unquestioned that the Chechens have a long history of anti-Russian and anti-Soviet activity, marked especially by the rebellions led by Sheikh Mansur and Imam Shamyl in the nineteenth century. The influence of Sufi movements in Chechnya has led to Chechen Islam being characterized by calls for ascetism, moral purification, and the unification of all Muslims in the Caucasus; combined with the traditional *teip* structure, Sufi brotherhoods have helped the Chechens to hold Russification and Sovietization at bay.[61] However, the Chechen experience cannot be put forward as representative of all Muslim nationalities. Many of those who cited Chechen resistance to Russian and Soviet rule as evidence of the Muslim threat to the Soviet Union failed to discuss countervailing tendencies.

A number of analysts also assumed that the maintenance or retention of an Islamic identity by Soviet citizens automatically translated into political dissidence and opposition, even when there was little evidence to support such an assertion.[62]

It also appears that a number of Westerners overestimated the influence of underground Islamic movements in the USSR, especially those that began to stir in the 1970s, which were influenced by developments in Iran and contacts in Afghanistan. Certainly, after decades of atheist persecution, and in the midst of a search for religious roots that began among certain segments of the Soviet intelligentsia, some turned to stricter forms of Islam in a search for purity of faith.[63] Such movements began to emerge publicly during the Gorbachev period, but what had not been expected or predicted by a number of Westerners was the ability of official Soviet and post-Soviet Islam to cope with such challenges.[64]

President Geidar Aliev of Azerbaijan, in a telling comment, pointed out that much of what shapes and defines the post-Soviet states, including those of the Muslim world, "was created in the Union."[65] Seven decades of Sovietization has led to a much higher degree of secularization and Westernization in Central Asia and the Caucasus than in the Middle East. Moreover, no consensus exists among the Muslim populations of this region that this is necessarily a bad thing.[66] The Soviet legacy, therefore, has played an important role in retarding the development of Islamist movements in the region, even when Soviet power itself began to crumble and fall during the 1980s.

ISLAM, GORBACHEV, AND THE BREAKUP OF THE USSR

Like Nikita Khrushchev before him, Mikhail Gorbachev, who became general secretary of the Communist Party of the Soviet Union in 1985, attempted to revive Communist fervor by increasing the pressure on religion. Gorbachev chose a visit to Tashkent in November 1986 to demand "an uncompromising battle against all religious phenomena."[67] This included renewed harassment of unofficial clergy and crackdowns on Islamic publication and education efforts.[68] Gorbachev also continued KGB-initiated efforts to infiltrate the ranks of the Muslim clergy and to send agents into the Muslim world to propagandize on behalf of the USSR.[69] An unpublished decree of the Central Committee of the Communist Party, promulgated in August 1986, set down measures to accelerate the struggle with Islam, seen as a hindrance to Soviet reform efforts.[70]

Linked to Gorbachev's antireligious campaign was a drive to shake up the Soviet establishment, particularly by ending the policy of "stability of cadres," which had enabled Communist leaders to build up patronage networks and solidify their positions of power and authority.[71] This had profound effects in Central Asia, where it is estimated that more than half of the Uzbek party and bureaucracy was replaced by 1986, and where, in the Khirghiz SSR, some 82 percent of the local Communist secretaries were purged.[72] Of course, a number of the people within the Communist elite, the so-called Muslim Communists, had used their positions to extend a certain degree of protection around some Muslim practices and institutions;[73] with their removal, it appeared as if Gorbachev was, in fact, trying to target the national minorities in order to accelerate their Russification and Sovietization. Gorbachev's famous blunder in Kiev in June 1985, when he referred to the USSR as Russia and then offered the excuse that the two were synonymous,[74] would have further raised suspicions about the goals of his policies.

Gorbachev, however, began to encounter resistance to his policies. In Kazakhstan in December 1986, popular discontent flared up into riots and violence when Gorbachev removed Dinmukhamed Kunayev as first secretary of the Communist Party in Kazakhstan and attempted to replace him with an ethnic Russian, Gennadii Kolbin. Kunayev, during his tenure as first secretary, had carried out a strong policy of Kazakhization within the republican system of education, in industry, in the media, and especially within the Communist Party. Fears among ethnic Kazakhs of creeping Russification led to days of clashes, which Giampaolo Capisani labels as the symbolic end of the *pax Sovietica* and the beginning of the end for the Soviet state. Certainly, the clashes, which produced an official death toll of seventeen in the capital city of Alma-Ata (Almaty), helped to galvanize local opinion to begin serious discussions about national sovereignty and the relationship of the republic to the federal Soviet center.[75]

Fears about the gradual elimination of national languages in favor of Russian (as the international language of communication within the USSR) also began to be expressed publicly and also provided a way for religious concerns to be voiced. In December 1988 protests by Uzbek students in Tashkent were accompanied by overtly religious demonstrations, such as the waving of green banners and the recitation of verses from the Quran.[76]

Initially, Gorbachev's call for *glasnost'* (openness) was supposed to be limited to encouragement of criticism when such efforts would aid the interests of reform, but by 1988, *glasnost'* began to take on a life of its own, as reporters and social groups began to articulate concerns and demands going far beyond a limited reform agenda, including those touching on religion.[77] Gorbachev and his circle in the leadership were also concerned about being able to reach out to the general population. A cautious note indicating a reassessment of the Soviet line toward religion was first sounded by an editorial in *Kommunist* in March 1988, which was critical of past Soviet policies on religion and stated the need to reexamine the question of the role of religion in a socialist society. This was followed by a roundtable meeting between Gorbachev and religious leaders in April 1988, at which Gorbachev proclaimed that Communists and believers did share "universal norms and customs" and that, as a result, there could be cooperation in furtherance of shared aims.[78]

The Soviet regime was thus prepared to permit a moderate Islamic revival. There were 200 or so mosques in operation in 1982, and that number grew to 600 by 1987, with another 48 Muslim communities registered in 1988. By July 1990 there were some 1,103 registered Muslim communities in the USSR. Moreover, the authorities permitted the Islamic institutions of higher learning in Tashkent to expand their enrollments, while another Islamic preparatory academy was permitted to open in Ufa and an Islamic college in Tajikistan was set up. Publication of Islamic literature was also accelerated.[79]

Growing democratization in Soviet society and a loosening of controls led to the first major shakeup in the Soviet Islamic establishment. Long-running dissatisfaction with the life and behavior of Shamsuddin Baba-khanov ibn Zeyudin, the head of the Spiritual Directorate for Kazakhstan and Central Asia, flared up into public demonstrations in Tashkent, Uzbekistan, in February 1989. After several days, Babakhanov was persuaded to retire by an Uzbek Communist leadership eager to prevent further disorder. On March 15, 1989, at a *kurultai* (assembly) of the Muslim religious board for Central Asia, the head of the Tashkent institute, Muhummad Sadiq Yusuf (Mama Yusupov), was elected.[80] Both Muhammad Yusuf and the head of the Spiritual Directorate for Transcaucasia, Allahshukur Pashazade, were subsequently elected as members of the Congress of People's Deputies, the quasi-democratically elected parliament assembled by Gorbachev.[81] Similar manifestations were seen in Dagestan in May 1989, where local protests flared up against the *mufti* in Makhachkala, the capital city. Ultimately, in January 1990 a congress elected a replacement.[82]

However, even with these changes, the official leadership could hardly be characterized as radical. Muhammad Yusuf, for example, urged Central Asian Muslims to fulfill their civic obligations, including military service, to the Soviet state, and continued to inveigh against superstitions and outmoded customs, such as the *kalym* (the bride-price).[83] After 1989, one of the growing preoccupations of the Soviet leadership by this point was the shoring up of the official Islamic establishment. Indeed, one of the goals of inserting KGB-controlled figures into leadership positions within the Islamic community was "for use in measures in the struggle with the reactionary part of the Muslim clergy."[84] Moreover, a number of the new privileges were reserved only for religious groups that registered with the state.[85]

Ferment thus continued within the ranks of Soviet Muslims, both religious and political. One of the first overtly political manifestations was the creation of the movement "Islam and Democracy of Uzbekistan," which held its founding congress in Alma-Ata (Almaty) on October 28, 1988.[86] Other grassroots Islamic movements, dubbed "Wahhabite" by the press, began to emerge in the Fergana valley in Uzbekistan.[87] As other

Muslim-oriented political movements began to arise throughout the Soviet Union, an all-Soviet organization was proposed—the Islamic Revival Party (IRP), which held its founding congress in Astrakhan, Russia, on June 10, 1990, with 150 delegates present from the North Caucasus, Tajikistan, Azerbaijan, and other Muslim areas. The party was clearly Islamist in orientation, calling for the establishment of *shariat* courts and the teaching of Islam in schools.[88] It looked to the writings of Qutb, al-Banna, and Mawdudi for inspiration.[89] However, the blended background of most Soviet Muslims, reflecting both Islamic and Western influences, was clearly evident. In addition to embracing Islamist ideas, the IRP also, at times, seemed to stand for Western-style liberal democracy. Abdullah Yusuf, the first deputy chairman of the IRP in Uzbekistan, declared,

> With our people, the notion of democracy means no restrictions . . . It would not be a one-party state; the franchise would be universal; the rights of ethnic and religious minorities would be protected; and private property would be honored.[90]

Other movements, such as the Islamic Democratic Party in Uzbekistan or the Alash party in Kazakhstan also gained prominence in 1990, advancing largely Islamist demands vis-à-vis the social and political order.[91] However, none of these movements succeeded in developing a mass following.

Nonetheless, the Soviet leadership thus began to voice concerns about Islamic fundamentalism. As the Soviet empire began to disintegrate, Gorbachev and his associates began to paint all opposition movements in Muslim areas "in the colors of radical Islam."[92] This was a tactic largely directed at the West to gain support for Gorbachev's efforts to hold the USSR together, by playing upon fears of the potential radicalization of the Muslim populations of the Soviet Union by pro-Iranian elements.[93]

However, the real threats to the integrity of the Soviet state came from secular, nationalist movements. Nationalism proved to be the prime motivator for informal movements and members of the Communist Party to put aside their differences and forge a consensus toward democratization and claiming a greater degree of sovereignty within the USSR (or outright independence). In Azerbaijan, for example, the Muslim element in the Popular Front movement was minimal; pro-independence groups were secular in orientation, and when religious figures were present at demonstrations or meetings, the Muslim clergy were joined by Orthodox Christian and Jewish religious leaders.[94] While Islamic movements surfaced throughout the region, the principal opposition political movements arose out of concern for economic and linguistic issues—these, not Islam, were responsible for the politicization of the populations of Central Asia and the Caucasus during Gorbachev's tenure.[95]

In fact, nationalism was more appealing, not only to the masses but even more so to the political, economic, and intellectual cadres in the various republics, because, as Valery Tishkov has noted, the nation-building process had created a powerful new stratum in Central Asian and Caucasian societies: the "administrative, creative, and scientific-technical intelligentsia."[96] This group, in particular, was not prepared to exchange the practical benefits of the existing republican structure to support the establishment of a vague Islamic-Turkestani community. This elite view also began to filter down to the popular level. By 1990, Muslim religious and political organizations in the USSR had begun to splinter and divide along national lines—the same lines demarcated by the Soviets during the 1920s and 1930s.[97]

Even the Islamic Revival Party, created as an all-Union, all-inclusive, pan-Muslim organization, began to split apart on national lines, first with the separation of the Tajik branch of the party from the whole. One of the Tajik leaders, Davlat Usmon, "voiced no interest in the creation of a supranational Islamic state. Apart from the fact that he considered such a state impracticable, he also saw it as undesirable because, to him, national differences mattered."[98] In Kyrgyzstan, there was a growing fear that pan-Islamic or pan-Turkic political movements were nothing more than disguises for the establishment of Uzbek supremacy in Central Asia or a tool for the Uzbekization of other groups in the region.[99]

Although leaders like Muhammad Yusuf (Yusupov) in Tashkent continued to put forward an ideal of Muslim unity (in 1991 he declared, "We used to be one people and we will be one people in the future, I hope. Common religion will help us to resolve disputes and conflicts."),[100] any remaining illusions about Muslim solidarity in the USSR were shattered by a series of intra-Muslim clashes between members of different ethnic and national groups. As Tishkov noted: "Interethnic relations in Central Asia and Kazakhstan have clearly deteriorated . . . The main cause is the upsurge in ethnic nationalism among the representative of the titular groups."[101] Violence erupted in clashes between Meskhetian Turks and Uzbeks in the Fergana valley of Uzbekistan in May–June 1989, between Uzbeks and Kyrgyz in the Osh district of Kyrgyzstan (May–August 1989), between Kazakhs and Lezghins in Western Kazakhstan (June 1989), between Tajik and Kyrgyz in the Isfara district of Tajikistan and the Baktin district of Kyrzystan (June–July 1989), and among the nationalities living in the Gorno-Badakshan region of Tajikistan and in Dushanbe, resulting, in the end, in hundreds of deaths and injuries. Common profession of Islam was not sufficient to forestall ethnic clashes,[102] despite the efforts of the Muslim establishment to try and calm tensions.[103] Instead, such clashes reinforced ethnic divisions among Central Asians.

The notion of a united Muslim wave rising up to sweep away the Soviet Union, therefore, dissolved before the reality of interethnic conflicts and the consolidation of popular movements behind national, rather than Islamic, principles. In fact, with the exception of Azerbaijan (and Chechnya, within the Russian Federation), most Muslim areas of the Soviet Union continued to support the continuation of the USSR. Muslim demands tended to focus on achieving greater status for their nationalities within a revived and reinvigorated Union (such as recognition of national languages, allowing for some public manifestation of Islam, or obtaining greater autonomy). In Uzbekistan, for example, Muslim clerics publicly supported efforts to hold the USSR together, and in the March 1991 referendum, Uzbek voters virtually unanimously voted to retain the Union.[104] Ferment in the Baltics, unrest in Georgia, and the emergence of a Russian elite and nationalism distinct from the Soviet center were the main causes of the disintegration of the Soviet Union; the Muslim regions proved to play little or no role in the chain of events that led to the Soviet collapse. The Central Asian republics only declared their independence from the USSR following the failed August 1991 coup, when it was clear that the Soviet Union was disintegrating. Far from being the bane of the Soviet state, Muslim Central Asia proved to be its last bastion.

POST-SOVIET ISLAM: GENERAL OBSERVATIONS

Even though Islam in the post-Soviet space is increasingly moving in different directions, there are still a number of general trends that can be identified as being characteristic of Islam in Eurasia, which can help to explain why Islamist movements have not been successful in gaining ground in the region.

The first is the continuing disintegration of any sort of unified Islamic presence, identity, or organization spanning the region. After the collapse of the Soviet Union, the Islamic Revival Party precipitously declined as an international/all-Eurasian movement. By the time of its Third Congress (held April 1992 in Saratov), only forty delegates were present.[105] The unified Spiritual Directorate for Central Asia fragmented into national administrations.[106] In the Caucasus and the Russian Federation, at least ten self-nominated *muftiyat* have appeared, often based on national and ethnic lines.[107] In all, it is now estimated that there are some forty Muslim spiritual administrations now functioning on the territory of the former Soviet Union, many with overlapping jurisdictional claims.[108]

Moreover, far from rejecting the Soviet-era national constructions, the current states, especially in Central Asia, are seeking to strengthen and deepen their national identities, at the expense of any sort of pan-Islamic or pan-Turkic sense of solidarity.[109] There have been continuing interethnic problems among the various Muslim nationalities as well, most notably tensions between the Uzbek authorities and the large Tajik population in Samarkand and Bukhara.[110] This process of nation-building includes recasting Islam in terms of national faiths. In Turkmenistan, President Saparmurat "Turkmenbashi" Niyazov has consistently stressed the national-ethnic character of Islam in that republic; his New Year's Address (2001) made it clear that "Turkmen society created its own specific rules and regulations."[111] Niyazov has advocated banning the publication of the *hadiths* (the collected sayings of the Prophet Muhammad) as being inconsistent with the Turkmen version of Islam, saying,

> The Turkmen do not believe in *hadiths*. The Turkmen people believe in the Koran. . . *Hadiths* are being published now. Our radio and television are quoting them. Don't do that. Most of them do not apply to our present traditions and religion.[112]

In Uzbekistan, President Islam Karimov extolled the universalist character of Uzbek culture, and proclaimed,

> An important step on the path to reawakening our historical memory and establishing our cultural and historical identity and integrity has thus been our encouragement of an Islamic revival within the context of Uzbekistan's internal transformation . . . That process vindicates the decision not to "import" Islam from outside, not to politicize Islam, and not to Islamize our politics.[113]

Indeed, some have touted using Uzbekistan's "rich heritage of classical Muslim spirituality" as "the best means of fighting against religious extremism," by stressing a particularly Uzbek or Central Asian approach to Islam that emphasizes peace and enlightenment.[114]

The second is the continuing orientation toward Europe and the West that distinguishes the Muslim areas of Eurasia from those in the Middle East. This tendency was pronounced even in the nineteenth century.[115] Although speaking specifically about Azerbaijan, Elin Suleymanov's comments apply, to some extent, to all of the post-Soviet areas. In drawing a distinction between the ethnically Azeri population in Iran and those living in the Republic of Azerbaijan, Suleymanov noted,

> While the identity of the South's population developed broadly within the Iranian, and subsequently Middle Eastern, framework, the population of the Republic of Azerbaijan clearly sees itself as part of the Caucasus and Eastern Europe, areas with which it shares common elements of historical experience and culture. Political processes . . . have also been similar to those in Eastern Europe and the post-Soviet space, and hence very different from the ones in Iran and the Middle East in general. This has resulted in different political thinking and priorities.[116]

A similar observation has also been made by Martha Brill Olcott in comparing Kazakhs in Kazakhstan versus their ethnic brethren in Iran, Mongolia, and China: "Seventy years of Soviet rule left Kazakhstan's Kazakhs closer to the European-dominated global culture than to their nomadic past."[117]

In contrast to the direct rejection of the West and its values that one can find in the Middle East, many Eurasian Muslims are much more comfortable viewing themselves as functioning as a bridge between East and West[118] and seeking meaningful ways to reconcile the Islamic and Western experiences in a viable synthesis. The most visible manifestation of this orientation has been in dress. Since 1990, there has been no real move to adopt any sort of Islamic dress code, especially for women, in the Caucasus or Central Asia, with the exception of certain rural regions (such as the Fergana valley). Western dress (for both men and women) has remained the norm, especially in the cities. In general, Central Asians aspire to a Western lifestyle.[119]

This has implications for how many Eurasian Muslims view the role of faith in society. Certainly, many expect that religion should play a prominent role in public life, but this does not translate into sentiments that Islamic law, for example, should be substituted for secular law.[120]

The third is the continuity in Muslim leadership between Soviet and post-Soviet periods. Talgat Tadzhuddin, mufti for the European territories of Russia and the CIS, and Allahshukur Pasha-Zade, chair of the Transcaucasian spiritual board, both moderate clerics appointed during Soviet times,[121] remain in their positions. In Tashkent, Muhammad Yusuf was demoted from his position in April 1993 (facing charges that he enjoyed close relations with the KGB) but he remained in the leadership as first deputy mufti to the new appointee, Muktarkhan Abdullaev, who enjoyed good relations with the Uzbek leadership.[122] Younger clergy appointed to official positions, such as Nasrullah ibn Ibadullah in Turkmenistan, have the reputation of being modernist in outlook.[123] Radical Islamists have thus had little ability to infiltrate the official structures of Islam in Eurasia, with some exceptions (such as in Tajikistan), and thus have been relegated to a place outside the mainstream.

Another factor that must be considered is the growing rift between natives and outsiders in Eurasian Islam. Initially, the arrival of Muslim activists and teachers from the Middle East and South Asia was welcomed by many as a Godsend for the restoration of Muslim educational and community life. Over time, however, Wahhabites and representatives of other Islamist organizations have begun to alienate local populations with their interpretations of Islam.[124] In particular, their "puritanical views are not shared by the majority of the Muslims of Central Asia who adhere to the Hanafi school of Islam noted for its general liberal orientation and its emphasis on private opinion and public consensus in administration and interpretation of Islamic principles."[125] Many Eurasian Muslim cultures also place great weight on *adat*—indigenous, pre-Muslim law and customs—and do not view the *sharia* as all-encompassing.[126] As Bruce Pannier noted,

> The Wahhabi movement has been looked upon with suspicion . . . the Wahhabis have been active in Central Asia and Muslim regions of the Caucasus. . . However, their presence . . . is resented by other sects, particularly the various Sufi orders which have been present in Muslim areas of the CIS for centuries . . . While some

people may be willing to accept Wahhabi interpretations of Islamic duty others are, and have been, satisfied with the religion the way it has been practiced in their region or even village for years, if not centuries. Sufi masters especially object to the arrival of these outsiders . . .[127]

In some cases, disputes between outsiders and natives has led to violence; in May 1997, in the village of Chabani-Makhi (Dagestan), armed clashes broke out between members of a Wahhabi organization and members of one of the Sufi brotherhoods (*tariqat*).[128]

Foreign sponsorship of Islamic educational centers, such as in Tatarstan, has also led to problems. Graduates of such *madrassahs*, when they become imams, "try to build community and spiritual life in the Arab way. They interfere with established national religious traditions and ceremonies, trying to mould the spiritual life of their flocks in accordance with Arab norms."[129] As a result, the head of the Muslim administration in Tatarstan, Gabdulla Galiullin, succeeded in having a decree enacted banning the activities of Arab Muslim movements in Tatarstan, and a careful policy in the placement of *imams* has been developed; if a candidate has studied abroad in the Middle East, he is given a trial period of a year before being confirmed in his position at a mosque.[130] Turkmenistan has gone even further, by expelling all foreigners engaged in religious activity, no matter whether Muslim or not.[131] Kazakhstan also expels "any foreigner not part of an official delegation who is caught 'propagating' Islam."[132]

A final point that must be considered is the attitude of Iran. Most outside observers automatically assumed that Iran would seek to overthrow the regimes of Central Asia and the Caucasus to install fanatical Islamists in power. This has not occurred, because Iran prefers political tranquility across its northern borders to risking the chaos and disruption that would result from any attempt at a radical Islamicization of Central Asian states.[133] Iran has no desire to create a vacuum and its attendant instability.[134] This does not mean that Iran is not interested in furthering its influence through political and economic deals, or by trying to influence the course and direction of Central Asian and Caucasian Islam (e.g. through missionary work, sponsoring the construction of mosques and schools, etc.) However, Iran's relationships with Central Asia and the Caucasus are based on pragmatic considerations, not ideology.

STATE ISLAM AND THE EURASIAN CONSENSUS

One of the key features of Islamic life across Eurasia is the fact that official or state Islam "has continued to play a significant role in shaping the ongoing Islamic revival by keeping a close watch on the activities of those Muslims who have chosen to return to the traditional ways of life after nearly 80 years of involuntary interruption."[135] Close state involvement in Muslim affairs has stymied the development of independent Muslim organizations and groups that might seek to challenge the *status quo*. While indigenous Muslim organizations are encouraged to register with the state, foreign Islamic groups are tightly regulated and supervised.[136] All of this has precedent in the imperial past; in the nineteenth century the tsarist government tried, with mixed success, to prohibit nonimperial subjects from holding any official positions within the Muslim establishment, to ban any foreign assistance to Muslim communities within the Empire, and to break the ties between the *ulema* of the Persian and Ottoman Empires and the Muslim leadership in the Caucasus and Central Asia.[137]

In Uzbekistan, the official *muftiyat* is promoted as a link between the Islam religious community and state, a type of transmission belt between the government and believers. President Islam Karimov has assumed the role of a social mediator and thus is perceived not only as a secular political leader, but also as a figure of authority within Uzbek Islam.[138] In Turkmenistan, a Council for Religious Affairs remains attached to the presidential apparatus, and all clerical appointments at all levels are closely supervised and monitored.[139] After independence, in both Kazakhstan and Uzbekistan, the official Muslim establishment also extended the hand of fellowship to those Muslim clerics and leaders who had functioned illegally during the Soviet period, giving them the opportunity, which many accepted, to become part of the official Islamic community.[140]

By taking the initiative on restoring a more visible Muslim presence in society, most Central Asian states and Muslim regions of Russia have neutralized or co-opted some of the forces that might have otherwise been drawn into an Islamist orbit. In Uzbekistan, for example, the government has presided over a modest Islamicization of society, extending state financial support for the construction of mosques and the restoration of shrines; it has permitted religious programming on state-run media and has exercised a modest degree of Islamic censorship, such as banning advertisements for alcohol or tobacco products. This has enabled the government to control the pace and scope of the Islamic revival in society.[141] In Turkmenistan, it is the state that controls the institutions of Islamic learning, thus allowing the government to exercise oversight functions.[142] Throughout the region, the bulk of the Hanafites have demonstrated their willingness to cooperate with the state in return for official establishment.[143] However, independent manifestations of Islam, and particularly any movement that seeks to utilize Islam to achieve political ends, is suppressed.

The Uzbek model has been followed, to some extent, by the other Islamic states and regions: Islam is allowed to emerge as a cultural and social force, and an Islamic veneer is imposed on society, but the state resolutely prevents any type of political Islam to emerge as a challenge to the basic structure of society.[144] This has been accomplished in large part by requiring that all schools, mosques, houses of worship, and other religious institutions must register with the state (with the proviso that unregistered organizations can be liquidated) and by drawing up legislation that explicitly defines what constitutes religious activity.[145] The continuing cooperation between local authorities and official Muslim clergy is cited as one of the major reasons Islamists have failed to make significant inroads in most Muslim regions of Eurasia.[146]

This, of course, is not to argue that there are no Islamists in Central Asia. There are, indeed, a number of illegal movements—notably the Islamic Movement of Uzbekistan (IMU) and the political party Hizb-ut Tahrir. Islamists have attracted support even from government functionaries. Although no reliable figures exist, Islamist activists have been numbered in the hundreds and low thousands, but they appear to be drawn largely from ethnic Uzbek populations both in Uzbekistan as well as in Kyrgyzstan and Tajikistan.[147] Yet the Islamists cannot be described as forming any sort of mass movement in any part of Central Asia or the former Soviet Union.

Another key development—one that was largely unanticipated by Western analysts who assumed that hostility and suspicion was the normal state of affairs between Muslims and Christians—has been the enunciation of the Eurasian consensus that sees Christianity and Islam as complementary faiths, based on common values, capable of cooperating to achieve social peace and harmony throughout Eurasia.[148]

The Eurasian consensus places a premium on social stability and harmony. It encourages the traditional religious groups, especially Orthodox Christianity and Islam, to accept each other's fundamental legitimacy vis-a-vis their specific ethnic and national demographic constituencies.[149] It also encourages support for the existing *status quo* as preferable to radical, disruptive changes, especially if initiated by outside competitors.[150] Thus, one of the leading Muslim political movements in Russia (*Refakh*) proclaims its intent to "strive for welfare not only for Muslims but for all citizens of Russia. We proceed—in full accord with our religion, incidentally—from the fact that all peoples are brothers . . . the peoples of Russia should not be fragmented, but united. It is unity that leads to welfare."[151]

Cooperation has been fostered by the ongoing interfaith dialogue underway between Orthodox and Muslim leaders, taking place under the auspices of the Moscow Patriarchate of the Russian Orthodox Church and the Islamic Republic of Iran. Orthodox and Muslim leaders meet on a regular basis through such institutions as the Inter-Religious Council, which brings together representatives of the traditional faiths of Eurasia.[152] Orthodox and Muslim clerics have found it especially in their mutual interests to cooperate to prevent foreign Muslim and Christian missionaries from having access to their respective flocks;[153] thus, Orthodox and Muslim communities have worked closely together in a number of areas to pressure governments to forbid missionaries entry into their regions.[154] Of critical importance has been the recognition by some Muslim leaders across Eurasia that their Orthodox Christian brethren are co-believers in the same God;[155] this stands in direct contrast to the viewpoint held by many Islamists that Christians are nonbelievers or idolaters. The statement, expressed by a Lezgin elder in the North Caucasus in the nineteenth century, that "the salvation of the soul can take place either through the Gospels or the Qur'an," is anathema to most Islamists.[156]

State officials routinely praise the efforts made by Orthodox and Muslim leaders to assist in peace-making efforts, and in helping to inculcate in society the "spirit of kindness, equality, and justice, the moral tenets that underlie all world religions."[157] Talgat Tadzhuddin, the leading Muslim leader in European Russia, has been one of the strongest proponents of the Eurasian consensus and its emphasison Orthodox-Islamic cooperation. Rather than espousing the unity of all Muslim believers in one state, he has instead endorsed the concept of a united Eurasian state. Speaking about the Russian Federation, he said,

> The Most High has united more than one hundred nations into one Fatherland. A Fatherland, like a mother, cannot be chosen. This is the will of the Most High. And it is not accidental, no, not at all, that in this time of disunity, He has so united us together. On this massive expanse of space live together in common accord and peace millions of Orthodox and other believers, and, God willing, this unity shall be preserved . . .[158]

Proponents of the Eurasian consensus, in order to further delegitimize Islamist groups, insist that they be seen as renegades, who are attempting to undermine the traditional beliefs and practices of Islam in Eurasia. It is also alleged by some that the activity of Islamist groups is being sponsored by foreign groups—including, interestingly enough, the United States—to sow dissension and to provoke conflict between Orthodox Christians and Muslims.[159]

The strength of official Islam, and the Eurasian social and political consensus that has developed, has largely retarded the development of Islamist forces. Indeed, even many of the supporters of Islamist movements have a "very vague notion of the ideology and goals."[160] Attempts to fuse Islamism with movements designed to foster national revival have also largely failed.[161] The main exceptions to this have been those regions that have experienced significant political and economic instability, particularly Chechnya and Tajikistan.[162] Islamism has also found fertile soil only in the mountain-valley regions of Eurasia, characterized by a higher degree of isolation and intolerance; in contrast, the Islam of the steppe and of the urban center has tended to be more pragmatic, open, and tolerant.[163] In

Central Asia, Islamism has arisen largely as a reaction to the economic stagnation and political authoritarianism that characterizes the new republics, rather than out of any heartfelt desire for the creation of an Islamist order.[164] Indeed, the Fergana valley—the main site of Islamist agitation in Central Asia—has an 80 percent unemployment rate; factories are shut down, and an ecological crisis brought about by over-irrigation is eroding the agricultural base of the region.[165] Contrary to predictions, Islamist movements have managed to acquire prominence only in those areas where the collapse of Soviet power has created such a vacuum that there are no viable alternatives. In terms of political units, there have been only two where Islamists had a serious opportunity to take power: the former Soviet republic of Tajikistan, and the Chechen republic, within the Russian Federation.

ISLAMISTS ASCENDANT? THE CASE OF TAJIKISTAN

The specter of an Islamist takeover in Tajikistan began to arise because of the unsettled and unstable nature of the transition in this republic. Moreover, Tajikistan's close geographic proximity with Afghanistan, as well as ties between groups in Tajikistan and their ethnic kin across the border, meant that there was considerable spillover from the civil wars in that country.

Unlike the other republics in Central Asia, either where communist authorities were able to tap and harness nationalist sentiment, or where noncommunists came to power in a power-sharing arrangement (as in Kyrgyzstan), the Party leadership in Tajikistan was rapidly delegitimized in the eyes of the population, yet made little effort to cultivate popular support.

The crisis began in January 1990[166] with a series of riots in Dushanbe, the capital, after reports began to circulate that thousands of Armenian refugees from Azerbaijan were to be resettled in the city, at a time when jobs and housing were both in short supply. Demonstrators rejected the assurances of Communist Party First Secretary Ghahar Makhkamov that this would not be the case. Public gatherings, sponsored by the nationalist movement *Rastokhez* (organized in September 1989 by Tohir Abdujabbor, an economist at the Tajik Academy of Sciences), turned violent, with rioters calling for radical political and economic reforms. Makhamov sought military reinforcements from the all-Union Ministry of the Interior (MVD) to put down the demonstrations; some 22 people were killed and 565 injured in several days of clashes.

Makhamov's over-reliance on brute force to maintain order, however, caused dissension within the ranks of the Communist Party itself. The deputy chair of the Council of Ministers, Buri Karimov, called for the leaders of the Tajik Communist Party to step down; on February 14, 1990, Makhamov and Prime Minister Ezatolloh Khayeyev tendered their resignations.

The Tajik Central Committee refused to accept these resignations, fearing that the entire edifice of the party-state in Tajikistan might collapse. Instead, Karimov himself and others who had denounced Makhamov were forced out of the party. In March 1990, the republican government banned opposition parties and movements from contesting the elections for the Supreme Soviet, creating a largely rubber-stamp legislature dominated by the Communists. In November 1990, Makhamov was elected as president of Tajikistan by this body.

However, Makhamov was fast losing any semblance of legitimacy. Two new political movements were organized in the republic in the fall of 1990: the western-oriented Democratic Party and the Tajik branch of the Islamic Revival Party (IRP). Although initially denied registration, the IRP was recognized as an official party in Tajikistan on October 26, 1991, and by the end of 1991 was said to have over 30,000 members[167] Makhamov supported the coup attempt against Mikhail Gorbachev in August 1991. The Supreme Soviet passed a resolution of "no confidence" in him, and massive demonstrations were organized by the Democratic Party and the IRP; as a result, he tendered his resignation as president on August 31, 1991.

The Communist leadership was divided as to how to respond to these developments. Acting President Ghaddredin Aslonov sought to follow the example of other Central Asian leaders in trying to co-opt opposition forces; Tajikistan declared its independence on September 7, 1991, and banned the Communist Party. However, the Supreme Soviet reacted by declaring a state of emergency. Aslonov resigned from office, and Rahman Nabiyev, the former Tajik Communist Party First Secretary, was recalled to public life by the Communist deputies of the Supreme Soviet to act as temporary president. After presiding over passage of an electoral law to select a president, Nabiyev resigned so as to run for office as a candidate. On November 24, 1991, Nabiyev was elected president with a majority of votes cast, although there were allegations of vote fraud.

Nabiyev was unable to consolidate his authority, however, and fresh challenges to Tajikistan's political stability erupted in March 1992 after Nabiyev fired the Minister for Internal Affairs, an ethnic Pamiri, and the mayor of Dushanbe, an opposition supporter, was arrested. A united opposition to Nabiyev and the Communists began to take shape, composed of the IRP, the Democratic Party, La'l-e Badakhshan (a movement seeking greater cultural and political autonomy for Pamiri peoples in the republic), and Rastokhez.

The creation of this grouping, which eventually evolved into the United Tajik Opposition, is critical because it marked a key point in the evolution of the IRP—it was now committed to a political alliance with nationalist, pro-Western, and secular movements. Up to this point, the IRP had been constituted as a traditional Islamist party. Its initial leaders, such as Dawlat Usman and Mullah Abdullah Mirsaidov, had promoted demands such as the implementation of Islamic law in the republic, traditional dress for women, and so on. However, when the former kazi for Tajikistan, Akhbar Taradjonzoda, entered the party, he and his followers acted as a moderating force within the IRP. Taradjonzoda reached out in two directions. One was to embrace leaders and practitioners of folk Islam in the republic, whose practices and beliefs were often denounced by Wahhabite purists. The second was to reach out to nationalists and other secularized political forces. By the end of 1991, the IRP had begun to revise its platform, shifting from a call to create an Islamic state to instead promote a Muslim revival among believers. In his analysis of IRP politics in Tajikistan, C. William Walldorf noted,

> In order to organize regionally excluded elements for the achievement of political power, the IRP leadership had to yield to a broad-based, Soviet-inspired social secularization . . . that generated Taradjonzoda's impulse to moderate party doctrine for the purpose of creating the broadest possible coalition of excluded opposition forces.[168]

In April 1992 opposition forces took sixteen deputies of the Supreme Soviet and two ministers hostage. They demanded the resignation of Safarli Kenjoyev, the chairman of the Supreme Soviet. When Kenjoyev temporarily resigned, Nabiyev introduced presidential rule on April 30, 1992, banning all demonstrations. In May, the opposition succeeded in taking control of most of the capital, Dushanbe, leading to a negotiated settlement—Nabiyev and the Communists were to share power with the parties making up the opposition—both democratic and Islamist. Dawlat Usman was appointed as a deputy prime minister in the new coalition government, and eight portfolios were distributed to opposition politicians within the cabinet.

However, outside the capital, pro-Communist and pro-opposition militias continued to fight each other for control of the countryside. This civil war had a pronounced regional character: Kulyab and the heavily industrialized regions around Khojend (Leninabad) were the strongholds of the Communists; the opposition was centered in the southern Kurgan Teppe region and the Gharm valley. The pro-Communist Tajik Popular Front (TPF) militia, dominated by Kulyabis and led by Sangak Safarov, moved into Kurgan Teppe in August 1992. The TPF maintained that the opposition was receiving arms and assistance from Islamist groups in Afghanistan, notably the *Hizb-e Islami* movement led by Gulbeddin Hekmatyar. In response to the advance of the TPF, the opposition militia took control of Dushanbe and on September 7, 1992, succeeded in capturing Nabiyev at the airport, forcing him to resign.

A caretaker government formed under Akbarshah Eskandarov but was unable to hold the coalition together. Moreover, the TPF took control over much of the southern portion of the republic. In November, Eskandarov resigned. The Supreme Soviet then convened in Khojend, abolished the office of president, and elected Emomali Rahmanov, a Kulyabi collective farm chairman, as the new head of state. In December 1992, forces loyal to Rahmanov captured Dushanbe. The opposition forces, under the rubric of the Popular Democratic Army, as the military wing of the political alliance came to be known, were driven into the Gharm valley and Gorno-Badakshan, while some 80,000 Tajiks fled as refugees. For a time in early 1993, the Gharm valley was proclaimed to be an independent Islamic republic, but by mid-year most of Tajikistan was under government control, with significant Russian and Uzbek military assistance being rendered to the Rahmanov regime. However, opposition forces were able to find sanctuary in Afghanistan and to continue the struggle with the regime. This raised the issue of whether or not Tajik refugees and opposition fighters were being radicalized in camps in Afghanistan, especially in those camps where "an atmosphere of secrecy surrounded the identity of NGO's active in the former which, combined with restricted access to the UNHCR [United Nations High Commissioner for Refugees] . . . suggested a desire on the port of the opposition to control carefully information, organizations, and individuals in the camps . . ."[169]

An agreement to end the fighting was signed in Tehran on September 17, 1994. However, fighting continued in a number of districts. Although Rahmanov was elected president in a nationwide election on November 6, 1994, the election was, in the words of Human Rights Watch, "marred by fear and flagrant fraud." Iran, Russia, and other Central Asian states tried to keep the peace process alive. Finally, in 1997, an agreement signed in Mashad, Iran, resolved the final issues surrounding the creation of a National Reconciliation Committee, which was composed of an equal number of government and opposition representatives and chaired by Rahmanov and Sayyid Abdullah Nouri (Nuri) of the IRP. The goal was to begin to include representatives of the opposition in all levels of the government and military. Eventually, a 30 percent quota was introduced for United Tajik Opposition representatives in government positions, and disbanding of militias began to take place.[170]

Since the end of the fighting, there has been little enthusiasm in Tajikistan for the forcible creation of an Islamic state. All major social and political actors are focused on the task of reconstruction and maintaining social peace. Certainly, there are few visible signs of Islamicization. Public consumption of alcohol continues. Mosques have not emerged as the principal center of social life, even in the villages, nor has there been any upsurge in Islamic education.[171] Meanwhile, an uneasy truce continues between the IRP and the excommunists grouped in the People's Democratic

Party. In a post–September 11 environment, the IRP has found itself under increasing pressure from Rahmonov and the Popular Democratic Party. In late 2002 in the northern Isfara district (of the Soghd province), the government began closing mosques and removing imams with IRP connections from their positions. IRP representatives have suggested that the government is trying to blur the lines between Islamist radicals and IRP moderates in an effort to undercut electoral support for the IRP.[172]

Another question that has been raised is the degree to which the IRP can in fact be classified as an Islamist party. The party has accommodated secularists and proponents of folk Islam within its ranks, as well as purists who want to reform Tajik Islam and move society along a more Islamic path. Certainly, the comments of one IRP leader, Sultan Hamad, after the New Year's Eve (2000/2001) bombing of Christian churches in Dushanbe, are not indicative of a traditionally Islamist outlook on questions of religious freedom and freedom of conscience:

> If these acts were carried out by people who, by such means, want to prevent people from accepting other religions, it is the wrong means, because it is a violation of the constitution, the basic law. I think it is against Islam as well—that is to say, imposing one's ideology on others is against Islamic principles.[173]

In fact, the IRP has found itself challenged by a more radical Islamist movement, in the form of Hizb-ut-Tahrir. Nuri himself has characterized this group as a threat to Tajikistan's stability and has not objected to a government crackdown on its activities. It is estimated that some 100 leaders and members have been imprisoned in the period between 1999 and 2002. Hizb-ut-Tahrir is said to have its primary base in the Uzbek-speaking population through their connections with relatives in the Fergana valley. However, Said Ahmedov, the head of the Tajik State Committee for Religious Affairs, maintains that Hizb-ut-Tahrir has limited prospects and a weak social base in Tajikistan. Moreover, it is not yet clear that those who want a greater Islamic presence in Tajik society are prepared to leave the IRP for a more shadowy and underground organization.[174] It is also not clear that supporters or potential members of Hizb-ut Tahrir are attracted to the movement because of its Islamist ideology; often, it is because Hizb-ut Tahrir represents an alternative to corruption or poor economic prospects. A spokesman for the group in Tajikistan acknowledged this, observing, "There is too much corruption and bad policies. There are no jobs; the economy is very bad."[175] Yet, whereas Islamists may be able to capitalize on popular discontent, they remain crippled by their inability to strike deep roots among the populace committed to their vision of an Islamic state for Tajikistan. Moreover, the bloodshed spilled during the Tajik civil war has had a sobering effect on elites and the masses throughout Central Asia. Even those dissatisfied with the *status quo* have little desire to unleash that sort of fratricidal struggle elsewhere in the region.

ISLAMISTS ASCENDANT? THE CASE OF CHECHNYA

As the USSR began to disintegrate, one of the peoples most cruelly oppressed by the Soviet system—the Chechens—saw the very real possibility of winning full political independence for themselves and breaking completely from the Muscovite orbit. Many assumed that the Chechens would seek to reestablish or recreate some version of the Imamate set up by Shamyl during the nineteenth century—a Chechen-dominated North Caucasian federation based on Islamic law and principles of governance. This was due to the strong influence of Sufi *tariqat* in the region, which helped to forge common identities, using religion, to overcome the division of Chechen society into clans (*teip*). Indeed, as Malise Ruthven has noted, these Sufi brotherhoods were "important sources of social and . . . political power" in the region, because the "common spiritual disciplines of the orders" as well as the "gradations of spiritual authority linking the leader with his followers" helped to lay the basis for concrete social action and armed resistance.[176]

Despite the whole-scale deportations of the Chechens (and the Ingush, their neighbors) from their homeland in 1944 on the direct orders of Josef Stalin (some 400,000 were exiled to Kazakhstan or other regions of Central Asia, and not permitted to return to the Caucasus until the 1950s), the traditional organizations of clan and Sufi brotherhood remained largely intact. Aslan Maskhadov, elected president of Chechnya in 1997, observed, "Even under Soviet power, when Soviet laws operated everywhere in the USSR, they resorted to the Shari'ah court in Chechnya. Every murder must be punished and every person must know that he is protected by Shari'ah law.[177]

As the Soviet Union disintegrated, the Chechens declared their independence on November 2, 1991. However, in the beginning, the radical Islamist vision held by some Chechens was not acceptable to the Chechen nation as a whole. The leaders were not utilizing fanatical Islam tactics, often only associating themselves with Islamic practice as a symbolic rallying cry for mobilizing forces. Former Soviet airborne general Dzhokhar Dudayev, who became Chechnya's first president in 1991, was not viewed by many as an authentic believer. His association with Islam was considered to be political and superficial,[178] and his agenda differed from the one put forward by some of the Sufi clans. Many of his opponents who questioned his Muslim faith often made reference to his actions with the Soviet military against *mujahideen* forces in the war in Afghanistan. Moreover, Dudayev indicated his desire to form a democratic secular government, ruling out the creation of an Islamic republic during the first two years of his presidency. Indeed, the first draft of a constitution for the Chechen Republic (Ichkeria) was imbued with the spirit of representative democracy of the presidential type and secular law. Islam and various traditional social institutions were relegated to a more ritual role: in the constitution there was no mention of Islam or Allah, and religious liberty for all citizens was recognized."[179]

Once the Russian federal government, however, decided to intervene militarily in the republic in 1994 to restore the authority of the central government, Islam began to play a more pronounced role in the political situation. In late 1994 Dudayev attempted to implement sharia law, largely in an attempt to draw Islamic support against Russia from such areas as the mountain clans of Chechnya.[180] As the conflict dragged on, it drew in Islamist fighters from the Gulf, Pakistan, and Jordan—itself home to a large Chechen diaspora community that had left the region after its final incorporation into the Russian Empire. The Chechen cause was also embraced by the international Islamist movement.[181]

All of this contributed to a growing Islamicization of life in Chechnya, although a number of the foreign Islamists (the Wahhabis) clashed with local Sufi elders over the proper interpretation of Islam.[182] Increasingly, the Chechen leadership moved to discard the secular rhetoric of the early Dudayev administration, a process that accelerated after the general's death. Shortly after the August 1996 cease-fire agreement negotiated by Russian security council secretary Aleksandr Lebed and Chechen General Aslan Maskhadov ended the first war, Maskhadov, who had directed Chechen military operations during the war, was elected president of Chechnya in a January 1997 election. In February of that same year, an amendment to the Chechen constitution declared Islam as the state religion. In November 1997, Chechnya was formally declared an Islamic republic and the leadership committed itself to enforcing Islamic mores (in terms of dress and behavior) on the entire population.[183] In February 1999 a presidential decree introduced a form of sharia law into the republic and the process to create a constitution that draws on the Quran, and sharia as well as Chechen customs and traditions.[184]

For some Chechen Islamists, these moves were insufficient. Even by the end of 1997, Maskhadov had begun to struggle with radical *mujahideen* and opposition groups. Prominent Chechen field commanders Shamil Basayev, Salman Raduyev, and Khunkar-Pasha Israpilov "asked the parliament and the court to impeach Maskhadov for 'treason,' by which they meant his pragmatic approach to relations with Moscow."[185] Maskhadov sought to diminish the differences with the opposition, and created a *Shura* (State Council), allowing them a small voice into the political system that would not damage his overwhelmingly strong presidential powers. Unsatisfied, the opposition called for the resignation of Maskhadov and created its own Shura, headed by Basayev, intent on delegitimizing Maskhadov's presidency.[186]

However, as with Islamists in the Middle East, the Chechen government found that Islamic slogans could not guarantee a stable administration. In fact, the inability of the Chechen government to enforce law and order between 1996 and 1999 discredited the Islamic nature of the regime with other Muslims in the former Soviet Union. Indeed, the repeated invocation of the Islamist basis of Chechen society was never put into practice. As a result, the failed Islamist state "did not win the residents of Chechnya fame in the rest of the North Caucasus as exemplary Muslims. Kidnappings, cattle rustling, and other forms of robbery, and the constant attacks from Chechen territory on border posts did not enhance the Chechen people's reputation."[187] It became increasingly clear that Chechnya was not becoming a beacon of Islamism for the rest of the North Caucasus; what populations wanted was not an Islamic moral order but basic guarantees of security. Agitation among other Muslim nationalities to break away from the Russian Federation and join Chechnya in the creation of an Islamic North Caucasian state fell on deaf ears. The main area for Chechen Islamist agitation, Dagestan, proved unreceptive, because "the population of Dagestan understands that their republic's inclusion in the Russian Federation is a guarantee of economic and social stability."[188]

Thus, in August 1999, Chechen Islamists led by Basayev launched an armed attack on Dagestan that was characterized by Chechen leader Movladi Udugov as an act of liberation of fellow Muslims. Very few Dagestanis, however, wanted to be liberated by the Islamists, and the local population rallied to the defense of Dagestan against the insurgents. Magomedkhan Magomedkhanov said the following of the Chechen Islamists:

> The Dagestanis recognized them as enemies, as aggressors. The people, including 30,000 armed volunteers, supported the Russian army. The call to establish an Islamic state in Dagestan was supported by only a few thousand Wahhabis in a handful of villages (Karamakhi, Chabanmakhi, and others). Dagestanis subsequently came to regard the latter as traitors. A clear and absolute majority of the Dagestani people supports the idea of a secular state.[189]

Along with the bombing of apartment buildings in a number of Russian cities attributed to the Chechen separatists, the incursion into Dagestan was used by the Russian federal government as a *causus belli* and the armed conflict between Chechen separatists and federal forces resumed and continues to the present day. Maskhadov forged new ties with the more radical Islamists, appointing Shamil Basayev as senior commander in Chechnya following the second Russian invasion.

Interestingly, Moscow has paid much greater attention to co-opting Chechnya's Islamic heritage in the creation of its own government for the republic. It remains to be seen whether the Moscow-backed provisional administration for Chechnya will be able to co-opt Chechen understandings of Islam in order to legitimize its position. The appointment of Hadj Ahmad Kadyrov, the mufti of Chechnya, as chief administrator by

Vladimir Putin was an attempt to find a pro-Russian leader who could utilize Chechnya's Islamic heritage in the reconstruction of the republic. Kadyrov has been outspoken in his opposition against the Wahhabite movements in Chechnya, denouncing from his pulpit the invasion of Dagestan led by Basayev in 1999 and ultimately choosing not to support Maskhadov in offering resistance to federal forces. Kadyrov believes that Chechens can reconstruct society, and lay the conditions for civil peace and economic prosperity, through cooperation with the Russian Federation, although conceding Chechnya should enjoy a great deal of internal autonomy.[190] In January 2003 Kadyrov, accompanied by Islamic religious leaders from other North Caucasian republics, undertook a tour of the Middle East to stress that the Russian government, in fighting against Chechen separatists, was not waging war on Islam.[191]

Hadj Ahmad Shamayev, Kadyrov's successor as mufti (after the latter resigned to take up his governmental post), believes that Chechens must accept certain realities about the present-day situation, and seek an accommodation with Russia, rejecting the ideology of the radicals.

> Every Muslim would want to see a fully Islamic state. But this will not succeed here . . . The Chechens are a proud people. A common language should simply be found with them. I blame our leaders, the Chechen politicians, not Russia for what has happened. I have visited Tatarstan. And I am [both] unhappy and glad because we could be living the same way. We failed to organize life that way.[192]

Pro-Moscow Chechens insist that the Maskhadov regime and more radical field commanders such as Basayev forged close ties with Islamists in the Arab world. One Chechen commander (Khattab), a Jordanian-born Chechen, had previously fought in Afghanistan against the Soviets and was invoked as an example of the ties binding the Chechen separatists and the international Islamist movement. The Chechen city of Urus-Marten was alleged to be the location of a terrorist training camp, and documentation was produced to show how Chechen rebels were receiving money, arms, and volunteers from the Persian Gulf. (Estimates of financial support range from $10 million to $200 million per annum.) Osama bin Laden's deputy, Ayman al-Zawahiri, visited Chechnya in 1996 to assess its possible value as a base for Al-Qaeda, while it is estimated that approximately two hundred of the thirteen hundred separatist soldiers are non-Chechen Muslims.[193] Yet other Chechen leaders argue that the aid from foreign Islamists is negligible and that radical Islamist views have little currency among the Chechens.[194]

The extreme destruction wrought in Chechnya as a result of the two wars and the dispersion of much of the population into refugee camps, makes it unclear what the future holds. On the one hand, continued dislocation and harsh treatment from federal forces means that the population could be further radicalized. Chechnya is likely to continue to be a failed republic whether it achieves full independence or autonomy within the Russian Federation, and thus it will be a continued center for instability in the North Caucasus. On the other hand, a weariness with war and a desire for reconstruction may lead to a peace settlement and the expulsion of more radical elements from Chechen society.

Indeed, it appears that the Russian government may have embarked on the Algerian solution to the Chechen problem, by promoting a treaty of accord not dissimilar to the Rome Accords, by moving ahead with a referendum in March 2003 to approve a new constitution for Chechnya and by holding new elections for local offices in December 2003, while continuing military operations against militants. Of especial significance has been the great effort by the Russian-backed administration to draw in Chechen intellectuals and elders into the dialogue about the proposed constitution for the republic.[195] Based in part on the Tatarstan constitution (one of the largest Muslim republics of the Russian Federation), the various drafts are, nonetheless, secular documents, not Islamic in nature.[196]

No matter what, the experience of de facto independence (1996–1999) points to an apparent failure of the Islamists to construct a viable regime capable of meeting the needs of the local populace or of serving as a model for other Muslim regions of the Russian Federation. The failure of the Islamists in Chechnya has had a sobering effect on other Muslim regions of the Caucasus and in fact has helped to reinforce secular governments.

THE ISLAMIST THREAT IN EURASIA: A REALISTIC ASSESSMENT

In the aftermath of the September 11 attacks on the United States, a good deal of attention has been paid to whether Central Asia and the Caucasus will become new centers for radical Islam. As Anna Matveeva observed,

> With ethnic separatism in decline in the former Soviet states, the question is whether Islamism will replace it as a new force for instability. In contrast to traditional Islam, which is deeply embedded in local conventions and beliefs, Islamist movements are explicitly anti-system, reformist, and determined to change the status quo. They are rooted in the insecurities and traumas of today, in social polarization and injustice. They also reflect the failures of official Islamic clergy who have effectively become extensions of the established secular leaderships.[197]

Yet, a distinction must be drawn between small groups able to operate in the margins of Central Asia and the Caucasus (e.g. inaccessible mountain areas) and the rise of full-fledged movements able to topple regimes. By the late 1990s, there was a great deal of anxiety about the ability of Islamist movements led by charismatic figures to exploit discontent in Central Asia in order to propel themselves into power. Much of this crystallized around the figure of Juma Namagani, the leader of the Islamic Movement of

Uzbekistan (IMU). Namagani, a former Soviet paratrooper who had fought in Afghanistan, left his native Uzbekistan in 1992 after President Karimov launched a major crackdown on Islamic movements. He fought with the IRP in Takikistan and formed the IMU in 1998 with the explicit intent of initiating a pan-Central Asian *jihad* against the existing regimes. The IMU was able to recruit some of the Tajik militants who were not integrated into the Tajik government and army following the 1997 peace accord. The Taliban offered sanctuary to Namagani, enabling him to use Afghanistan as a base of operations (and also to play a role in the shipment of narcotics from Afghanistan into Central Asia for eventual delivery to the West). The IMU also benefited from close links with the international Islamic movement, as its ranks were joined by Chechens, Uighurs, Pakistanis and Arabs as well as Central Asians. Namagani also found the Uzbek diaspora in Saudi Arabia (created after 1917 when conservative Uzbeks left their homeland) an important bridge to tap into sources of support and funding in Saudi Arabia and the Gulf.[198]

The IMU was behind the bombings in Tashkent on February 16, 1999 that were an attempt to decapitate the regime of Islam Karimov (and which killed 16 and injured 128). The IMU also began a series of armed incursions in 1999 and 2000 from Afghanistan across Tajikistan and Kyrgyzstan in an effort to try and raise the flag of rebellion in Uzbekistan. Yet, although the IMU could launch raids and engage in guerilla operations, it was not entirely clear that they could move beyond opposition to the *status quo* and take power. The IMU under Namagani was skillful in exploiting discontent, but even among some of the IMU's supporters, the goal was to get rid of the current regimes rather than create an Islamic order.[199] The opposition could foment protests but it was not clear that they could provide any real alternative to the existing regimes. Ahmed Rashid concluded that

the political aims of the IMU remain shrouded in secrecy and the nature of their Islamic beliefs and what kind of Islamic state they envisage is also unknown. "The IMU's weakness is that [*jihad*] is their only criterion, they have no political structure to speak of," says Moheyuddin Kabir [deputy leader of the Tajik IRP, senior aide to IRP leader Abdullah Nuri]. The most remarkable facet of life in the Kartagan and Tavildera valleys is the lack of overt Islamicisation compared to Afghanistan or Pakistan . . .[200]

The activities of the IMU also galvanized the states of Central Asia to rebuild their ties to Moscow and to seek military and technical aid; fears about the military and security threat posed by Islamists led Uzbekistan to conclude a five-year security agreement with Russia (December 11, 1999).[201] In fact, some have alleged that the threat to Central Asia was vastly overstated, "because the presence and continuation of this threat justify the Russian military presence in Central Asia."[202]

After the September 11 attacks, the situation changed even further. Namagani himself was killed in Afghanistan and most of the 1,300 IMU fighters left Central Asia to fight with the Taliban in Afghanistan, where most were captured or killed by allied forces. The states of Central Asia have also been the beneficiary of expanded American security and economic assistance that has greatly bolstered their ability to deal with Islamic radicalism. With thousands of American troops now based in Central Asia and Afghanistan, with border patrols vastly augmented, and with new American–Russian–Central Asian intelligence cooperation, the IMU's supporters have been scattered. Efforts to unite different Islamists into a single, pan-Central Asian organization have run into enormous logistical (as well as ideological) difficulties. Surviving IMU fighters may end up taking refuge with Gulbuddin Hekmatyar in Afghanistan rather than launching new military strikes in Central Asia.[203]

Indeed, one feature of post 9/11 Central Asia has been a renewed wave of arrests directed against anyone who might seek to challenge the existing regimes. To some extent, Central Asian states appeared to have adopted the Egyptian model—tight government control over official Islam and harsh repression of underground movements. In particular, Muslim activities occurring outside the sanction of the official Muslim boards have drawn the especial attention of the security services.[204] One cannot also underestimate the resiliency of the regimes in Central Asia and their ability to deal decisively with threats to their existence, especially amidst a largely politically apathetic population. In fact, the regimes have shown great deftness and skill at being able to accommodate some Muslim demands without making any concessions on major issues affecting the distribution of power or resources. Thus, while it is possible that, in the coming years, Central Asian state structures may be colored by a faint whiff of Islamic green,[205] the emergence of a new radical Central Asian caliphate espousing radical Islam remains highly unlikely.

NOTES

1. David K. Willis, *Klass: How Russians Really Live* (New York: Avon, 1985), 242.

2. Giampaolo R. Capisani, *The Handbook of Central Asia: A Comprehensive Survey of the New Republics* (London: I. B. Tauris, 2000), vii, 84–85.

3. M. Nazif Shahrani, "Islam and Political Culture in Central Asia," in *The Politics of Religion in Russia and the New States of Eurasia*, ed. Michael Bourdeaux (London: M. E. Sharpe, 1995), 274.

4. Some 61 percent of Russians surveyed chose Islamic fundamentalism as the leading threat to the Russian Federation. See *Vneshnaia Politika Rossii: Mneniia Ekspertov* (Moscow: Russian Independent Institute for Social and Nationality Problems, 2001), 20.

5. John Gunther, *Inside Russia Today,* rev.ed. (New York: Harper and Row, 1962), 508. Some of the principal works on Islam in the Soviet Union have included Alexandre Bennigsen and S. Enders Wimbush, *Muslims of the Soviet Empire: A Guide* (London: Hurst, 1985), and Alexandre Bennigsen and Chantal Lemercier-Quelquejay, *Islam in the Soviet Union,* trans. Geoffrey E. Wheeler and Hubert Evans (New York: Praeger, 1967).

6. Alexandre Bennigsen and Marie Broxup, *The Islamic Threat to the Soviet State* (New York: St. Martin's Press, 1983), 48; Mehdrdad Haghayeghi, *Islam and Politics in Central Asia* (New York: St. Martin's Press, 1995), 9.

7. In 1959, "Muslims" (that is, people belonging to traditionally Muslim nationalities) comprised some 12% of the Soviet population; had the USSR remained intact, it was estimated that by 2000 nearly one in three Soviet citizens would have been of Muslim origin.

8. Michael Rywkin, *Moscow's Muslim Challenge: Soviet Central Asia* (London: M. E. Sharpe, 1982), viii–ix.

9. Ravil Bukharaev, *Islam in Russia: The Four Seasons* (New York: St. Martin's Press, 2000), 14.

10. Evgeniy Abdullaev, "The Central Asian Nexus: Islam and Politics," *Central Asia: A Gathering Storm?,* ed. Boris Rumer (Armonk, NY: M. E. Sharpe, 2002), 248.

11. For example, the Tatars, a settled, urban nation, have lived within the Russian Empire and the USSR for five centuries; the Chechens, a rural mountain people divided into clans, did not convert to Islam until the seventeenth to eighteenth centuries and did not fully come under Russian rule until 1864, and even then enjoyed a great deal of autonomy. Residents of Bukhara and Khiva are heirs to a flourishing Muslim civilization and were never directly under Russian rule at all, being incorporated into Soviet controlled territory only in 1920.

12. Agnes Kefeli, "The Role of Tatar and Kriashen Women in the Transmission of Islamic Knowledge, 1800–1870," in *Of Religion and Empire: Missions, Conversion, and Tolerance in Tsarist Russia,* eds. Robert P. Geraci and Michael Khodarkovsky (Ithaca, NY: Cornell University Press, 2001), 262, 264, 272–73.

13. Quoted in Rene Grousset, *The Empire of the Steppes: A History of Central Asia,* trans. Naomi Walford (New Brunswick, NJ: Rutgers, 1970, 1999), 416.

14. Approximately 470,000 Muslims, for example, emigrated from the Caucasus once it came under Russian imperial control (Austin Jersild, *Orientalism and Empire: North Caucasus Mountain Peoples and the Georgian Frontier, 1845–1917* (Montreal: McGill-Queen's University Press, 2002), 23–28), a process, by the way, complemented by the emigration of Eastern Christians (Serbs, Greeks, and Armenians) into Russian-controlled areas.

15. For example, the traditional distrust between Shiite and Sunni Muslim, along with the existence of other Muslim sectarians, prevented the formation of a joint Muslim effort to expel the Russians from Transcaucasia during the nineteenth century. In particular, distrust of Sufi movements on the part of mosque-based Shiite and Sunni clergy was to play a role in helping to stem the tide of anti-imperial uprisings. Cf. Firouzeh Mostashari, "Colonial Dilemmas: Russian Policies in the Muslim Caucasus," *Of Religion and Empire,* 235; and Nikolas K. Gvosdev, *Imperial Policies and Perspectives Toward Georgia, 1760–1819* (New York: St. Martin's Press, 2000), 122.

16. Bennigsen and Broxup, 68.

17. Bukharaev, 13–14.

18. Paul Werth, *At the Margins of Orthodoxy* (Ithaca, NY: Cornell University Press, 2002), 262.

19. Bennigsen and Broxup, 37; Bukharev, ix–x.

20. Haghyaeghi, 16–18, 26–27; Donna E. Arzt, "Proselytizing and the Muslim *Umma* of Russia: Historical Heritage or Ethno-National Threat?" *Proselytism and Orthodoxy in Russia: The New War for Souls*, eds. John Witte, Jr. and Michael Bordeaux (Maryknoll, NY: Orbis, 1999), 112–113.

21. Valery Tishkov, *Ethnicity, Nationalism, and Conflict in and after the Soviet Union: The Mind Aflame* (Thousands Oaks, CA: SAGE Publications, 1997), 191.

22. Quoted in James Critchlow, "Islam and Nationalism in Soviet Central Asia," in *Religion and Nationalism in Soviet and East European Politics*, ed. Pedro Ramet (Durham, NC: Duke Press Policy Studies, 1984), 108.

23. Haghayeghi, 9–10; Bukharaev, 13–14.

24. Robert D. Kangas, "State Building and Civil Society in Central Asia," in *Political Culture and Civil Society in Russia and the New States of Eurasia*, ed. Vladimir Tismaneanu (London: M. E. Sharpe, 1995), 274.

25. Shoshana Keller, "Conversions to the New Faith: Marxism-Leninism and Muslims in the Soviet Empire," *Of Religion and Empire*, 319.

26. Bennigsen and Broxup, 48.

27. Haghayeghi, 19–21; Bennigsen and Broxup, 47–48.

28. Haghayeghi, 21.

29. Keller, 331.

30. Haghayeghi, 23.

31. Igor Torbakov, "Tajik-Uzbek Relations: Divergent National Historiographies Threaten To Aggravate Tensions," *Eurasianet*, June 12, 2000, at http://www.eurasianet.org.

32. Geoffrey Hosking, *The First Socialist Society: A History of the Soviet Union From Within* (Cambridge, MA: Harvard University Press, 1985), 241.

33. Ibid., 241–243.

34. Pedro Ramet, *Cross and Commisar: The Politics of Religion in Eastern Europe and the USSR* (Bloomington, IN: Indiana University Press, 1987), 36.

35. Hosking, 243, see also Artz, 114.

36. Hosking, 447.

37. Keller, 332.

38. Artz, 113–114.

39. Ibid, 113.

40. Keller, 330, 332.

41. Hosking, 240–241, 446; Keller, 333; Artz, 113–115.

42. Haghyaeghi, 37.

43. Ibid, 38–39.

44. Bennigsen and Broxup, 114.

45. Haghayeghi, 37.

46. Bennigsen and Broxup, 143.

47. Ramet, 36.

48. Bennigsen and Broxup, 144.

49. Chantal Lemercier-Quelquejay, "From Tribe to *Umma*," *Central Asian Survey* 3:3 (1984), 21–22.

50. Quoted in Haghayeghi, 66.

51. Rywkin, 106.

52. Ramet, 36.

53. Haghayeghi, 26–28; Hosking, 237. On the level of Soviet political control over Muslim activities, however, see "Father George," *God's Underground*, ed. Gretta Palmer (New York: Appleton-Century-Crofts, Inc., 1949), 229–230.

54. Bennigsen and Broxup, 72.

55. Critchlow, 115.

56. Hosking, 445.

57. See "Father George," 223–224.

58. Hosking, 445–446.

59. Ibid, 432.

60. Rywkin, 198.

61. See Tishkov, especially 189–193.

62. John Anderson, *Religion, State, and Politics in the Soviet Union and Successor States* (Cambridge University Press, 1994), 95.

63. A. A. Iarlykapov, *Problema Wahhabizma na Severnom Kavkaze* (Moscow: Russian Academy of Sciences, 2000), 5.

64. This included relaxing restrictions on official, aboveground Muslim communities and giving Party leaders in Muslim republics some flexibility in choosing how to implement central directives regarding religion. See Anderson, 130–131.

65. "In the First Person. Everything Will Be Restored. Only Peace is Needed," *Rossiiskaia Gazeta*, August 20, 1994, 1.

66. See the comments about the differences that have emerged between Azeris in Iran, living within the framework of an Islamic republic and within the Middle East, versus Azeris, who experienced seven decades of Soviet rule and a century of being incorporated into the Russian Empire, in Fereydoun Safizadeh, "On Dilemmas of Identity in the Post-Soviet Republic of Azerbaijan," in *Caucasian Regional Studies*, 3:1 (1998), archived at http://poli.vub.ac.be/publi/crs/eng/0301-04.htm.

67. Haghayeghi, 55.

68. Ibid, 56–57.

69. Felix Corley, *Religion in the Soviet Union: An Archival Reader* (New York: New York University Press, 1996), 368–369.

70. Anderson, 144.

71. Gordon B. Smith, *Soviet Politics: Continuity and Contradiction* (New York: St. Martin's, 1988), 325–330.

72. Haghayeghi, 50–51.

73. Anderson, 95. For example, the first secretary of the district Party committee in Samarkand, who had been removed, provided assistance for the renovation of a holy site, whereas the former deputy chairman of the regional council (*sovet*) had diverted state funds and equipment for the construction of a mosque. Haghayeghi, quoting the report of Rafiq Nishanov, first secretary of the Uzbek Communist Party (1988), 66.

74. Smith, 310.

75. Capisani, 1–3.

76. Haghayeghi, 66.

77. Anderson, 146.

78. Ibid.

79. Haghayeghi, 68; Artz, 118; Anderson, 172–173.

80. Haghayeghi, 66–67; Anderson, 183.

81. Anderson, 171.

82. Ibid, 183.

83. Ibid, 143.

84. Corley, 369.

85. Artz, 118.

86. Haghayeghi, 85.

87. Shirin Akiner, "Uzbekistan and the Uzbeks," in *The Nationalities Question in the Post-Soviet States*, ed. Graham Smith (London: Longman, 1990, 1996), 343.

88. Haghayeghi, 86–87.

89. C. William Walldorf, Jr. "Towards a Nuanced Conception of Political Islam: The Case of Tajikistan," in *Transformations of 1989–1999*, 171.

90. Ibid, 71.

91. Ibid, 85–86.

92. Rafik Osman-Ogly Kurbanov and Erjan Rafik-Ogly Kurbanov, "Religion and Politics in the Caucasus," in *The Politics of Religion in Russia*, 234.

93. Ibid, 235.

94. Elin Suleymanov, "Azerbaijan, Azerbaijanis, and the Search for Identity," in *Analysis of Current Events* 12:1 (2001), 10, 11–12.

95. Haghayeghi, 103.

96. Tishkov, 115.

97. Anderson, 183.

98. Muriel Atkin, "Tajikistan: Reform, Reaction, and Civil War," in *New States, New Politics: Building the Post-Soviet Nations*, ed. Ian Bremmer and Ray Taras (Cambridge: Cambridge University Press, 1997), 618.

99. Eugene Huskey, "Kyrgyzstan: The Politics of Demographic and Economic Frustration," in *New States, New Politics*, 664.

100. Tishkov, 107–108.

101. Ibid, 128.

102. Ingvar Svanberg, "Kazakhstan and the Kazakhs," in *The Nationalities Question*, 322; Haghayeghi , 192–201, Tishkov, 47, 128. For further information on the deadly Osh conflict between Kyrzgyz and Uzbeks, see the case study in Tishkov, 135–154.

103. Anderson, 143.

104. Gregory Gleason, "Uzbekistan: The Politics of National Independence," in *New States, New Politics*, 579.

105. Haghayeghi, 87.

106. Kazakhstan established its own *muftiyat* in 1990; Uzbekistan followed suit by creating the *muftiyat* of Mawarannahr. By 1994, Turkmenistan and Kyrgyzstan set up their own separate administration; Tajikistan had already taken this step in 1993. Capisani, 126–127; see also Abdullaev, 263.

107. In 1992, for example, the "Spiritual Directorate of Muslims in the Republic of Tatarstan" severed all links and ties to the larger directorate in Ufa, just as the political movement to achieve greater sovereignty for Tatarstan within the Russian Federation was increasing in strength and popularity. See Sergei Filatov, "Tatarstan: at the Crossroads of Islam and Orthodoxy," *Religion, State and Society*, 20:3/4 (1998), 268.

108. Aleksandr Vladimirov, "Terror for Allah's Glory," in *Rossiiskaia Gazeta* (internet edition), July 6, 2001.

109. Abdullaev, 263–264. See Torbakov for a discussion on how current Uzbek and Tajik scholars are both engaged in "anchoring" their current nation-states in the historical past; the Uzbeks, by claiming the history of the territory, and the Tajiks, by focusing on the ethno-linguistic identity of the people living in the region. Neither side is interested in resurrecting a common or shared identity based on profession of Islam. The lack of any sort of Islamic or Turkic solidarity was recently lamented in an article by Rauf Mirqadirov ("Moscow Hangs a Millstone Around Azerbaijan's Neck," *Zerkalo*, May 25, 2001), which pointed out that Azerbaijan is increasingly becoming isolated in the region, and cannot turn to its half-brothers (the other Turkic-Islamic states of the former Soviet Union) for assistance.

110. Haghayeghi, 197.

111. "Turkmen Head in New Year Message Applauds Economic Growth," *Turkmenistan Daily Digest*, January 2, 2001, at http://www.eurasianet.org.

112. "Turkmen President Urges Approval of Nation's Spiritual Books," *Turkmenistan Daily Digest*, January 13, 2000, at http://www.eurasianet.org.

113. Islam Karimov, *Uzbekistan on the Threshold of the Twenty First Century* (Cambridge, MA: Uzbekiston, 1997, 1998), 91–92

114. Botyr Ochilovf, "Islam in Uzbekistan," in *Perihelion* (30 September–6 October 2002).

115. Austin Jersild notes, "The idea of 'Europe' was a powerful notion . . . Even the children of Shamil [the great Muslim rebel leader of the northern Caucasus] were to be incorporated into not just this world of privilege but also a world united by their common assumptions about Enlightenment and the prospect of progress in Russia and the transformation of its backward frontier in particular," 147.

116. Suleymanov, 11.

117. Martha Brill Olcott, *Kazakhstan: Unfulfilled Promise* (Washington, DC: Carnegie Endowment for International Peace, 2002), 177.

118. Suleymanov, 9.

119. Haghayeghi, 99. For a discussion of the differentiation between Uzbeks of the Fergana valley, who adhere more closely to traditionally Islamic norms, and Uzbeks, particularly in the major cities, see Lawrence Markowitz, "State, Society, and Identity in Uzbekistan: Differentiation among Ferghana Valley Uzbeks," in *The Transformations of 1989–1999*, 53–70.

120. For example, a 1998 survey among Muslim believers in Kazakhstan revealed that while 30 percent agreed with the statement that the government should be based on Islamic law, 55 percent preferred to be ruled by secular legislation. Olcott, 212.

121. Tadzhuddin (born 1948) and Pasha Zade (born 1949) were described by Bennigsen and Broxup as clerics of high training involved in trying to reconcile Islam with Soviet modernity (72) and were cited as representative of the moderation of Eurasian Islam.

122. Anderson, 184.

123. Annette Bohr, "Turkmenistan and the Turkmen," in *The Nationalities Question*, 358–59.

124. Vladimirov.

125. Haghayeghi, 95.

126. Jersild, 69.

127. Bruce Pannier, "Russia: Dagestan's Religious Tensions—Analysis," in *Radio Free Europe/Radio Liberty*, May 19, 1997, archived at http://www.stetson.edu/~psteeves/relnews/dstanpannier1905.html.

128. Ibid.

129. Filatov, 271.

130. Ibid.

131. Felix Corley, "Turkmenistan Crushes Religious Minorities," *Turkmenistan Daily Digest*, January 25, 2001, at http://www.eurasianet.org.

132. Olcott, 207.

133. Atkin, 619.

134. See Paul Goble, "The Roots of Russian-Iranian Rapprochement," *RFE/RL Newsline*, March 25, 1999, at http://www.rferl.org/newsline/1999/03/5-NOT/not-250399.html, and Nikolas K. Gvosdev, "Iran's Eurasian Strategy," *Analysis of Current Events*, 13:2 (2001), 1, 3.

135. Haghayeghi, 157.

136. Fahmi Huwaydi, "Neither the Fundamentalists nor the Arabs Are the Source of Tension in Central Asia," *Al-Sharq al-Aswat*, October 2, 2000, 9.

137. Firouzh Mostashari, "Colonial Dilemmas: Russian Policies in the Muslim Caucasus," in *Of Religion and Empire*, 243–247.

138. Capisani, 125.

139. Bohr, 358.

140. Haghayeghi, 160.

141. Akiner, 345, Haghayeghi, 160–161.

142. Bohr, 358–59.

143. Bakhtiar Babadzhanov, "Islam in Uzbekistan," in *Central Asia: A Gathering Storm?*, 321.

144. Gleason, 590.

145. Haghayeghi, 159.

146. Vladimirov.

147. Abullaev, 286–287.

148. See, for example, "Kazakhstan Preparing for a Papal Visit," *Zenit*, July 5, 2001, for a discussion on how Kazakh citizens of all faiths—Christian and Muslim alike—see the Pope as the conveyor of common values shared by both monotheistic faiths.

149. See, for example, the discussion over the difference between Islam as a Tatar-national phenomenon versus Islam as a religion seeking converts among ethnic Ukrainians. Gyorgy Lederer, "Islam Takes Root in Ukraine," *Eurasianet.org*, April 6, 2001, at http://www.eurasianet.org.

150. Nikolas K. Gvosdev, "Tolerance versus Pluralism: The Eurasian Dilemma," *Analysis of Current Events*, 12:7–8 (2000), 7–10.

151. Tatyana Roshchina, "Only Unity Leads to Welfare," *Rossiisakaia Gazeta* (internet version), March 17, 2000, 3.

152. For a discussion on these developments, see Nikolas K. Gvosdev, "When Mullahs and Metropolitans Meet: The Emerging Orthodox-Islamic Consensus in Eurasia," *Orthodox News*, Vol. 3, no. 7 (2001).

153. Mikhail Pozdnyayev, "Great Clerical Revolution," *Obshchaya Gazeta*, 52/1, December 31, 1997–January 14, 1998, 10.

154. Filatov, 270.

155. Roshchina, 3.

156. Quoted in Jersild, 51.

157. Lyudmila Barkina, "Rushaylo Urges N. Caucasus Orthodox, Muslim Leaders to Cooperate," *ITAR-TASS*, June 28, 2000; cited in *World News Connection: Central Eurasia*, FBIS-SOV-2000-0628 (June 28, 2000).

158. Cited in Gvosdev, "When Mullahs and Metropolitans."

159. See, for example, Vladimir Kucherenko, "Dagestan: Firing on Our Own People?" *Rossiiskaia Gazeta*, September 7, 1999, 2; cited in *World News Connection: Central Eurasia*, FBIS-SOV-1999-0908 (September 8, 1999).

160. Abdullaev, 261.

161. In Kazakhstan, for example, the nationalist movement *Jeltoqsan* tried to link issues related to "decolonization" of Kazakhstan with proposals to institute Islamic law; however, by 1993, this movement was in decline. Similarly, in Tajikistan, the nationalist movement *Rastokhez* recognized the primacy of Islam in Tajik culture but insisted that the state would have to remain ideologically and religiously neutral. Cf. Haghayeghi, 107, 115.

162. Vladimirov.

163. Abdullaev, 274.

164. Ahmed Rashid, "CA Fears Renewed Insurgency," *The Nation* (Lahore internet edition), April 5, 2001.

165. Ibid.

166. A good summary of events in Tajikistan is provided by Haghayeghi, 142–152. See also the report issued by Human Rights Watch ("Tajikistan: Tajik Refugees in Northern Afghanistan," *Human Rights Watch*, 8:6(D), May 1996. (A copy of this report is archived at http://www.hrw.org/reports/1996/Tajik.htm.)

167. Haghayeghi, 88.

168. Walldorf, 177.

169. See the Human Rights Watch report "Tajikistan: Tajik Refugees in Northern Afghanistan," cited previously.

170. "End of Tajik Civil War Boosts Iran-Russia Friendship," *IPS-Inter Press Service*, February 24, 1997; see also Muso Dinorshoyev, Interview by B. Turekhanova, *Agenstvo Politicheskikh Issledovaniy (Almaty)*, January 10, 2001.

171. Rashid.

172. Igor Rotar, "Government Tries to Clamp Down, As Islam's Influence Builds in Northern Tajikistan," *EurasiaNet*, November 12, 2002.

173. "Tajik Islamic Party condemns New Year's eve church explosions," report of Iranian radio *Mashad*, broadcast on January 3, 2001, and carried in *Tajikistan Daily Digest*, January 3, 2001, at http://www.eurasianet.org.

174. Davron Vali, "Banned Islamic Movement Increasingly Active in Tajikistan," *Eurasia Insight*, September 5, 2002 (http://www.eurasianet.org/departments/insight/articles/eav090502.shtml).

175. Abdullaev, 261.

176. Malise Ruthven, *Islam: A Very Short Introduction* (New York: Oxford University Press, 1997), 124–125.

177. Valerii Batuyev, "Interview with Aslan Maskhadov: 'I Must Speak About Chechnia's Independence'," *Argumenty i Fakty*, January 28, 1997.

178. David Damrel, "The Religious Roots of Conflict: Russia and Chechnya," *Religious Studies News*, 10:3 (1995), 10.

179. Tishkov, 208. A copy of the 1992 Chechen constitution can be accessed online at http://www.uni-wuerzburg.de/law/cc00000_.html.

180. John Dunlop, *Russia Confronts Chechnya: Roots of a Separatist Conflict* (New York: Cambridge University Press, 1998), 149.

181. See, for example, the appeal of *Lashkar-e Tayyaba* in Pakistan, for fighters and financial support Charles Recknagel, "Russia: Islamic Countries Unlikely to Help Chechnya," *Radio Free Europe/Radio Liberty*, November 19, 1999; archived at http://www.rferl.org/nca/features/1999/11/F.RU.991119132655.html.

182. Recknagel.

183. Edward Walker, "No War, No Peace in the Caucasus: Contested Sovereignty in Chechnya, Abkhazia, and Karabakh," in *Crossroads and Conflict: Security and Foreign Policy in the Caucasus and Central Asia*, Gary K. Bertsch and others, eds. (New York: Routledge, 2000), 155.

184. Justin Miller, "Ethnic and Religious Minorities and their Search for Justice: The Case of Chechnya," in *Civil Society and the Search for Justice in Russia*, eds. Christopher Marsh and Nikolas K. Gvosdev (Lanham, MD: Lexington, 2002), 156.

185. Anna Matveeva, *The North Caucasus: Russia's Fragile Borderland* (London: Royal Institute of International Affairs, 1999), 94.

186. Miller, 156.

187. Magomedkhan M. Magomedkhanov, "Will Dagestan Go the Way of Chechnya?" *EurasiaNews*, December 10, 1999, and archived at http://www.eurasianews.com/1210magomedkhanov.htm.

188. Ibid.

189. Ibid.

190. See "Kadyrov Comments on His Work as Head of Chechen Civil Administration," *Interfax*, November 5, 2000, and "Chechen Leader Predicts Rapid Economic Recovery," *Interfax*, March 28, 2001.

191. "Chechen Administration Head Says Russia Not Waging War on Islam," *ITAR-TASS*, January 26, 2003.

192. "New Chechen Muslim Leader Says Wahhabism Unacceptable for Chechnya," *Interfax*, October 17, 2000.

193. Cf. news reports in *Al-Sharq al-Awsat*, January 7, 2000; *The Sunday Telegraph*, January 9, 2000; *The Wall Street Journal*, July 2, 2002; and the *Baltimore Sun*, October 30, 2002.

194. The Chechen diaspora in Jordan, for example, has denied providing funding for the separatists. See their statement as released by *Interfax*, January 27, 2003.

195. *ITAR-TASS* report, January 27, 2003.

196. *ITAR-TASS* report, December 5, 2002.

197. Anna Matveeva, "The North Caucasus: Analysis of Current Events," *WriteNet Paper* no. 17, 1999, http://www.unhcr.ch/refworld/country/writenet/wn17_99.htm.

198. Babadzhanov, 322; Rashid.

199. "Imprisoning Islam," *Transitions Online*, April 4, 2001, at http://www.tol.cz.

200. Rashid.

201. Dinorshoyev.

202. Huwaydi, 9.

203. Zamira Eshanova, "Central Asia: Are Radical Groups Joining Forces?" *Radio Fee Europe/Radio Liberty,* October 11, 2002.

204. Antoine Blua, "Uzbekistan: Case Highlights Plight of Religious Minorities in Central Asia," *Radio Free Europe/Radio Liberty,* November 9, 2002.

205. Boris Rumer, "The Search for Stability in Central Asia," in *Central Asia: A Gathering Storm?,* 33.

Chapter 7

Some Thoughts on Islamist Failures in Sudan and Afghanistan

The 1990s were not entirely a period of setbacks for radical Islamists. Although the campaigns to win power in Algeria and Egypt failed, the radicals did manage to take control of two states on the periphery of the Middle East—Sudan and Afghanistan.[1] Even though the countries themselves were poor and impoverished, the apparent victory of Sunni-based Islamist movements in these two states was very important to Islamists throughout the region, especially those for whom Iran—a Shiite theocracy—was not a model to be emulated but a heretical regime to be despised.[2] Sudan and Afghanistan also became focal points for the international Islamist movement, as radicals from all over the world traveled to live (and many to train in) authentically Islamic regimes.

These two states, therefore, allowed other Islamists—as well as outside observers—to track how radical Islamists would put their theories and slogans into practice and how the solutions put forth by radical political Islam would actually function as policy. After all, Islamists themselves insisted that "the only way to know whether the 'Islamic solution' is workable is to provide them the opportunity to implement their vision."[3] Looking at this record (or lack thereof), Graham Fuller concluded that "some skepticism is due . . . about the ability of Islamists to run effective and moderate governments, especially when the three Islamic state models to date—Iran, Sudan and the Taliban's Afghanistan—have all failed dramatically in this area."[4]

SUDAN: TRAJECTORY OF FAILURE

In Sudan, the driving force behind the Islamist movement was the charismatic scholar Hassan al-Turabi (born 1932). In 1964, Turabi created the Islamic Charter Front (ICF), which drew upon the ideology and outlook of the Egyptian Muslim Brothers but mimicked the Communist Party in its organization.[5]

Turabi believed that Islam could provide a comprehensive plan for the social, political, and economic development of the country, as opposed to other systems. He commented,

> Arab socialism was a very important slogan but there was no content to it, except perhaps a vague belief in Arab unity, and in Arab integrity or Arab independence. But it did not tell you a lot about how the Arab economy should be managed or how government should be structured in a typical Arab society. And the nationalist movement aspired simply to national independence. This just meant changing a British administrator by putting in his place a Sudanese administrator. Once independence was achieved, these movements looked bankrupt. They were not prepared for anything else. They were completely consumed in the business of national struggle and how to achieve national independence.[6]

However, on May 25, 1969, the Free Officers' Movement led by then Colonel Jaafar an-Nimeiri overthrew the republic and created a Revolutionary Command Council. Like similar groups of officers in Egypt and Libya, the Sudanese officers wanted to create a progressive and nationalist regime and as such found themselves pitted against both conservative Muslims (especially the brotherhoods) and the Communists. As part of the consolidation of power, many leading Muslim figures were imprisoned, among them Turabi.

In 1977, Nimeiri began to reverse course and proclaimed the need for national reconciliation. Seeking greater legitimacy for his regime, he had permitted elections and now reached out to the Islamists. Turabi was released from prison and became Sudan's attorney general. As in Egypt under Sadat, Sudan began to Islamify itself as a way to gain popular support and to undercut leftist forces. The greater Islamic coloration of the regime was also a way for Nimeiri to rally support in trying to fend off separatist challenges posed by the largely non-Muslim south. In 1983, Nimeiri declared that sharia would now become the law of the land—this act coincided with the resumption of the civil war, as southerners protested the whittling away of the autonomy provisions guaranteed to them under the 1972 settlement that had ended the first civil war.

In seeking to displace the Communists, Nimeiri turned to Islamists to help staff professional positions in government, the economy, the military, and academia. As Kepel concluded, "In other words, the conquest of the state by an 'enlightened elite' eventually made it possible for Turabi to bring his Islamist project to fruition."[7] Fearing the rise in Turabi's influence, Nimeiri tried to repress the Islamists, and for a short time in 1985 Turabi was once again imprisoned. However, Nimeiri himself was overthrown in a coup later that year.

Turabi then created a new political party, the National Islamic Front (NIF), in order to contest parliamentary elections and to push Sudan further along the Islamist path. Yet, in free elections, Turabi's movement came in third place, receiving the support of approximately 18 percent of the electorate. Continued fighting between the central government and southerners seeking greater autonomy and the collapse of the Sudanese economy (in 1986, the IMF had declared Sudan to be bankrupt) strengthened Turabi's conviction that the only way for Sudan out of its political and economic morass was the Islamist path. When the government announced on June 30, 1989, that it was suspending the application of Islamic law as a prelude for reconciliation with the south (leading to the creation of a more liberal and pluralist system), Turabi's disciples within the military hierarchy, led by Omar Hassan al-Bashir, took control of the government. (Although Turabi was widely viewed as the power in the post-1989 regime, he took no official executive title, but retained his position as head of the NIF and took the post of speaker of parliament.)

This was the signal for the NIF to unleash its militias and street activists to begin a purge of Sudanese society, especially in organizing and running unofficial torture centers referred to as ghost houses. The new government banned all other political parties and movements, purged the civil service and the judiciary of non-Islamists, and accelerated the military campaign against the southern separatists.[8]

Turabi also used his new authority to try and project his vision of Islamism throughout the Islamic world. He set up an alternative to the Saudi-sponsored Organization of the Islamic Conference, the Popular Arab and Islamic Conference, which held meetings in April 1991, December 1993, and March–April 1995. "These gave Turabi a forum with which to establish his own presence on the international scene through the media, which he handled with consummate skill, and to strengthen his hold on his own country."[9] Moreover, these conferences allowed Turabi to assume some degree of leadership within the international Islamist movement, because Khartoum could serve as a place for Islamists to meet and find refuge.[10] (The most famous of these international Islamists, of course, was Osama bin Laden.)

Yet, as Turabi himself admitted, the NIF did not have any concrete policies for Sudan. "So people came out with a new model which they thought would approximate Islam. They don't know how it will work in practice."[11] Yet vaunted slogans such as "Islam is the solution" could not substitute for practical action. Between 1983 and 1999 some 1.2 million people died in Sudan as a result of the civil war and the accompanying famines, and the prolonged conflict ended up costing Sudan $1.5 million per day.[12]

The appalling conditions in which southern Sudanese existed—facing starvation, genocide, and the slave trade—did much to erode the international image of Sudan and its Islamist government.[13] More importantly (for the purposes of this book), however, the dictatorship set up by the NIF demonstrated to mainly Muslims that an Islamist-inspired regime could not create a government based upon consensus, nor could it apply Islamic law and principles to create a prosperous economy. Of particular concern was the NIF's savage repression of other Islamic parties in Sudan, whose leaders and activists were constantly arrested, whose newspapers were shut down, and whose ability to enter the public square was severely limited.

The NIF thus found itself subject to criticism on Islamic grounds. Some imams criticized the actual performance of the government, especially its failure to control rising prices or to prevent the deterioration of public services. Yet other Muslim parties believed that the NIF had distorted Islamic values in its conduct of state affairs. Interestingly, the Muslim Brotherhood split from the NIF, considering the latter to have become too absorbed in its quest for worldly power. Other political parties with roots in the traditional brotherhoods, notably the Umma party led by former Prime Minister Sadiq al-Mahdi (who served from 1986 until the 1989 coup), have been harassed and their leaders frequently detained. The government particularly took umbrage at the *Ansar al-Sunna* movement (a movement akin to the Saudi Wahhabis), which challenged the Islamic credentials of the NIF.[14]

Yet the regime could not hide the evidence of its failure to create a utopia. Following the feast of Eid in 1995, Sadiq al-Mahdi spoke from the pulpit of his mosque in Omdurman, where he lambasted the NIF government as a "total failure" and held it responsible for the "unparalleled corruption" running rampant in the country. Later that year, in September, student protestors in Khartoum chanted "No to traders of religion" and, more ominously, "The people are hungry."

The NIF was also not capable of producing a more equitable economic system. Instead, it used force and repression to try and reorganize the economy. "As a result of this political instability, perceived risks of the economic environment have increased, especially during the early years of the 1989 military regime, which used extreme political repression, unheard of in the modern history of Sudan, as well as extreme predatory economic measures favoring party loyalists and discriminating against traditional entrepreneurs."[15] Sudan was kept afloat largely due to its oil industry, which continued to attract some foreign investment.

Matters came to a head in December 1999. Bashir imposed a state of emergency, dissolved parliament, and ousted Turabi as speaker of parliament after Turabi tried to shepherd measures through parliament that would have limited the president's power. Although Turabi continued to have a strong base of support within the legislature, Bashir had solidified his control over army, police, and security services, who backed his action. On December 24, he ruled out any political reconciliation with Turabi, saying, "We will not allow a return to duplicity in government decisions and we will not allow anyone to usurp the state institutions and the authority of the head of state." Furthermore, he denounced the excesses that had been promulgated by Turabi.[16] Turabi remains under house arrest and a number of key figures in his People's Congress party are in prison. Ironically, as in other countries such as Egypt, members of Turabi's party are having their terms of detention extended under emergency provisions.[17]

Although Bashir has never renounced the Islamist label (although he increasingly describes himself as a pragmatist), Sudan post-Turabi has shifted gears in a much more moderate direction, anticipating developments that have occurred in other Islamist-based movements in the Middle East. In 2002, Bashir's National Congress government approved legislation aimed at establishing a democratic state with respect for all religions and beliefs and would shift sharia from being a part of national legislation to becoming a duty of the Muslim community. Bashir also reached out to the opposition Umma party, proposing a power-sharing arrangement, and pledged constitutional amendments that would guarantee freedom of the press, freedom to stage demonstrations, and a ban on the abuse or political exploitation of religion.

Bashir appears to recognize that only the establishment of a durable peace with the southern separatists, based on substantial autonomy, can help to revitalize Sudan's economy. On top of this, his finance minister, Al-Zubayr Ahmad Hasan, has stressed the importance of continuing to privatize the economy and providing the stability necessary to encourage foreign investment. More than $500 million in investment came into Sudan in 2001, and he attributed this "to the economic stability that was established in the past few years, and to the government's liberalization policies."[18]

Sudan still has a long way to go to heal the scars produced by dictatorship and civil war. Yet it is striking the degree to which the post–December 1999 government has moved away from Islamist rhetoric. In March 2003, according to an assistant to President Bashir, Mubarak al-Fadil,

We entered into an agreement and called it the national program. It stipulated the adoption of political pluralism and democracy as the basis for the rule and peace . . . You should talk about the post December-1999 stage and the developments that followed it. The regime at this stage . . . embarked on major political changes at the domestic and foreign policy levels. At the domestic policy level, there is officially and constitutionally a transformation toward pluralism . . .[19]

AFGHANISTAN: AN ISLAMIST CAMBODIA?

The origins of the Taliban (students) movement is well known and can be easily summarized here. The Taliban arose from the Afghan refugee population (largely ethnic Pashtuns) that had studied in the fundamentalist Deobandi *madrassas* in Baluchistan as the war with the Soviets raged during the 1980s. Following the Soviet withdrawal in 1989, the war in Afghanistan continued: first against the Soviet-backed regime of Najibullah and then, in 1992, between various *mujaheddin* factions. The Taliban came to the attention of the interior minister of Pakistan during the government of Benazir Bhutto, Major General Nasrullah Babar, who saw the Taliban as a force for suppressing and pacifying Afghanistan (and to extend Pakistani influence in Afghanistan). With Pakistani support, the Taliban, under the leadership of the "one-eyed mullah," Muhammad Omar, consolidated a base around Kandahar, succeeded in taking control of much of the southern part of Afghanistan during 1995, and took Kabul in September 1996.[20]

The Deobandi origins of the Taliban are crucial for understanding their approach to governance. The Deobandi movement, initially established in 1867 following the establishment of the British *raj* in the Indian subcontinent, preached a type of withdrawal from the larger state and society into self-contained communities marked by strict adherence to the precepts of Islamic law. Thus, as Kepel concluded, "The Deobandi culture opposed ordinary public services, being traditionally focused on organizing the community in the meticulous respect for dogma without regard to the state."[21] The Deobandis were also known for militancy. Certainly, this feature was useful in whipping up support for a jihad against the Soviets. It also meant that the Deobandis were lavishly supported by Saudi Arabia in its efforts to counter Shiite influence in Pakistan and Afghanistan and by Pakistani intelligence as a way to funnel recruits into Kashmir for a deniable "war of attrition" against India.[22]

Because of the legacy of foreign involvement in Afghan affairs, it is difficult to ascertain how much popular support the ideals espoused by the Taliban actually had within Afghan society. Certainly, the Taliban capitalized on sentiments among the population that were weary of constant war and desired stability. As Elie D. Krakowski noted, "The Taliban, under a religious guise, were promising peace, security and development"[23]—not dissimilar to the promises made by other Islamist movements. The fact that the Taliban were primarily ethnic Pashtuns and had ousted from Kabul a government primarily composed of other ethnic minorities also played a role. Yet, it is also clear that without significant logistical and financial support from outside backers, the Taliban would have been unlikely to gain control over most of Afghanistan.[24] This tendency accelerated as Afghanistan became the central sanctuary and base of operations for Al-Qaeda. By 2001, between one-fifth and one-quarter of the Taliban's combat strength came from non-Afghans who had flocked to the country to take part in jihad—and the presence of these outsiders "served to prop up the constantly faltering Taliban military effort."[25]

Even a superficial examination of the Islamic Emirate of Afghanistan, however, reveals the complete poverty of the Deobandi Islamist ideology in constructing and maintaining a modern state. Afghanistan could not even be compared to Sudan or Iran, which, although operating on the basis of an Islamist ideology, nonetheless maintained the machinery of a modern government. Other than its armed forces and morals police, the Taliban had little state infrastructure. The Taliban survived from foreign assistance and from the tolls levied on commerce transiting Afghanistan; but it had no program for economic development. Justice was understood primarily as enforcing strict adherence to public codes of behavior.[26] Otherwise, the Taliban regime understood its purpose as organizing for war against the enemies of the faith. During its existence, the Taliban regime attracted those who wished to train for jihad and survived, in some sense, as a dumping ground where other Muslim countries could export their radicals, but the Taliban experiment in Afghanistan had little influence on the development of other Islamist movements in terms of providing any guidance in how society was to be administered. The Islamic Emirate was geared primarily for fighting; and after vanquishing most of its enemies within Afghanistan (with the exception of the territory that remained under the control of the Northern Alliance), it sought to spread jihad to other venues. However, down to the final days of the regime, it was unable to feed its own people and had to rely on international charitable associations, including, ironically, Christian charities, to fend off starvation among Afghans. An outsider observer concluded,

The Taliban has shown themselves to be incompetent administrators and unable to deliver on their various promises beyond a modicum of security. Even that security has begun to be increasingly weighed against the Taliban's mounting repression, intolerance and self-defeating harassment of those who would help with humanitarian aid. War weariness has been magnified by the deepening drought and famine . . .[27]

The extent to which Afghanistan under the Taliban failed to promote even the basic welfare of the population under its care is made all the more evident by what has been achieved in the post-Taliban era, even though full stability has yet to be achieved in the country. Hamid Karzai, speaking in Kuala Lampur in February 2003, noted that "over three million boys and girls returned to school as a result of the back to school campaign. Over 1.9 million refugees and thousands of internally displaced persons have returned to their homeland. An independent human rights commission is established to investigate violations of human rights and develop domestic human rights institutions."[28]

When Kandahar fell on December 6, 2001, the Taliban regime, for all intents and purposes, came to an end. Although Taliban militias continue to operate and harass the post-Taliban interim government, without significant foreign sponsorship and aid, they are likely to remain an annoyance rather than a real contender for power. Since Taliban Afghanistan also, to some extent, acted as a "basket for all the rotten eggs," a number of Arab and Central Asian Islamist fighters chose to remain and fight on behalf of the regime and so were neutralized as well.

With the fall of the Taliban in 2001, the second (and last) experiment in Islamist governance in a largely Sunni nation came to an end. Officially, Afghanistan remains an Islamic state—its designation from 1992 to 1997—yet the government has made it clear that it understands this to mean the promotion of "democracy, rights of self-determination and rule of law,"[29] not an attempt to set up a seventh-century utopian religious community. Although Afghanistan faces serious challenges in the years ahead, it is looking for inspiration not only from its Muslim heritage but the Western experience as well.

NOTES

1. Michael Scott Duran, "Somebody Else's Civil War," *Foreign Affairs* (January/February 2002), 33.

2. For one example, see the profile on Usbat al-Ansar, a radical Islamist organization in Lebanon, and its view on Iran, in *Al-Safir*, February 7, 2003 (internet version).

3. Faisal Kutty, "Islamists and the West: Co-existence or Confrontation?"*Washington Report* (January 1996), 34.

4. Graham Fuller, "The Failure of Political Islam," *Foreign Affairs* (March/April 2002), 52.

5. Gilles Kepel, *Jihad: The Trail of Political Islam*, trans. Anthony F. Roberts (Cambridge, MA: Harvard University Press, 2002), 178.

6. "Islam, Democracy, the State and the West: A Round Table with Dr. Hasan Turabi," held May 10, 1992, Tampa, FL (co-sponsored by the World and Islam Studies Enterprise and the University of South Florida).

7. Kepel, 180.

8. For greater detail, please consult "Sudan: In the Name of God," *Human Rights Watch* 6:9 (November 1994).

9. Kepel, 184.

10. See Turabi's interview in *Al-Nahar*, November 3, 1995, 10.

11. "Islam, Democracy, the State and the West."

12. BBC News, "Analysis Sudan: A Political and Military History," February 21, 1999.

13. See, for example, Donald Petterson, former U.S. ambassador to Sudan, in his *Inside Sudan: Political Islam, Conflict and Catastrophe* (Boulder, CO: Westview Press, 1999).

14. For more details, consult *Behind the Red Line: Political Repression in Sudan* (Washington, DC: Human Rights Watch, 1996).

15. See the May 2002 report, "Explaining Sudan's Economic Growth Performance," prepared by Abdel Gadir Ali of the Arab Planning Institute (Kuwait) and Ibrahim A. Elbadawi of the World Bank, 12.

16. Bashir's comments appeared in *Al-Sharq al-Awsat*, December 24, 1999 (internet version).

17. See the report in *Al-Quds al-Arabi*, October 28, 2002, 2.

18. See his interview in *Al-Sharq al-Awsat*, October 14, 2002, 13.

19. See his interview in *Al-Sharq al Awsat*, March 1, 2003, 8.

20. See Dennis Kux, "The Pakistani Pivot," *The National Interest* (Thanksgiving 2001), 51; and Ahmed Rashid, "The Taliban: Exporting Extremism," *Foreign Affairs* (November/December 1999), 23–25.

21. Kepel, 229; Rashid, 26–28.

22. Rashid, 28.

23. Elie D. Krakowski, "Bin Laden, the Taliban and the Future of Afghanistan," *Middle East Insight* (November/December 2001), 26.

24. See Julie Sirrs, "Lifting the Veil on Afghanistan," *The National Interest* (Thanksgiving 2001), esp. 47.

25. Krakowski, 26.

26. Kepel, 229–232.

27. Krakowski, 26.

28. "Statement" by His Excellency Hamid Karzai, President of the Transitional Islamic State of Afghanistan at the 13th Nonaligned Movement Summit in Kuala Lumpur (February 24, 2003).

29. Ibid.

Conclusion

Daniel Pipes and Edward Said are not known for sharing the same position on most issues, but both of these observers of the Muslim world have come to the same conclusion: radical Islamism, although it can continue to inspire militant opposition and terrorist attacks, cannot provide a working, alternate model for organizing society. Pipes argues that "Islamism (or fundamentalist Islam) must fail because of its inherent weaknesses,"[1] and Said concurs: "Political Islam has generally not done well wherever it has tried through Islamist parties to take state power."[2]

This assessment was also reached by a Sudanese Islamist scholar, Abdel Wahab al-Effendi. On December 29, 1999, he penned an editorial for the London based newspaper *Al-Quds al-Arabi*, trying to analyze the failures of the Islamist movement. He concluded that Islamist movements had been most successful as opposition forces, where they could "bask in the glow of martyrdom," but had egregiously failed, once in power, to provide a stable and workable form of government capable of addressing the challenges faced by ordinary Muslims.[3] This explains, in part, the shift in tactics by the international Islamist movement, away from challenging regimes in the Muslim world to trying to provoke the United States. Speaking of the September 11 attacks, Michael Scott Doran concludes,

> The attacks were a response to the failure of extremist movements in the Muslim world in recent years, which have generally proved incapable of taking power (Sudan and Afghanistan being the major exceptions). In the last two decades, several violent groups have challenged regimes such as those in Egypt, Syria and Algeria, but in every case the government has managed to crush, co-opt or marginalize the radicals.[4]

The growing ideological (not to mention financial) bankruptcy of the Islamic Republic of Iran was the first major setback for Islamists. The Iranian attempt to reconcile Islamic imperatives with the exigencies of modern society has resulted in contradictions that Iran's theocrats seem incapable of resolving. Frightened of the possibility that the free market will unleash forces beyond their control, the clerics refuse to loosen the reins of Iran's command economy. Equally fearing the ramifications of a truly democratic political system, the regime controls both legislation and candidates for office. The mullahs now face a new generation that neither experienced the revolution nor has any evident commitment to its ideals. The demands of Iran's youth for the elimination of suffocating cultural restrictions, as well as for fundamental economic reform and political freedom, threaten the very identity of the Islamic Republic. In fact, for Iran to avoid collapsing into civil strife it must adopt some basic secular tenets. This task may be possible, as growing numbers within Iran's elite seem to recognize Islam's limited utility as a template for governance.

In Algeria, after nearly a decade of civil war, the Algerian military has effectively defeated the Islamist insurgency, although not without great cost in lives. But the Islamist movement lost popular support well before its collapse. The Algerian state succeeded because its actions were supported by the citizenry. In successive presidential and parliamentary elections (albeit elections managed by the military), Algerians have been given an opportunity to cast their ballots for multiple parties and candidates—including ones with Islamist agendas and platforms. The Algerian economy, through substantial international efforts and the revival of the oil market, has gradually recovered. In essence, the Algerian state rehabilitated itself by succeeding in two areas that the Islamists failed: providing a coherent economic plan and a mechanism that increased popular participation in the political process.

In Egypt, the brutal tactics employed by Hosni Mubarak to combat the Islamists did much to destroy their influence. At the same time, the ranks of the radicals have never been replenished because the majority of Egyptians concluded that their problems would not be solved by the violent overthrow of the state. Support for militant Islam has gradually dwindled as the Islamists failed to provide a rationale for even the most disillusioned youth to battle Egypt's security apparatus.

In the Balkans, Islamism had a certain appeal after the collapse of the communist system produced an ideological and spiritual void. Interest in the Islamist option also increased as a result of the civil wars in Bosnia and Kosovo, which also provided the opening for radical Islamists from the Middle East and southwestern Asia to enter the region. Yet the absolute majority of the Muslim populations of the Balkans have their eyes on eventual integration into Europe, not association with the traditional Muslim world—validating the proverb often cited by Osama bin Laden that when a weak and a strong horse are seen side-by-side, a person chooses the strong. Europe represents peace and prosperity, and, assuming that the project of European integration continues in the next two years to encompass Muslim-majority areas (absorbing a reunified Cyprus and initiating accession talks with Turkey), then the blandishments of the radicals will fall on largely deaf ears.

The Central Asian and Caucasian states of the former Soviet Union have paid careful attention to the models demonstrated by the authoritarian regimes of the Middle East in coping with Islamism—co-opting certain items of the Islamist agenda while selectively engaging in repression of those elements that have tried to exist beyond the control and purview of the state. The failure of Islamists to construct stable or just orders in either Chechnya or Tajikistan also has had a certain chilling effect on both the elites and the mass populations of the region. The greatest danger is that the authoritarian regimes of Central Asia will not provide sufficient venues for constructive opposition and thus drive people into the hands of the radicals.

This work has concentrated on radical political Islam in the Middle East, the Balkans, and the former USSR, but its conclusions can be tested in what happens in the years to come in the Muslim states of southeast Asia and western Africa, where the cycle is just beginning. The apparent initial success of Islamist movements in Nigeria or Malaysia, therefore, must be evaluated in light of the following propositions.

First, radical Islamist movements are *reactions* to political and economic dislocations caused by modernization and liberalization, especially to perceived inequities in access to political power and economic opportunity. Linked to this is the perception that the *traditional*, orthodox Islamic establishment is unable or unwilling to address these concerns. Akbar Taradjonzoda, the former kazi of Tajikistan and a leader in the IRP, observed, "If our supporters grew militant, they did so in reaction to the government repression, discrimination, violence, and doubletalk."[5] Islamist movements attract those who believe that the *status quo* in government and the economy precludes them from achieving their rightful potential, and these movements draw power and legitimacy by framing these questions in terms of Islamic justice and morality. Islamists are dual revolutionaries: they oppose the existing socio-economic structure and also critique traditional Islam for its seeming inability to promote change. However, the utopian vision of the Islamists—rooted in an ahistorical version of Islam—is also their Achilles' heel.

Second, Islamist movements often gain momentum because the regime in power ignores the Islamists or tacitly renders support to them, usually in an effort to undercut secularists or progressive forces. In Iran, the Shah's American advisors focused on pro-Soviet leftists, not the clerics, as the primary threat to the regime. Indeed, throughout much of the Middle East, the United States viewed Islamists as potential allies against what they considered Godless Soviet communism, an approach subsequently adopted in the decision to support Islamist guerillas in Afghanistan against a Soviet-backed regime. In Algeria, Islamists were able to use the quasi-patronage of the state's de facto chief Muslim cleric to install their preachers in mosques around the country and to use the country's Muslim establishments as a way to organize at the grassroots level. Egypt's Anwar Sadat used the Islamists, particularly on university campuses, as a way to combat leftist and progressive movements—and a similar approach occurred in Sudan. In contrast, in a state like Tunisia, strict state control and supervision over the staffing of mosques and over Islamic educational institutions have enabled the regime to marginalize radical elements and to deny them the space in which to organize and thrive. This model has also been embraced by the successor states in Central Asia, which have resisted any efforts to loosen state control over Muslim religious activities.[6]

Third, Islamist movements often begin as broad-based coalitions dissatisfied with the status quo and desirous of creating a just Islamic order to replace failed policies linked with Westernization (economic modernization, socialism, nationalism, and so on). When these movements exist in pure opposition, it is easy to find common ground among diverse groups in acceptance of abstract principles. As an Islamist movement draws closer to attaining power (or after a successful seizure of power), however, fissures inevitably open up between those who maintain that strict adherence to ideology will produce results versus those who are more pragmatic in their assessments or willing to make compromises. Thus, in Iran, the Islamists were able to organize a large anti-Shah coalition; only after Khomeini came to power were more moderate elements purged. In Algeria, a schism developed within the FIS between those prepared to accept the legitimacy of the electoral system versus those who saw elections merely as a tool to seize control of the machinery of the state. Usually, radical elements rise to the fore when a crisis discredits more moderate pragmatists. The cancellation of the Algerian elections, the increased repression in Egypt, the outbreak of civil and external war in Iran, Tajikistan, and Bosnia—all of these factors emboldened radicals who disdained any sort of compromise and helped to stoke the fervor of the true believers. In turn, moderation can rise to the fore in periods of relative peace or in the exhausted aftermath of bitter struggles. The moderation of the IRP in Tajikistan today, in contrast to its utopian radicalism a decade ago, is partly a reflection of the bloody civil war that country endured.

Fourth, even though Islamism appeals to those on the margins of power and wealth, because of their stress upon righteousness, Islamist parties can easily lose legitimacy when they cannot produce the just and moral order that they have promised. Palestinian refugees in Jordan, for example, may find Islamism's slogan that "Islam is the solution" to be seductive, living in conditions of squalor and political disenfranchisement.[7] Yet, the "Dilemmas of institutional decay, maldistribution of wealth, and the absence of democracy were simply beyond the ken of the Islamists' empty ideological formulations."[8] The rhetoric of a new order for Sudan, based upon Islamic principles, gave way to a corrupt military dictatorship, leading many to question whether such a regime could in fact deliver the justice it promised.[9] In Iran, the Islamists created a command economy that suffered from numerous and irreparable defects and was plagued by corruption at every level. Indeed, Iran's hard-line clerics are among the most corrupt actors on the Iranian political scene, actively creating institutions to maintain their privileges at the expense of the collective good. The soldiers of faith in Algeria and Egypt, proclaiming their "vision of probity and justice," in practice behaved as a criminal gang, extorting the local population to sustain their campaign of violence and terror. Disillusionment leads to the discrediting of Islamist claims that it alone can deliver a more perfect order—and can often lead to repression and violence, as Islamists seek to use force and intimidation to retain power.[10]

Moreover, the descent into corruption can have a profound demonstration effect. One reason why Iranian-inspired Islamist parties have found little support in Azerbaijan—despite the corruption of the existing regime and a common Shiite interpretation of Islam—has been the discrepancies observed between the official rhetoric of the Islamic Republic and the behavior of ordinary Iranians who cross the border into secular Azerbaijan.[11] The growing perception that Islamist revolutionaries in Algeria and Egypt were not idealistic soldiers of the faith but murderous robbers helped to drive the pious middle and business classes back into the embrace of the existing regimes.

The fifth point is the connection between Islamism and violence. As a militant ideology, Islamism has often thrived in conditions of strife—whether internal civil conflicts (as in Egypt, Sudan, Algeria, Bosnia, or Tajikistan) or external war (as in Iran or Chechnya). Under the conditions of stress produced by conflict, Islamists try to rally support under the guise of shared struggle. With the coming of peace, however, the rhetoric of jihad and sacrifice loses its appeal.

Indeed, the need for violence and struggle is often transformed and directed by radical Islamists against their own domestic opponents. This tendency is amplified by the practice of many radical groups to attack not only non-Muslims, but other Muslims who disagree with their interpretation or application of Islamic law or principles. Al-Effendi lamented in his editorial that Islamists failed to resolve conflicts peacefully and often abandoned the democratic principles that they claimed to cherish. In an interesting turn of events, the group that is most aggressively persecuted in the Islamic Republic are not ardent secularists but clerics who defy the regime's religious postulations and who have a more moderate vision of religious democracy in place of the revolutionary theocracy created by the mullahs. In a similar vein, in Algeria and Egypt, radical Islam saved its wrath for moderate religious figures, who were qualified best to challenge its spurious claims.[12] The practice of Islamists to kafirize their opponents (that is, to declare them unbelievers or pagans)[13] further widens the gap between the radicals and the mainstream—a process that is most visible on university campuses throughout the Muslim world.[14] Yet, the logic of excommunication (*takfir*) led some Islamists, such as the Algerian *amir* Zouabri, to declare all Algerians outside the ranks of the GIA to be impious and excommunicated from the community of true Muslims.[15] Similarly, the radical group *Usbat al-Ansar* (which operates in Lebanon) has proclaimed that "all Arab and Muslim governments, without exception" are guilty "of blasphemy."[16]

This desire for separation is also reflected in the efforts of radical leaders to try and make their followers distinctive even among other Muslims by encouraging distinct forms of the *hijab* for women, to the point of rejecting traditional forms of modest dress as un-Islamic, as well as specific types of clothing and beard-trimming for men. Indeed, radical Islamists have used dress and appearance as a way to demonstrate "adherence to their political movement."[17] The stress on separation is seen as necessary "because anything beyond the barest contact with the barbarousness of contemporary life threatened to corrupt these young, authentic Muslims."[18]

Separation from an unclean and sinful world reinforces the worldview of the radicals that they are fighting for a new Islamic order, but it raises a very practical yet real political problem. With such an attitude of derision for the realities of modern life as well as for the traditional forms of Islam, the Islamists are rarely ever in the majority. Even if they won initial support from the broad mainstream due to their critique of the status quo, the Manichean division of society into us versus them (plus the violence that often accompanies this approach) is profoundly alienating to the majority.[19] To win and hold political power, therefore, they must secure the acquiescence of the populations over which they hope to govern.

For some Islamists, the solution is found in continued violence and mass terror—the use of the machinery of the state to suppress the unrighteous and stifle dissent. Sudan, Iran under Ayatollah Khomeini, and Afghanistan under the Taliban are all examples of how Islamists created military dictatorships and recast civil or external wars as jihads between the true Muslims and non- or pseudo-Muslims as a way to legitimize authority and root out domestic opposition. An excellent analogy can be drawn with the period of war communism in Russia during its civil war, when the exigencies of the military struggle fired ideological purity and facilitated mass repression against opponents of the regime. One could also point to the fact that many of the more radical Islamist leaders who engaged in whole-scale violence were young men, often with little higher education and few economic prospects, who had few tangible assets to lose.[20]

Certainly, the appeal to the cleansing violence of a jihad against the unrighteous will resonate with the disenfranchised and the poor. Yet no regime or political movement can maintain a state of perpetual war—it will either be overthrown eventually or it must begin to explore reform as a way to meet popular aspirations. Utopian revolutionary movements, especially those that seize power, eventually reach the point of Thermidor—a stage when radical forces are displaced by more moderate ones. Economic crisis and war fatigue are powerful inducements to moderation. This process is aided by the fact that one of the mainstays of Islamist movements— the devout middle class—is increasingly "looking for an acceptable form of access to the system" rather than the complete destruction of society.[21]

In political systems that are competitive or semicompetitive in nature, Islamists are subject to the polls, and therefore must be prepared to either accept permanent minority status or try to broaden their appeal by forming coalitions with other groups. As John Esposito noted,

> It must be recalled that the membership of Islamic organizations generally constitute a numerical minority, not a majority of the population . . . the realities of a more open marketplace and having to compete for votes (coming to power and having to rule amidst diverse interests) could force Islamic groups (as they often do secular political parties) to adapt or broaden their ideology and programs in response to domestic realities, diverse constituencies, and interests.[22]

In places like Jordan, Kuwait, and Morocco, therefore, the existence of a parliamentary system has acted as a moderating force on Islamist movements, drawing them into dialogue with secular and nationalist parties.

Ultimately the most powerful antidote to radical Islam, beyond immediate palliatives of state-sponsored controls, may be greater pluralism and competition of ideas. Radical Islamism is an ideology of wrath, directed against an existing order. So long as the political order remains closed, the radical guerrillas will have a place in society, as their defiance of the oppressive order and their criticism of the stagnant rule of the autocrats will have resonance with a segment of the populace. In an open arena of competition, radical Islam will find its ideas contested by a range of alternatives, from secular liberalism to moderate Islam. It is unlikely that the radicals can sustain their base of support in light of such systematic dissection of their creed. Radical Islamists have found it exceedingly difficult to transform their slogans into a governing dogma. The intellectual poverty of this movement makes an ideal ideology of opposition but an impossible and unrealistic alternative to mainstream ideologies. In the last several years, some Islamists have renounced their utopian vision in favor of more moderate approaches. The attempts to form a moderate Center Party in Egypt in 1995, or the creation of the Islamic Action Front in Jordan, are reflections of the fact that Muslim populations do not want utopia but rather open political and economic systems.[23]

Indeed, one of the most interesting cases of Islamist evolution has been in Turkey, where the remnants of banned Islamist parties came together to form the Justice and Development Party (AKP), which won a plurality of the votes in the 2002 parliamentary elections. While claiming that the party is rooted in Islamic values, its leader, Recep Tayyip Erdogan, insists that the party is not a radical movement but a conservative, pro-values group similar to European Christian Democrats. Erdogan believes that the AKP can successfully integrate Muslim ethics with liberal democracy and has committed his party to undertake the reforms necessary to bring Turkey into full membership within the European Union. In fact, Erdogan and other Islamist leaders like Abdullah Gul who initially espoused very radical sentiments now have "advocated a much more moderate approach. Thus, some radicals were willing to work within the system to achieve systemic change in society and politics . . ."[24]

Gul has been a leading figure among the Young Ones within the ranks of Turkish Islamism, seeking to move the party away from an Islam-referenced party to what he has termed a "new politics" based on a "more universally-understood democracy." When the Virtue Party, a predecessor to the AKP, was banned in June 2001, Gul and Erdogan parted company with more conservative elements. The moderates created the AKP, whereas the conservative Islamists formed the Felicity (Saadet) party. The Turkish election results demonstrated that fusing Islamic values with liberal principles is more likely to attract support than espousing a spartan utopian vision of a lost Golden Age.

Given that "Islamist participation in electoral politics does not mean necessarily that they would win an absolute majority of votes,"[25] for polls and surveys throughout the Islamic world indicate that Islamist-based parties would poll between 15 and 35 percent of the vote, Islamists would most likely emerge as an opposition force or one partner among several in a coalition. Although having a strong influence on public life, Islamist parties committed to the democratic process would have little opportunity to fully implement their programs.

This, in turn, may lead to an interesting synthesis between Islamism and liberalism, of the type being charted by thinkers such as Soroush in Iran or Hassan Hanafi in Egypt. Such a synthesis would not automatically embrace all of the concepts of the Enlightenment; rather, it would seek to balance reverence for Islamic values with the individual's desire for self-expression. It would embrace limits on personal freedom consistent with the notion of preserving community stability. However,

Even though an Islamic democracy will resist certain elements of post-Enlightenment liberalism, it will still be a system that features regular elections, accepts dissent and opposition parties, and condones a free press and division of power between branches of the state.[26]

The problem, however, is how this process can come about—the evolution of radical utopian movements into moderate political parties. All of the countries in this study were (or still are) autocratic polities at the time Islamist forces began to organize. Only in Bosnia (and to a lesser extent in Iran) have Islamists had ongoing experience with regular, competitive elections. Yet even in the current autocratic political societies of the Middle East, political parties and civic and professional associations (such as teachers' unions, lawyers' guilds, and so on), although they may have little impact on the direction of state policy, do perform the traditional function of mediating between the rulers and the masses. Most of these organizations are run on democratic and competitive lines, where the rank and file membership elects the leaders (in competitive elections), and their platforms are subject to member participation and consensus. As such, despite their relative political impotence, Arab civic organizations, especially those that exist in places like Egypt and Jordan, have proven to be an important moderating force, tempering the pronouncements of the radicals and allowing more moderate elements to rise to the fore. The close of the twentieth and the beginning of the twenty-first century also has seen the transfer of power in much of the Muslim world to younger, better educated, more technocratic leaders—Mohammed VI of Morocco, Abdullah of Jordan, the rulers of the Gulf states, and so on— who are actively seeking to create new forms of governance that can reconcile Islamic values and traditions while embracing political and economic modernity. All of this is having its impact. As Mumtaz Ahmad pointed out,

They [Islamists] have also incorporated democratic practices and institutions in their policies, demands and praxis. The Pakistani, Bangladeshi, Turkish, Malaysian, Egyptian, Jordanian, Algerian, Tunisian and Moroccan Islamists have already accepted the Islamic legitimacy of popular elections, the electoral process, the multiplicity of political parties and even the authority of the popularly-elected parliament to legislate not only on socio-economic matters but also on Islamic doctrinal issues . . . Even on the issue of a woman holding political office in an Islamic government, Islamists seem to have revised their earlier position.[27]

In the end, the best solution to containing the forces of radical Islam may be the democratic system firmly anchored in a respect for pluralism and the rule of law.

NOTES

1. Letter to the Editor, *The National Interest*, no. 64 (Summer 2001), 135.

2. Edward W. Said, *Covering Islam: How the Media and the Experts Determine How We See the Rest of the World*, rev. ed. (New York: Vintage Books, 1981, 1997), xxxv.

3. Gilles Kepel, *Jihad: The Trail of Political Islam*, trans. Anthony F. Roberts (Cambridge, MA: Harvard University Press, 2002). Kepel discusses the Al-Effendi article at some length, see 360–62.

4. Michael Scott Doran, "Someone Else's Civil War," *Foreign Affairs* (January/February 2002), 34.

5. Quoted in Mehdrdad Haghayeghi, *Islam and Politics in Central Asia* (New York: St. Martin's Press, 1995), 207.

6. This raises a separate issue. State control over Islam may be an effective way to retard the growth of radicalism if it is deftly handled, but it clashes with Western concepts of freedom of religion and freedom of assembly. It is ironic that a number of radical Islamist leaders found refuge in the West, claiming religious persecution for refusing to submit to the authority of the state. For a deeper discussion of this issue, see Olivier Roy, "EuroIslam: The Jihad Within?" and David Martin Jones, "Out of Bali: Cybercaliphate Rising," both in *The National Interest*, no. 71 (Spring 2003). In particular, the United States can send out extremely contradictory signals, on the one hand encouraging governments to crack down on radical movements yet at the same time demanding that regimes respect the right to free assembly and privacy, even when the exercise of such rights benefits the radicals. See comments of Nikolas K. Gvosdev, "Realism and Human Rights," held at The Nixon Center, August 28, 2002, and available at http://www.nixoncenter.org/realism_and_human_rights.htm.

7. Anthony Shahid, "Anger and Islam Rise in Jordan," *Washington Post*, January 28, 2003, A1.

8. Ray Takeyh, "Islamism: R. I. P." *The National Interest*, no. 63 (Spring 2001), 102.

9. Lawrence Davidson, *Islamic Fundamentalism* (Westport, CT: Greenwood Press, 1998), 108.

10. For example, the "morals police" in Iran that attempts to shore up the Islamic credentials of the regime by focusing on externalities such as dress, even as the deeper promises of the Revolution to provide economic justice and political democracy are not met. See Davidson, 41.

11. Freydoun Safizadeh, "On Dilemmas of Identity in the Post-Soviet Republic of Azerbaijan," *Caucasian Regional Studies*, 3:1, (1998), archived at http://poli.vub.ac.be/publi/crs/eng/0301-04.htm.

12. This practice has drawn the ire of Algerian President Bouteflika, who observed that, "regarding the Islamists and their movement, I would like to stress that the entire Algerian people are Muslims." See Bouteflika's interview in *Al-Sharq al-Aswat*, September 12, 2000.

13. John Esposito, *The Islamic Threat: Myth or Reality?*, 2nd ed. (Oxford: Oxford University Press, 1992, 1995), 238–239.

14. Henry Munson, Jr., *Islam and Revolution in the Middle East* (New Haven, CT: Yale University Press, 1988), 95–98.

15. Kepel. 273.

16. *Al-Safir*, February 7, 2003.

17. "Algerian Officer Discusses Terorrism," *al-Sharq al-Awsat*, November 4, 1997, 16.

18. Daniel Benjamin and Steven Simon, *The Age of Sacred Terror* (New York: Random House, 2002), 71.

19. One of the terms used by the general public to describe radical Islamists has been "the people of the cave"—pointing to their hermitlike separation from society and because some have literally chosen to leave society to dwell in caves. Ibid.

20. One could point to the relative youth of the leaders of the GIA in Algeria, often men in their twenties or thirties, or the composition of the Islamic Movement of Uzbekistan, under the leadership of a young former paratrooper.

21. Kepel, 359.

22. Esposito, *Islamic Threat*, 251.

23. Kepel, 359.

24. Jenny B. White, *Islamist Mobilization in Turkey* (Seattle: University of Washington Press, 2002), 118.

25. Mustapha Kamel Al-Sayyid, *The Other Face of the Islamist Movement* (Washington, DC: Carnegie Endowment for International Peace, 2003), 24.

26. Ray Takeyh, "Faith-Based Initiatives," *Foreign Policy,* November/December 2001, 70.

27. Mumtaz Ahmad, "Islam and democracy: the emerging consensus," *Milli Gazette,* October 2, 2002 (Internet version).

Selected Bibliography

Abdo, Geneive. "Days of Rage in Tehran," *Middle East Policy* (October 1999).

———. "Electoral Politics in Iran," *Middle East Policy* (June 1999).

———. "The Fragility of Khatami's Revolution," *The Washington Quarterly* (Fall 2000).

———. *No God but God: Egypt and the Triumph of Islam.* Oxford: Oxford University Press, 2000.

———. "Re-Thinking the Islamic Republic: A Conversation with Ayatollah Hussein Ali Montazeri," *Middle East Journal* (Winter 2001).

Abdullaev, Evgeniy. "The Central Asian Nexus: Islam and Politics," in *Central Asia: A Gathering Storm?* ed. Boris Rumer. Armonk, NY: M. E. Sharpe, 2002.

Abrahamian, Evrand. *Khomeinism: Essays on the Islamic Republic.* Berkeley: University of California Press, 1993.

Absood, Wassim. "The Militant Islamist Threat to Egypt," at http://www.info-manage.com/nonproliferation/najournal/militantislamegypt.html <accessed February 14, 2003>.

Adelkhah, Fariba. *Being Modern in Iran.* New York: Columbia University Press, 2000.

Addi, Lahourai. "Algeria's Army, Algeria's Agony," *Foreign Affairs* (July/August 1998).

———. "Algeria's Tragic Contradictions," *Journal of Democracy* (Spring 1996).

———. *L'Algerie et la Democrite: Pouvoir et Crise du Politicque dans l'Algerie Contemporaire.* Paris, 1995.

Ajami, Fouad. "The Sorrows of Egypt." *Foreign Affairs* (September/October 1995).

Akiner, Shirin. "Uzbekistan and the Uzbeks," in *The Nationalities Question in the Post-Soviet States,* ed. Graham Smith. London: Longman, 1990, 1996.

Al-Ahnaf, Mustapha. *L'Algerie par ses islamistes.* Paris: Karthala, 1991.

"Algerian Officer Discusses Terrorism." *Al-Sharq al-Awsat,* November 4, 1997.

Al-Sayyid, Mustapha Kamel. *The Other Face of the Islamist Movement.* Washington, DC: Carnegie Endowment for International Peace, 2003.

Alwall, Jonas. *Muslim Rights and Plights: The Religious Liberty Situation of a Minority in Sweden.* Lund: Lund University Press, 1998.

Amuzegar, Jahangir. "Iran's Post-Revolutionary Planning: The Second Try," *Middle East Policy* (March 2001).

Anderson, John. *Religion, State and Politics in the Soviet Union and Successor States.* Cambridge: Cambridge University Press, 1994.

Ansari, Ali. *Iran, Islam and Democracy: The Politics of Managing Change.* London: Royal Institute of International Affairs, 2000.

Arzt, Donna E. "Proselytizing and the Muslim *Umma* of Russia: Historical Heritage or Ethno-National Threat?" in *Proselytism and Orthodoxy in Russia: The New Way for Souls*, eds. John Witte, Jr. and Michael Bordeaux, 108–140. Maryknoll, NY: Orbis, 1999.

Atkin, Muriel. "Tajikistan: Reform, Reaction, and Civil War." *New States, New Politics: Building the Post-Soviet Nations.* Eds. Ian Bremmer and Ray Taras. Cambridge: Cambridge University Press, 1997.

Babadzhanov, Bakhtiar. "Islam in Uzbekistan," in *Central Asia: A Gathering Storm?* ed. Boris Rumer. Armonk, NY: M. E. Sharpe, 2002.

Bakhash, Shaul. "Iran's Remarkable Election," *Journal of Democracy* (October 1998).

———. "Iran's Unlikely President," *New York Review of Books* (November 5, 1998).

de Ballaigue, Christopher "The Struggle for Iran," *New York Review of Books* (December 16, 1999).

Banac, Ivo. "Bosnian Muslims: From Religious Community to Socialist Nationhood and Postcommunist Statehood," in *The Muslims of Bosnia-Herzegovina: Their Historic Development from the Middle Ages to the Dissolution of Yugoslavia*, ed. Mark Pinson. Cambridge, MA: Harvard University Press, 1994.

Barisic, Marko. "Muslims—Destroyers of Bosnia?" *Vjesnik*, March 5, 1997.

Barkina, Lyudmila. "Rushaylo Urges N. Caucasus Orthodox, Muslim Leaders to Cooperate," *ITAR-TASS*, June 28, 2000.

Belhaj, Ali. *Fasl al-kalam fi muwajhat al-hukkam.* Algiers, 1989.

———. "Qui est responsable de la violence?" *El –Mousqid* (November 1990).

Benjamin, Daniel, and Steven Simon. *The Age of Sacred Terror.* New York: Random House, 2002.

Bennigsen, Alexandre and Marie Broxup. *The Islamic Threat to the Soviet State.* New York: St. Martin's Press, 1983.

———, and Chantal Lemercier-Quelquejay. *Islam in the Soviet Union.* Trans. Geoffrey E. Wheeler and Hubert Evans. New York: Praeger, 1967.

———, and S. Enders Wimbush. *Muslims of the Soviet Empire: A Guide.* London: Hurst, 1985.

Bennoune, Mahfoud. "The Industrialization of Algeria: An Overview," in *Contemporary North Africa*, ed. Halim Barakat. Washington, DC: Center for Contemporary Arab Studies, 1985.

Binder, David. "In Yugoslavia, Rising Ethnic Strife Brings Fears of Worse Civil Conflict," *The New York Times*, November 1, 1987.

Blua, Antoine. "Uzbekistan: Case Highlights Plight of Religious Minorities in Central Asia," *Radio Free Europe/Radio Liberty*, November 9, 2002.

Bohr, Annette. "Turkmenistan and the Turkmen," in *The Nationalities Question in the Post-Soviet States*, ed. Graham Smith. London: Longman, 1990, 1996.

Boroumand, Ladan and Roya. "Is Iran Democratizing? Reform at an Impasse," *Journal of Democracy* (October 2000).

Bougarel, Xavier. "Bosniaks Under the Control of Panislamists (Part I)," *Dani*, June 18, 1999, and hosted at http://www.cdsp.neu.edu/info/students/marko/dani/dani9.html.

Boroujerdi, Mehrzad. "The Paradox of Politics in Post-Revolutionary Iran," in *Iran at the Crossroads*, eds. John Esposito and R. K. Ramazani. New York: Palgrave Macmillan, 2000.

Bringa, Tone. *Being Muslim the Bosnian Way: Identity and Community in a Central Bosnian Village*. Princeton, NJ: Princeton University Press, 1995.

Brumberg, Daniel. "Dissonant Politics in Iran and Indonesia," *Political Science Quarterly* (Fall 2000).

———. "Is Iran Democratizing," *Journal of Democracy* (October 2000).

———. *Reinventing Khomeini: The Struggle for Reform in Iran*. Chicago: University of Chicago Press, 2001.

Buchta, Wilfried. *Who Rules Iran?* Washington, DC: Washington Institute for Near East Studies, 2000.

Buffington, Minoo and Milton Buffington. *Meet Mr. Khatami, The Fifth President of the Islamic Republic*. Washington, DC: Middle East Insight, 1998.

Bukharaev, Ravil. *Islam in Russia: The Four Seasons*. New York: St. Martin's Press, 2000.

Burgat, Francois. *The Islamic Movement in North Africa*. Austin: University of Texas University Press, 1993.

Capisani, Giampaolo R. *The Handbook of Central Asia: A Comprehensive Survey of the New Republics*. London: I.B. Tauris, 2000.

Chehabi, H. E. "The Political Regime of the Islamic Republic of Iran in Comparative Perspective," *Government and Opposition* (Fall 2000).

Chistelow, Allan. "Three Islamic Voices in Contemporary Nigeria," in *Islam and the Political Economy of Meaning*, ed. William R. Roff. Berkeley: University of California Press, 1987.

Choueiri, Youssef M. *Islamic Fundamentalism*. Rev. ed. London: Pinter, 1990, 1997.

Cohen, Lenard J. "Bosnia's 'Tribal Gods': The Role of Religion in Nationalist Politics," in *Religion and the War in Bosnia*, ed. Paul Mojzes. Atlanta: GA: Scholars Press, 1998.

———. *Broken Bonds: The Disintegration of Yugoslavia*. Boulder, CO: Westview Press, 1993.

Connelly, Matthew. "Déjà vu All Over Again: Algeria, France and Us," *The National Interest* (Winter 1995–96).

———. *A Diplomatic Revolution: Algeria's Fight for Independence and the Origins of the Post–Cold War Era*. Oxford: Oxford University Press, 2001.

Cordes. "The Communitarian Case for Bosnia's Partition," in *The Transformations of 1989–1999: Triumph or Tragedy?* ed. John S. Micgiel. New York: East Central European Center, Columbia University, 2000.

Corley, Felix. *Religion in the Soviet Union: An Archival Reader*. New York: New York University Press, 1996.

Coulson, N. J. "The State and the Individual in Islamic Law," in *The Traditional Near East*, ed. J. Stewart-Robinson. Englewood Cliffs, NJ: Prentice-Hall, Inc., 1966.

Critchlow, James. "Islam and Nationality in Soviet Central Asia," in *Religion and Nationalism in Soviet and East European Politics*, ed. Pedro Ramet. Durham, NC: Duke Press Policy Studies, 1984.

Dabashi, Hamid. *Theology of Discontent: The Ideological Foundation of the Islamic Revolution in Iran*. New York: New York University Press, 1993.

Davidson, Lawrence. *Islamic Fundamentalism*. Westport, CT: Greenwood Press, 1998.

Dillman, Bradford. *State and Private Sector in Algeria: The Politics of Rent-Seeking and Failed Development*. Boulder: University of Colorado Press, 2000.

Dinorshoyev, Muso. Interview by B. Turekhanova. *Agenstvo Politicheskikh Issledovaniy (Almaty)*, January 10, 2001.

"Distinctions between the Two Notions of Religious Democracy and Liberalism," *Dowran-e Emruz*, December 10, 2000.

Doran, Michael Scott. "Someone Else's Civil War," *Foreign Affairs* (January/February 2002).

Duijzinas, Ger. *Religion and the Politics of Identity in Kosovo*. New York: Columbia University Press, 2000.

Eickelman, Dale F. "Changing Interpretations of Islamic Movements," in *Islam and the Political Economy of Meaning*, ed. William R. Roff. Berkeley: University of California Press, 1987.

————, and James Piscatori. *Muslim Politics*. Princeton: Princeton University Press, 1996.

Entelis, John. *Algeria: The Revolution Institutionalized*. Boulder: University of Colorado Press, 1986.

————. *Islam, Democracy and the State in North Africa*. Indiana: Indiana University Press, 1997.

————. "Islam, Democracy and the State: The Reemergence of Authoritarian Politics in Algeria," in *Islamism and Secularism in North Africa*, ed. John Ruedy. New York: St. Martin's Press, 1994.

————. "Political Islam in Algeria: The Nonviolent Dimension," *Current History* (January 1995).

————. "Sonatrach: The Political Economy of an Algerian State Institution," *Middle East Journal* (Winter 1999).

Esfandiari, Haleh. "Is Iran Democratizing? Observations on Election Day," *Journal of Democracy* (October 2000).

Esfandiari, Khalil. "Reformists Seek a Religion That Does Not Interfere in Supervision and Policies," *Resalat*, August 28, 2000.

Eshanova, Zamira. "Central Asia: Are Radical Groups Joining Forces?" *Radio Free Europe/Radio Liberty*, October 11, 2002.

Esposito, John. *Islam and Politics*. Syracuse: Syracuse University Press, 1984.

————. *The Islamic Threat: Myth or Reality?* 2nd ed. Oxford: Oxford University Press, 1992, 1995.

————, and John O. Voll. *Islam and Democracy*. Oxford: Oxford University Press, 1996.

Fairbanks, Stephen. "Iran's Democratic Efforts," *Middle East Policy* (October 1997).

————. "Iran: No Easy Answers," *Journal of International Affairs* (Spring 2001).

————. "A New Era for Iran?" *Middle East Policy* (September 1997).

————. "Theocracy versus Democracy: Iran Considers Political Parties," *Middle East Journal* (Winter 1998).

Fandy, Mamoun. "Egypt's Islamic Group: Regional Revenge?" *Middle East Journal* 48:4 (1994).

Farhi, Farideh. "Reform and Resistance in the Islamic Republic of Iran," in *Iran at the Crossroads*, eds. John Esposito and R.K. Ramazani. New York: Palgrave Macmillan, 2000.

Filatov, Sergei., "Tatarstan: at the Crossroads of Islam and Orthodoxy," *Religion, State and Society,* 20:3/4 (1998).

Fine, John V. A. "Medieval and Ottoman Roots of Modern Bosnia," in *Muslims of Bosnia-Herzegovina: Their Historic Development from the Middle Ages to the Dissolution of Yugoslavia,* ed. Mark Pinson. Cambridge: Harvard University Press, 1994.

Frantz, Fanon. *The Wretched of the Earth.* New York: Grove Press, 1968.

Friedman, Francine. "The Bosnian Muslim National Question," in *Religion and the War in Bosnia,* ed. Paul Mojzes. Atlanta: GA: Scholars Press, 1998.

Fuller, Graham E. "The Future of Political Islam," *Foreign Affairs* 81:2 (March/April 2002).

Gasiorowski, Mark. "The Power Struggle in Iran," *Middle East Policy* (Winter 1998).

Gellner, Ernest. "The Unknown Apollo of Biskra: The Social Base of Algerian Puritanism," *Government and Opposition* (Summer 1974).

Gleason, Gregory. "Uzbekistan: The Politics of National Independence," in *New States, New Politics: Building the Post-Soviet Nations,* eds. Ian Bremmer and Ray Taras. Cambridge: Cambridge University Press, 1997.

Glenny, Misha. *The Balkans: Nationalism, War, and the Great Powers, 1804–1999.* New York: Viking, 2000.

———. *The Fall of Yugoslavia: The Third Balkan War.* Revised edition. New York: Penguin Books, 1993.

Goble, Paul. "The Roots of Russian-Iranian Rapprochement," *RFE/RL Newsline,* March 25, 1999, at http://www.rferl.org/newsline/1999/03/5-NOT/not-250399.html

Goftar, Ali Kosh. "Reactionism or Realism?" *Resalat,* March 17, 2001.

Gordon, David. *The Passing of French Algeria.* New York: Oxford University Press, 1987.

Grousset, Rene. *The Empire of the Steppes: A History of Central Asia.* Trans. Naomi Walford. New Brunswick, NJ: Rutgers University Press, 1970, 1999.

Gunther, John. *Inside Russia Today,* rev. ed. New York: Harper and Row, 1962.

Gutic, R. "Arafat—Alija's Adviser," *Vecernje Novosti,* June 24, 1997.

Gvosdev, Nikolas K. *Imperial Policies and Perspectives Toward Georgia, 1760–1819.* New York: St. Martin's Press, 2000.

———. "Iran's Eurasian Strategy," *Analysis of Current Events,* 13:2 (2001), 1–5.

———. "Tolerance versus Pluralism: The Eurasian Dilemma," *Analysis of Current Events,* 12:7–8 (2000), 7–10.

———. "When Mullahs and Metropolitans Meet: The Emerging Orthodox-Islamic Consensus in Eurasia," *Orthodox News,* Vol. 3, no. 7 (2001).

Haddam, Anwar. "The Political Experiment of the Algerian Islamic Movement," in *Power-Sharing Islam?* ed. Azzam Tamimi. London: Liberty Press, 1993.

Hafez, Mohammad. "Armed Islamist Movements and Political Violence in Algeria," *Middle East Journal* (Fall 2000).

Haghayeghi, Mehrdad. *Islam and Politics in Central Asia.* New York: St. Martin's Press, 1995.

Hammond, Andrew. "Between the Ballot and the Bullet: Egypt's War Against Terrorism," *World Press Review Online* (November 14, 2001).

Hamzeh, A. Nizar. "Islamism in Lebanon: A Guide," *Middle East Review of International Affairs* 1, no. 3 (1997). Available online at: http://www.bin.ac.il/SOC/besa/meria/journal/1997/issue3/jv1n3a2.html.

Harbit, Mohammad. *L'Algerie et son Destin-Croyants et Citoyens.* Paris: MediasAssocies, 1993.

———. *Le FLN, Mirages et realities.* Paris, 1980.

Hayden, Robert M. "The Use of National Stereotypes in the Wars in Yugoslavia," in *The Balkans: A Religious Backyard of Europe,* ed. Mient Jan Faber. Ravenna: Longo Press, 1995.

Heywood, Colin. "Bosnia under Ottoman Rule, 1463–1800," in *Muslims of Bosnia-Herzegovina: Their Historic Development from the Middle Ages to the Dissolution of Yugoslavia,* ed. Mark Pinson. Cambridge: Harvard University Press, 1994.

Hooglund, Eric. "Khatami's Iran," *Current History* (February 1999).

Hosking, Geoffrey. *The First Socialist Society: A History of the Soviet Union from Within.* Cambridge, MA: Harvard University Press, 1985.

Humbaraci, Arslan. *Algeria: A Revolution That Failed.* New York: Frederick Praeger, 1964.

Hunter, Shireen. "Is Iranian Perestroika Possible without Fundamental Change?" *Washington Quarterly* (Autumn 1998).

Huntington, Samuel P. "The West: Unique, Not Universal," *Foreign Affairs* 75, no. 6 (1996):28–46.

Huskey, Eugene. "Kyrgyzstan: The Politics of Demographic and Economic Frustration," in *New States, New Politics: Building the Post-Soviet Nations,* eds. Ian Bremmer and Ray Taras. Cambridge: Cambridge University Press, 1997.

Huwaydi, Fahmi. "Neither the Fundamentalists nor the Arabs Are the Source of Tension in Central Asia," *Al-Sharq al-Aswat,* October 2, 2000.

Iarlykapov, A. A. *Problema Wahhabizma na Severnom Kavkaze.* Moscow: Russian Academy of Sciences, 2000.

Ibrahim, Saad Eddin. "Crises, Elites and Democratization in the Arab World," *Middle East Journal* (Spring 1993).

"Imprisoning Islam." *Transitions Online,* April 4, 2001, at http://www.tol.cz.

"In the First Person. Everything Will Be Restored. Only Peace is Needed," *Rossiiskaia Gazeta,* Augsut 20, 1994, 1.

Irwin, Zachary T. "The Fate of Islam in the Balkans: A Comparison of Four State Policies," *Religion and Nationalism in Soviet and East European Politics.* Ed. Pedro Ramet. Durham, NC: Duke Press Policy Studies, 1984.

"Islamic Revolution Devotees Society, on Eve of 22 Bahman: Enemy's Method is Subversion From Within." *Resalat,* February 7, 2001.

Israeli, Raphael, trans. "The Charter of Allah: The Platform of the Islamic Resistance Movement," in *The 1988–89 Annual of Terrorism,* ed. Y. Alexander, 99–134. The Hague: Martinus Nijhoff, 1990.

———. "State and Religion in the Emerging Palestinian Entity," *Journal of Church and State,* 44:2 (Spring 2002).

Izetbegovic, Alija. *The Islamic Declaration: A Programme for the Islamization of Muslims and the Muslim Peoples.* Sarajevo: Mala muslimanska biblioteka/Bosna, 1990.

Jahanbkhash, Forough. *Islam, Democracy and Religious Modernism.* London: Brill Academic Publishers, 2001.

Jersild, Austin. *Orientalism and Empire: North Caucasus Mountain Peoples and the Georgian Frontier, 1845–1917.* Montreal: McGill-Queen's University Press, 2002.

Jones, David Martin. "Out of Bali: Cybercaliphate Rising," *The National Interest,* no. 71 (Spring 2003).

Kamrava, Mehran. "The Civil Society Discourse in Iran," *British Journal of Middle Eastern Studies* (2001).

Kangas, Robert D. "State Building and Civil Society in Central Asia," in *Political Culture and Civil Society in Russia and the New States of Eurasia*, ed. Vladimir Tismaneanu. London: M. E. Sharpe, 1995.

Karimov, Islam. *Uzbekistan on the Threshold of the Twenty First Century.* Cambridge, MA: Uzbekiston, 1997, 1998.

Kefeli, Agnes. "The Role of Tatar and Kriashen Women in the Transmission of Islamic Knowledge, 1800–1870." *Of Religion and Empire: Missions, Conversions, and Tolerance in Tsarist Russia*, eds. Robert P. Geraci and Michael Khodarkovsky. Ithaca, NY: Cornell University Press, 2001.

Keller, Shoshana. "Conversions to the New Faith: Marxism-Leninism and Muslims in the Soviet Empire," in *Of Religion and Empire: Missions, Conversions, and Tolerance in Tsarist Russia*, ed. Robert P. Geraci and Michael Khodarkovsky, Ithaca, NY: Cornell University Press, 2001.

Kepel, Gilles. *Jihad: expansion et déclin de 'islamisme.* Paris: Gallimard, 2000.

———. *Jihad: The Trail of Political Islam.* Trans. Anthony F. Roberts. Cambridge, MA: Harvard University Press, 2002.

———. *Muslim Extremism in Egypt: The Prophet and Pharaoh.* Berkeley: University of California Press, 1986.

Khatami, Muhammad. *Hope and Challenge: The Iranian President Speaks.* New York: Global Publications, 1997.

"Khatami's Programs for the Next Four Years: The Second Phase of Reform," *Hambastegi*, May 27, 2001, 1.

Kian-Thidbaut, Azadeh. "Political and Social Transformations in Post-Islamist Iran," *Middle East Report* (Fall 1999).

Kirk, George E. *A Short History of the Middle East.* 7th revised edition. New York: Frederick A. Praeger, 1964.

Krakowski, Elie D. "Bin Laden, the Taliban and the Future of Afghanistan," *Middle East Insight* (November/December 2001).

Kramer, Martin. "Islamist Bubbles," *The National Interest*, no. 68 (Summer 2002).

De Krnjevic-Miskovic, Damjan. "Assessing Militant Islamist Threats in the Balkans," *Strategic Regional Report* 7:6 (2002).

Kucherenko, Vladimir. "Dagestan: Firing on Our Own People?" *Rossiiskaia Gazeta*, September 7, 1999.

Kumar, Radha. *Divide and Fall? Bosnia in the Annals of Partition.* London: Verso, 1997.

Kurbanov, Rafik Osman-Ogly, and Erjan Rafik-Ogly Kurbanov. "Religion and Politics in the Caucasus," in *The Politics of Religion in Russia and the New States of Eurasia*, ed. Michael Bourdeaux. London: M. E. Sharpe, 1995.

Kutty, Faisal. "Islamists and the West: Co-existence or Confrontation?" *Washington Report* (January 1996).

Labat, Severine. *Les Islamistes algeriens entre les urnes et le maquis.* Paris: Seuil, 1995.

Laremont, Ricardo Rene. *Islam and the Politics of Resistance in Algeria, 1782–1992.* Trenton: Africa World Press, 2000.

Lazerg, Marina. *The Emergence of Class in Algeria.* Boulder: University of Colorado Press, 1976.

Lederer, Gyorgy. "Islam Takes Root in Ukraine," *Eurasianet.org*, April 6, 2001, at http://www.eurasianet.org.

"Legitimacy in the Islamic Republic System." *Khorasan*, March 12, 2001.

Lemercier-Quelquejay, Chantal. "From Tribe to *Umma*," *Central Asian Survey* 3:3 (1984).

Lubeck, Paul M. "Islamist Responses to Globalization: Cultural Conflict in Egypt, Algeria, and Malaysia," in *The Myth of Ethnic Conflict: Politics, Economics and Cultural Violence*, eds. Beverly Crawford and Ronnie D. Lipschutz. Santa Cruz, CA: University of California Press, 1998.

Lubonja, Fatos. "Reinventing Skanderbeg: Albanian Nationalism and NATO Neo-colonialism," in *Kosovo: Contending Voices on Intervention*, ed. William Joseph Buckley. Grand Rapids, MI: William B. Eerdmans, 2000.

Madani, Abassi. *Azmat al-fiar al-hadith wa mubarryrat al-hal al-islami*. Algiers, 1989.

Magas, Branka. *The Destruction of Yugoslavia: Tracing the Break-Up, 1980–1992*. London: Verso, 1993.

Magomedkhanov, Magomedkhan M. "Will Dagestan Go the Way of Chechnya?" *EurasiaNews*, December 10, 1999, and archived at http://www.eurasian-ews.com/1210magomedkhanov.htm.

Makram-Ebeid, Mona. "Egypt's 2000 Parliamentary Elections," *Middle East Policy* VIII:2 (June 2001).

Malashenko, Alexei V. "Islam versus Communism: The Experience of Coexistence," in *Russia's Muslim Frontiers: New Directions in Cross-Cultural Analysis*, ed. Dale F. Eickelman, 63–78. Bloomington: Indiana University Press, 1993.

Malley, Robert. *The Call from Algeria: Third Worldism, Revolution and the Turn to Islam*. Berkeley: University of California Press, 1996.

Maloney, Suzanne. "Election in Iran: New Majlis and a Mandate for Reform," *Middle East Policy* (June 2000);

Markowitz, Lawrence. "State, Society, and Identity in Uzbekistan: Differentiation among Ferghana Valley Uzbeks," in *The Transformations of 1989–1999: Triumph or Tragedy?* ed. John S. Micgiel. New York: East Central European Center, Columbia University, 2000.

Martin, Vannessa. *Creating an Islamic State: Khomeini and the Making of a New Iran*. London: I.B. Tauris and Co., 2000.

Martinez, Luis. *La Guerre civile en Algerie*. Paris: Karthala, 1998.

Marusic, Mario. "Warnings About 'Tolerance of Corruption' in Bosnia-Herzegovina Were Issued Long Time Ago," *Vjesnik*, December 3, 1998.

Masoud, Tarek. "Misreading Iran," *Current History* (January 1998).

McCarthy, Justin. "Ottoman Bosnia, 1800–1878," in *The Muslims of Bosnia-Herzegovina: Their Historic Development from the Middle Ages to the Dissolution of Yugoslavia*, ed. Mark Pinson. Cambridge: Harvard University Press, 1994.

Menashri, David. "Shiite Leadership: In the Shadow of Conflicting Ideologies," *Iranian Studies* (1980).

Mernissi, Fatema. *Islam and Democracy*. Trans. Mary Joe Lakeland. Cambridge, MA: Perseus Publishing, 2002.

Mertus, Julie A. *Kosovo: How Myths and Truths Started a War*. Berkeley: University of California Press, 1999.

Miller, Judith. "Faces of Fundamentalism: Hassan al-Turabi and Muhammed Fadlallah." *Foreign Affairs* 73:6 (1994).

Miller, Justin. "Ethnic and Religious Minorities and Their Search for Justice: The Case of Chechnya," *Civil Society and the Search for Justice in Russia*, eds. Christopher Marsh and Nikolas K. Gvosdev. Lanham, MD: Lexington Books, 2002.

Milosevic, Aleksandar. "Terrorism Without (State) Borders," *Vjesnik*, July 1, 1996.

Mirqadirov, Rauf. "Moscow Hangs a Millstone Around Azerbaijan's Neck," *Zerkalo*, May 25, 2001.

Mitchell, Richard. *The Society of the Muslim Brothers*. Oxford: Oxford University Press, 1969.

Moin, Baqer. *Khomeini: Life of the Ayatollah*. New York: St. Martin's Press, 1999.

Mojzes, Paul. "The Camouflaged Role of Religion in the War in Bosnia and Herzegovina," *Religion and the War in Bosnia*, ed. Paul Mojzes. Atlanta: GA: Scholars Press, 1998.

Mortimer, Robert. "Algeria: The Dialectic of Elections and Violence." *Current History* (May 1997).

———. "Islam and Multiparty Politics in Algeria." *Middle East Journal* (Fall 1991).

———. "Islamists, Soldiers and Democrats: The Second Algerian War," *Middle East Journal* (Winter 1996).

Mostashari, Firouzeh. "Colonial Dilemmas: Russian Policies in the Muslim Caucasus," in *Of Religion and Empire: Missions, Conversion, and Tolerance in Tsarist Russia*, eds. Robert P. Geraci and Michael Khodarkovsky, Ithaca, NY: Cornell University Press 2001.

Mowlana, Hamid. "Tomorrow and the Next Four Years," *Keyhan*, June 7, 2001.

Mozaffari, Mehdi. "Islam and Civil Society," in *Islam: State and Society*, eds. Klaus Ferdinand and Mehdi Mozaffari, 105–116. London: Curzon Press, 1988.

Mumtaz, Ahmad. "Islam and Democracy: The Emerging Consensus," *Milli Gazette*, October 2, 2002 (Internet version).

Munson, Henry, Jr. *Islam and Revolution in the Middle East*. New Haven, CT: Yale University Press, 1988.

Murray, Roger, and Tom Weingraf, "The Algerian Revolution," *New Left Review* (December 1963).

Norton, Augustus Richard. "The Future of Civil Society in the Middle East," *Middle East Journal* (Spring 1993).

Ochilov, Botyr. "Islam in Uzbekistan," *Perihelion* (30 September–6 October 2002).

Olcott, Martha Brill. *Kazakhstan: Unfulfilled Promise*. Washington, DC: Carnegie Endowment for International Peace, 2002.

Olsen, Gorm Rye. "Islam: What Is Its Political Significance? The Case of Egypt and Saudi Arabia," in *Islam: State, and Society*, eds. Klaus Ferdinand and Mehdi Mozaffari, 127–142. London: Curzon Press, 1988.

Ottaway, David and Marina. *Algeria: The Politics of Socialists Revolution*. Berkeley: University of California, 1970.

Palmer, Peter. "Religions and Nationalism in Yugoslavia: A Tentative Comparison Between the Catholic Church and the Other Communities," *The Balkans: Nationalism, War, and the Great Powers, 1804–1999*. New York: Viking, 2000, 159.

Pannier, Bruce. "Russia: Dagestan's Religious Tensions—Analysis," *Radio Free Europe/Radio Liberty*, May 19, 1997, archived at http://www.stetson.edu/~psteeves/relnews/dstanpannier1905.html.

Patai, Raphael. *The Arab Mind*. Revised edition. New York: Scribner, 1983.

Pazzanita, Anthony. "From Boumedienne to Benjedid: The Algerian Regime in Transition," *Journal of South Asia and Middle Eastern Studies* (Summer 1992).

Pecanin, Senad. "We Are Living the Islamic Declaration," *Dani*, October 15, 1999, and hosted at http://www.cdsp.neu.edu/info/students/marko/dani/dani23.html.

Petterson, Donald. *Inside Sudan: Political Islam, Conflict and Catastrophe.* Boulder, CO: Westview Press, 1999.

Pierre, Andrew J. and William B. Quandt, "Algeria's War on Itself," *Foreign Policy*, no. 99 (Summer 1995).

Pinson, Mark. "The Muslims of Bosnia-Herzegovina under Austro-Hungarian Rule, 1878–1918," in *Muslims of Bosnia-Herzegovina: Their Historic Development from the Middle Ages to the Dissolution of Yugoslavia*, ed. Mark Pinson. Cambridge, MA: Harvard University Press, 1994.

Piscatori, James P. *Islam and the Political Process.* Cambridge: Cambridge University Press, 1983.

Poulton, Hugh. "Muslim Identity and Ethnicity in the Balkans," in *Kosovo: Contending Voices on Balkan Interventions*, ed. William Joseph Buckley. Grand Rapids, MI: William B. Eerdmans, 2000.

Quandt, William. *Between Ballots and Bullets: Algeria's Transition from Authoritarianism.* Washington, DC: The Brookings Institution, 1998.

———. *Revolution and Political Leadership: Algeria, 1954–1968.* Cambridge, MA: MIT Press, 1969.

"Rafsanjani Assesses Islamic Government Two Decades After Revolution." *Hokumat-e Eslami* (Winter 2001).

Rajee, Farhang. "A Thermidor of Islamic Yuppies," *Middle East Journal* (Spring 1999).

Ramet, Pedro. *Cross and Commisar: The Politics of Religion in Eastern Europe and the USSR.* Bloomington, IN: Indiana University Press, 1987.

Rashid, Ahmed. "CA Fears Renewed Insurgency," *The Nation* (Lahore internet edition), April 5, 2001.

———. "The Taliban: Exporting Extremism," *Foreign Affairs* (November/December 1999).

Recknagel, Charles. "Russia: Islamic Countries Unlikely to Help Chechnya," *Radio Free Europe/Radio Liberty*, November 19, 1999; archived at http://www.rferl.org/nca/features/1999/11/F.RU.991119132655.html.

Reed, Stanley. "The Battle for Egypt," *Foreign Affairs* (September/October 1993).

Roberts, Hugh. "Algeria's Ruinous Impasse: An Honorable Way Out," *International Affairs* (Summer 1995).

———. "Algerian State and the Challenge of Democracy," *Government and Opposition* (Fall 1992).

———. "Doctrinaire Economic and Political Opportunism in the Strategy of Algerian Islamism," in *Islamism and Secularism in North Africa*, ed. John Ruedy. New York: St. Martin's Press, 1994.

———. "From Radical Mission to Equivocal Ambition: The Expansion and Manipulation of Algerian Islamism, 1979–1992," in *Accounting for Fundamentalism: The Dynamic Character of Movements*, eds. Martin Marty and Scott Appleby. Chicago: University of Chicago Press, 1994.

———."Radical Islamism and the Dilemma of Algerian Nationalism," *Third World Quarterly* (April 1988).

———. "The Struggle for Constitutional Rule In Algeria," *The Journal of Algerian Studies* (1998).

Roff, William R. "Islamic Movements: One or Many?" in *Islam and the Political Economy of Meaning*, ed. William R. Roff. Berkeley: University of California Press, 1987.

Rohde, David. *A Safe Area*. London: Pocket Books, 1997.

Roshchina, Tatiana. "Only Unity Leads to Welfare," *Rossiisakaia Gazeta* (internet version), March 17, 2001.

Ross, Christopher. "Political Islam: Myths, Realities, and Policy Implications." Speech delivered to the Salzburg Conference of Near Eastern Affairs Public Affairs Officers, September 21, 1993.

Rotar, Igor. "Government Tries to Clamp Down, As Islam's Influence Builds in Northern Tajikistan," *EurasiaNet*, November 12, 2002.

Rouadjia, Ahmed. "Discourse and Strategy of the Algerian Islamist Movement," in *Islamist Dilemma: The Political Role of Islamist Movements in Contemporary Arab World*, ed. Laura Guzaaone. London: Ithica Press, 1995.

———. "Doctrine et discours du Cheikh Abassi," *Peuples Mediterraneens* (52–3).

Roy, Olivier. "The Crisis of Religious Legitimacy in Iran," *Middle East Journal* (Spring 1999).

———. "EuroIslam: The Jihad Within?" *The National Interest*, no. 71 (Spring 2003).

———. *The Failure of Political Islam*. Cambridge, MA: Harvard University Press, 1994.

Ruedy, John. *Islamism and Secularism in North Africa*. New York: St. Martin's Press, 1994.

———. *Modern Algeria: The Origins and Development of a Nation*. Indiana: Indian University Press, 1992.

Rumer, Boris. "The Search for Stability in Central Asia," in *Central Asia: A Gathering Storm?* ed. Boris Rumer. Armonk, NY: M. E. Sharpe, 2002.

Rummel, Lynette. "Privatization and Democratization in Algeria," in *State and Society in Algeria*, eds. John Entelis and Philip Naylor. Boulder: University of Colorado Press, 1995.

Ruthven, Malise. *Islam: A Very Short Introduction*. New York: Oxford University Press, 1997.

Rywkin, Michael. *Moscow's Muslim Challenge: Soviet Central Asia*. London: M.E. Sharpe, 1982.

Safizadeh, Fereydoun. " On Dilemmas of Identity in the Post-Soviet Republic of Azerbaijan," *Caucasian Regional Studies*, 3:1, (1998), archived at http://poli.vub.ac.be/publi/crs/eng/0301-04.htm.

Said, Edward W. *Covering Islam: How the Media and the Experts Determine How We See the Rest of the World*. Rev. ed. New York: Vintage Books, 1981, 1997.

Sanson, Henri. *Laicite islamique en Algerie*. Paris: CNRS, 1983.

Savyon, Avelet. "Iranian Intellectuals Against Khamenei—Dr. Qassem Sa'adi: 'Your Regime Is Illegitimate, Your Foreign and Domestic Policies Are Failing and Despotic,'" MEMRI *Inquiry and Analysis Series—No. 125* (February 28, 2003).

Schevill, Ferdinand. *A History of the Balkans: From the Earliest Times to the Present Day*. New York: Barnes and Noble, 1995.

Schirazi, Asghar. *The Constitution of Iran: Politics and the State in the Islamic Republic*. London: I. B. Tauris and Co., 1997.

Sciolino, Elaine. *Persian Mirrors: The Elusive Face of Iran*. New York: Touchstone Books, 2000.

Sells, Michael A. "Vuk's Knife: Kosovo, the Serbian Golgotha, and the Radicalization of Serbian Society," in *Kosovo: Contending Voices on Balkan Interventions*, ed. William Joseph Buckley. Grand Rapids, MI: William B. Eerdmans, 2000.

Shahrani, M. Nazif. "Islam and Political Culture in Central Asia," in *The Politics of Religion in Russia and the New States of Eurasia*, ed. Michael Bourdeaux. London: M. E. Sharpe, 1995.

Shala, Blerim. "Because Kosovars Are Western, There Can Be No Homeland without a State," in *Kosovo: Contending Voices on Balkan Interventions*, ed. William Joseph Buckley. Grand Rapids, MI: William B. Eerdmans, 2000.

"A Short Exposition of the Tasks and Goals of an Islamic State," *Russia and the Muslim World* 4, no. 94 (2000).

Silverstein, Paul A. "'No Pardon': Rage and Revolt in Algeria," *Middle East Insight* (September/October 2001).

Smith, Gordon B. *Soviet Politics: Continuity and Contradiction*. New York: St. Martin's, 1988.

Smith, Patrick. "The Indigenous and the Imported: Khatami's Iran," *The Washington Quarterly* (Spring 2000).

Soroush, Abolkarim. *Reason, Freedom, and Democracy in Iran*. New York: Oxford University Press, 2000.

Stadler, Constance. "Democratization Reconsidered: The Transformation of Political Culture in Algeria," *Journal of North African Studies* (Fall 1998).

Starrett, Gregory. *Putting Islam to Work: Education, Politics, and Religious Transformation in Egypt*. Berkeley: University of California Press, 1998.

Stone, Martin. *The Agony of Algeria*. New York: Columbia University Press, 1997.

Suleymanov, Elin. "Azerbaijan, Azerbaijanis, and the Search For Identity," *Analysis of Current Events*, 13:1 (2001).

Sutton, Keith and Ahmed Aghrout and Salah Zamiche. "Political changes in Algeria: An Emerging Electoral Geography," *Maghreb Review* (1992).

Svanberg, Ingvar. "Kazakhstan and the Kazakhs," in *The Nationalities Question in the Post-Soviet States*, ed. Graham Smith. London: Longman, 1990, 1996.

"Symposium: Resurgent Islam in the Middle East," *Middle East Policy* 3:2 (1994).

Takeyh, Ray. "Faith-Based Initiatives," *Foreign Policy*, November/December 2001, 70.

———."God's Will: Iranian Democracy and the Islamic Context," *Middle East Policy*, VII:4 (October 2000), 41–49.

———."Iran's Emerging National Compact," *World Policy Journal* (October 2002).

———."Islamism: R.I.P." *The National Interest*, no. 63 (Spring 2001): 97–102.

———."The Lineaments of Islamic Democracy," *World Policy Journal* (Winter, 2001/2002).

———.*The Origins of the Eisenhower Doctrine: The US, Britain and Nasser's Egypt*. New York: St. Martin's Press, 2000.

———."Re-Imagining US-Iranian Relations," *Survival* (Fall 2002).

Taseva, Marija. "Islamisation and Its Contemporary Consequences," in *The Balkans: A Religious Backyard of Europe*, ed. Mient Jan Faber. Ravenna: Longo Press, 1995.

Tishkov, Valery. *Ethnicity, Nationalism, and Conflict In and After the Soviet Union: The Mind Aflame*. Thousand Oaks, CA: SAGE Publications, 1997.

Torbakov, Igor. "Tajik-Uzbek Relations: Divergent National Historiographies Threaten to Aggravate Tensions," *Eurasianet*, June 12, 2000, at http://www.eurasianet.org.

"Turkmen Head in New Year Message Applauds Economic Growth," *Turkmenistan Daily Digest*, January 2, 2001, at http://www.eurasianet.org.

"Turkmen President Urges Approval of Nation's Spiritual Books," *Turkmenistan Daily Digest*, January 13, 2000, at http://www.eurasianet.org.

Vakili, Valla. *Debating Religion and Politics in Iran: The Political Thought of Abdulkarim Soroush*. New York: The Council on Foreign Relations, 1997.

Vali, Davron. "Banned Islamic Movement Increasingly Active in Tajikistan," *Eurasia Insight*, September 5, 2002 (http://www.eurasianet.org/departments/insight/articles/eav090502.shtml).

Vandewalle, Dirk. "At the Brink," *World Policy Journal* (Fall 1992).

———. "Islam in Algeria: Religion, Culture and Opposition in a Rentier State," in *Political Islam: Revolution, Radicalism or Reform*, ed. John Esposito. Boulder: University of Colorado Press, 1997.

Vatin, Jean-Claude. "Religious Resistance and State Power in Algeria," in *Islam and Power*, eds. Alexander S. Cudsi and Ali Hilal Dessouki. Baltimore: Johns Hopkins University Press, 1981.

Velikonja, Mitja. "Liberation Mythology: The Role of Mythology in Fanning War in the Balkans," in *Religion and the War in Bosnia*, ed. Paul Mojzes. Atlanta: GA: Scholars Press, 1998.

Vladimirov, Aleksandr. "Terror for Allah's Glory," *Rossiiskaia Gazeta* (Internet edition), July 6, 2001.

Vneshnaia Politika Rossii: Mneniia Ekspertov. Moscow: Russian Independent Institute for Social and Nationality Problems, 2001.

Vrcan, Srdjan. "The Religious Factor and the War in Bosnia and Herzegovina," in *Religion and the War in Bosnia*, ed. Paul Mojzes. Atlanta: GA: Scholars Press, 1998.

Walldorf, C. William, Jr. "Towards a Nuanced Conception of Political Islam: The Case of Tajikistan," *Transformations of 1989–1999: Triumph or Tragedy?* ed. John S. Micgiel. New York: East Central European Center, Columbia University, 2000.

Weaver, Mary Ann. "The Novelist and the Sheikh," *New Yorker* (January 30, 1995).

Werth, Paul. *At the Margins of Orthodoxy*. Ithaca, NY: Cornell University Press, 2002.

Wiberg, Hakan. "Divided Nations and Divided States," in *The Balkans: Nationalism, War, and the Great Powers, 1804–1999*. New York: Viking, 2000.

Wikotrowicz, Quintan. "State Power and the Regulation of Islam in Jordan," *Journal of Church and State* 41, no. 4 (1999).

Willis, David K. *Klass: How Russians Really Live*. New York: Avon, 1985.

Willis, Michael. "Algeria's Other Islamists: Abdallah Djaballah and the Ennahda Movement," *Journal of North African Studies* (Fall 1998).

———. *The Islamists' Challenge in Algeria: A Political History.* New York: NYI Press, 1996.

Woodward, Bob. *Veil: The Secret Wars of the CIA, 1981–1987.* New York: Pocket Books, 1988.

Woodward, Susan L. *Balkan Tragedy: Chaos and Dissolution after the Cold War.* Washington, DC: The Brookings Institution, 1995.

Wright, Robin. "Deadline Tehran: A Revolution Implodes," *Foreign Policy* (Fall, 1996).

———. "Iran's Greatest Political Challenge: Abdol Karim Soroush," *World Policy Journal* (Summer 1997).

———. "Islam, Democracy and the West," *Foreign Affairs* (July/August 1992).

———. *The Last Great Revolution.* New York: Vintage Books, 2000.

———. *Sacred Rage.* New York: Simon and Schuster, 1985, 2002.

Yesfsah, Abdelkader. *Processus de Legitimation du Pouvoir Militaire et la Construction de l'Etat en Algerie.* Paris, 1982.

Zaman, Muhammad Qasim. *The Ulama in Contemporary Islam: Custodians of Change.* Princeton: Princeton University Press, 2002.

Zebiri, Kate. "Islamic Revival in Algeria: An Overview," *The Muslim World* (October 1993).

Zeghidour, Slimane. "Entretien avec Abbasi Madani," *Politique Etrangere,* 49 (1990).

Zomija, Alenko. "Everyday Life Proves That Stories about Equality of Croats Are False," *Vjesnik,* August 27, 1997.

———. "Train and Equip Program Is Getting Stuck," *Vjesnik,* September 26, 1996.

Zoubir, Yahia. "Algerian Islamists' Conception of Democracy," *Arab Studies Quarterly* (Summer 1996).

———. "The Painful Transition from Authoritarianism in Algeria," *Arab Studies Quarterly* (Summer 1993).

———. "Stalled Democratization of an Authoritarian Regime: The Case of Algeria," *Democratization* (Summer 1995).

Zubaida, Sami. *Islam, the People and the State: Political Ideas and Movements in the Middle East.* London: I. B. Tauris, 1993.

Index

About the Authors

RAY TAKEYH is Professor of National Security Studies at the National Defense University and Adjunct Scholar at the Center for American Progress. He is author of *The Origins of the Eisenhower Doctrine: The U.S., Britain and Nasser's Egypt, 1953–57.*

NIKOLAS K. GVOSDEV is Executive Editor of *The National Interest* and a senior fellow for strategic studies at The Nixon Center. His most recent work is *Civil Society and the Search for Justice in Russia.*